# The William Stallings Books on Computer and Data Communications Technology

## HANDBOOKS OF COMPUTER-COMMUNICATIONS STANDARDS

*(Available from Howard W. Sams & Company, Macmillan Computer Book Publishing Division)*

### Volume 1

#### The Open Systems Interconnection (OSI) Model and OSI-Related Standards, Second Edition

A description of the master plan for all computer-communications standards: the OSI model. The book also provides a detailed presentation of OSI-related standards at all 7 layers, including HDLC, X.25, ISO internet, ISO transport, ISO session, ISO presentation, Abstract Syntax ONE (ASN.1), and common application service elements (CASE).

### Volume 2

#### Local Area Network Standards, Second Edition

A detailed examination of all current local network standards, including logical link control (LLC, IEEE 802.2), CSMA/CD (IEEE 802.3), token bus (IEEE 802.4), token ring (IEEE 802.5), and fiber distributed data interface (FDDI, ANS X3T9.5).

### Volume 3

#### The TCP/IP Protocol Suite, Second Edition

A description of the protocol standards that are mandated on all DOD computer procurements and are becoming increasingly popular on commercial local network products, including TCP, IP, FTP, SMTP, and TELNET.

*All of these books provide a clear tutorial exposition, a discussion of the relevance and value of each standard, an analysis of options within each standard, and an explanation of underlying technology.*

*See last page for additional Stallings titles.*

# The Business Guide to Local Area Networks

William Stallings, Ph.D.

## HOWARD W. SAMS & COMPANY

A Division of Macmillan, Inc.
11711 North College, Suite 141, Carmel, IN 46032 USA

*For Tricia, as always.*

International Standard Book Number: 0-672-22728-2
Library of Congress Catalog Card Number: 89-64075
Acquisitions Editor: *Scott Arant*
Development Editor: *C. Herbert Feltner*
Manuscript Editor: *Susan Pink, TechRight*
Illustrator: *T. R. Emrick*
Cover Artist: *Garry Nichols*
Indexer: *Joelynn Gifford*
Compositor: *Shepard Poorman Communications Corporation*

*Printed in the United States of America*

**Trademarks**

# Contents

# Preface

The local area network (LAN) has come to play a central role in information distribution and office functioning in businesses and other organizations. The major factor driving the widespread introduction of the LAN has been the proliferation of small computer systems, especially personal computers but also workstations and minicomputers.

With the dropping price of LAN hardware and software, LANs have become more numerous and larger, and they have taken on more functions in the organization. After the LAN is installed, it quickly becomes almost as essential as the telephone system. At the same time, there is a proliferation of LAN types and options and a need to interconnect a number of LANs at the same site and with LANs at other sites. Because of the importance of these requirements, decisions on the purchase and day-to-day management of LANs cannot be left to technicians. Nontechnical staff and management personnel have an urgent need for a broad, reasonably detailed understanding of this technology and the products it has spawned.

The objective of this book is to meet that need. It presents the essential technical material in a way that is useful to readers who do not have a data communications background. Throughout the book, technical details are tied to the requirements that the LAN is intended to satisfy. Where alternative technical approaches are available (for example, different transmission media), the book discusses the relative merits of each approach and which environments and applications are matched by a particular technical option. Thus, the book is not simply a recitation of the technological ingredients of LANs. Rather, it is an explanation of that technology viewed from the perspective of its use to meet actual business needs.

The material presented in the book is supplemented by a number of case studies. These are short narrative descriptions of actual LAN projects undertaken by various companies. The case studies highlight practical problems in choosing, installing, and running a LAN, and the approaches that can be taken to overcome these problems.

An important element that helps structure the presentation is the essential role of standards. The proliferation of personal computers and other computer systems inevitably means that the manager will be faced with the need to integrate equipment from a variety of vendors. The only way to manage this requirement effectively is through standards. Increasingly, vendors are offering products and services that conform to international standards. This book addresses the key groups of standards that are shaping the marketplace and defining the choices available to the decision maker.

The book begins with an overview of the trends that have led to the proliferation of LANs. The discussion centers on the information movement requirements of an organization. These requirements, together with the evolving mix of computers on the scene, dictate a networking solution. Further, the nature of the information movement tells us something about the capabilities and structure of an overall networking solution.

With this background, the book introduces and surveys LAN technology. The discussion then moves to a description of specific LAN product configurations (for example, a token ring system using shielded twisted pair). The discussion is structured on existing LAN standards, because virtually all new products, and most existing ones, conform to one of the standards.

Next, the higher level issues of network software, network operating systems, and network services are addressed. This is followed by an examination of the key requirement of internetworking. There must be a way to link LANs to each other in the same building, to wide area networks, and to remote LANs.

Next, two essential topics that cut across all LAN technologies are addressed: security and network management. Various approaches and the requirements they address are introduced.

With all of this material covered, it is time to examine the process of selecting a LAN or set of LANs to meet the requirements of an organization. The discussion looks at the techniques for generating a statement of information processing requirements, then translating that into a set of LAN requirements that can be used as criteria for evaluating alternative approaches and products.

The book concludes with an examination of future requirements for LANs, although the future has become very short term in this context. A revolutionary shift in the form of information used by organizations—involving substantial reliance on fixed image and video (moving image) forms—is already taking place. This "visual revolution" has substantial implications for LANs developed in the near future, and these issues will be explored.

Other books by the author may be of interest to readers. *Local Networks: An Introduction, Third Edition* (1990, Macmillan) is a textbook as well as a reference book for professionals. It examines the technology of local area networks and digital private branch exchanges (PBX) in considerable detail. *Handbook of Computer-Communications Standards, Volume II: Local Area Network Standards, Second Edition* (1990, Howard W. Sams) is a detailed description and analysis of the various standards for LANs. *Local Network Technology, Third Edition* (1988, IEEE Computer Society Press, P.O. Box 80452, Worldway Postal Center, Los Angeles, CA 90080; telephone 800-272-6657) is a collection of reprints of many of the recent, important papers and technical journal articles on local area networks. Finally, a set of videotapes that cover LAN technology is available from Media Services, Boston University, 565 Commonwealth Avenue, Boston, MA 02215; telephone 617-353-3227.

# Chapter 1

# Introduction

T HE FIRST EXPERIMENTAL LOCAL AREA NETWORKS (LANs) appeared in the early 1970s. By the late 1970s, a number of LAN products were commercially available. In the 1980s, a need was felt to standardize LANs, and the work involved proceeded rapidly. The first significant LAN standards appeared in 1985, and these achieved almost instant support from both vendors and customers of LANs. Meanwhile, the growth in the number of LANs and the number of devices connected to LANs grew explosively. By the late 1980s, the need for LANs in the corporate environment was almost universally accepted, and the hot technical issues concerned not the connection of devices to each other through a LAN, but the techniques required to interconnect multiple LANs!

Local area networks have moved rapidly from the experimental stage to commercial availability. Figure 1-1 shows that the cost of connecting to LANs has dropped rapidly as the total value of shipments has risen. Because LANs meet important business needs, and because costs have fallen, LAN penetration into customer sites has been rapid. Figure 1-2 gives an idea of the extent of this penetration, in terms of both the percentage of companies that use LANs and the percentage of personnel that use LANs at those companies.

It should be clear from these two figures that LANs are an important feature of the business landscape, and one whose importance is growing. Furthermore, some difficult issues raised in the procurement and management of LANs are not found in other technologies. First, a wide variety of LANs are available to the user. The differences are due to not just the services offered but also the fundamental technology itself. Second, because LANs have become so inexpensive, it is relatively easy for a department-level or midlevel manager to make a procurement decision and get a LAN that serves a small part of the organization. Inevitably, however, these small LANs need to be interconnected to provide business-wide communication. If there are differences in the underlying technology of the various LANs in an organization, interconnection is difficult. Thus, it becomes important for those involved with LAN

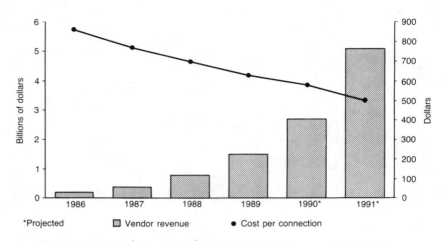

**Figure 1-1.** Trends in general-purpose LANs. *(Source: Frost & Sullivan, January 1988.)*

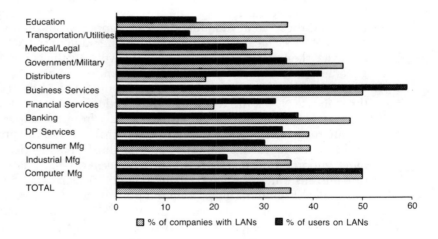

**Figure 1-2.** LAN penetration by industry. *(Source: Datamation, March 1988.)*

planning, procurement, management, and, yes, LAN use, to understand the technology of LANs. The purpose of this book is to provide that understanding.

This section is an introduction to LANs. We begin with a brief and general description of LANs, then discuss the reasons behind the extraordinary growth in LANs. Next, we discuss the types of applications that have driven the LAN marketplace. Finally, we assess the importance of LANs in the business organization.

# What Is a Local Area Network?

A data communication network is a facility that interconnects a number of data-transmitting devices, such as computers and terminals, and allows for the exchange of data among those devices. The term *local area network (LAN)* refers to a communication network with the following characteristics:

- The network is confined to a small area, typically a single building or a cluster of buildings.
- The network consists of a shared transmission medium.
- The data rate on the network is high, anywhere from 1 million bits per second (1 Mbps) to 100 Mbps.
- The devices on the network are peers. That is, any device can initiate data exchange with any other device.

## The Multidrop Line

To understand the nature of the LAN, it is worthwhile to look at an ancestor, the multidrop line. A multidrop line allows a number of terminals to share the same communications link with a host computer.

Let us illustrate this principle with a simple application. Consider the support of a number of 1200-bps terminal devices by a host computer. Two alternative approaches are shown in Figure 1-3. In Figure 1-3a, we see the simplest approach, which is to provide a direct, point-to-point link between each terminal and the host system. This requires a single I/O port for each terminal and a single transmission line for each terminal. Now, if all the terminals are in the same room as the computer, the transmission line cost is negligible. A substantial cost, however, is associated with the number of I/O ports on the host system. If the terminals are scattered throughout the building, the cost of stringing cable can be substantial. Furthermore, if a terminal is moved from one office to another, recabling is required for that terminal.

An alternate, shown in Figure 1-3b, is the multidrop line. The multidrop line takes advantage of the fact that a typical terminal is transmitting only a

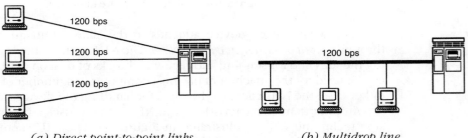

*(a) Direct point-to-point links.*        *(b) Multidrop line.*

**Figure 1-3.** Terminal connection alternatives.

fraction of the time. All these terminals can share a single line into the host system. The host controls the transmission process by polling each terminal in turn for data. The same 1200-bps line may be sufficient to support as many as a dozen terminals. There is clearly a savings in I/O port costs: the host computer needs only a single port to service many terminals. There is also a potential savings in cable installation costs because less cable is used.

There are some limitations to this approach. For one thing, all the devices must operate at the same data rate. You cannot mix different types of terminals that operate at different data rates on the same cable. Also, communication is only between host and terminal. This type of configuration typically does not allow data exchange directly between two terminals. In the days of large host computers, when all users accessed the central computer by a terminal, this arrangement worked very well. In today's office, with personal computers, minicomputers, workstations, and digital fax machines, this approach is inadequate, as we will see.

## A Simple LAN

In contrast to the multidrop line, consider the arrangement in Figure 1-4. As before, there is a shared transmission medium. In this case, all the devices attached to the medium are considered peers. Any device can transmit to any other device.

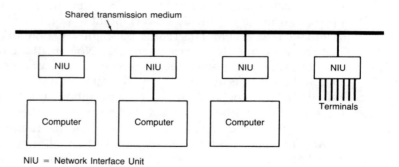

**Figure 1-4.** A simple local area network.

With a LAN, each device attaches to the shared transmission medium through a *network interface unit (NIU)*. The NIU contains the logic for accessing the LAN and for sending and receiving blocks of data on the LAN. The NIU can be used for the attachment of a host computer or a number of terminals. In either case, the NIU contains the logic for handling the devices attached to it.

An important characteristic of the NIU is that it uses a buffered transmission technique. This is illustrated in Figure 1-5. The NIU captures transmissions intended for one of the devices attached to it. That transmission is at the data rate of the medium. In Figure 1-5, the data rate is 10 Mbps. When the block of data is captured, it is stored temporarily in an input buffer. It is then delivered to the attached device, *at the data rate of the attached device*. In this example, that rate is 56 Kbps.

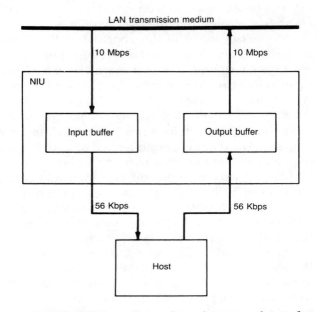

**Figure 1-5.** Buffered transmission through a network interface unit.

Thus, the LAN is much more powerful than the multidrop line. It permits peer communication. It allows the interconnection of devices that transmit and receive at different data rates. And, at the high data rates typically found on shared media, it can support hundreds or even thousands of devices.

# The Need for Local Area Networks

Figures 1-1 and 1-2 dramatize the explosive growth in the use of LANs. Having given a preliminary definition of LANs, we can return to the question of why they have become so popular. The reasons behind the rapid development in LAN use can be classed under two general headings: wire replacement and computer networking.

## Wire Replacement

Although it appears to be a mundane issue, one of the most difficult problems in data communications is wiring. For two devices to communicate, a physical signal path must be between them. The common and traditional situation has been the need to connect dispersed terminal users to one or more central data processing resources. Within a building, this requirement has generally been met with a nonshared hardware approach: A wire is strung from each terminal to the central facility. To reduce wiring demand, multidrop lines or mutliplexers are sometimes used in larger buildings.

The disadvantage of this approach is its inflexibility. Moving a terminal usually requires rewiring and may require pulling new cable. This is expensive and time-consuming. Also, if a terminal or a terminal multiplexer is wired into a particular host, the terminal user can access only that host. This is sometimes countered by the use of a patch panel in the computer room.

With more than one building, the problem is more severe. Not only must the intrabuilding requirements be met, but interbuilding communication is required. The traditional solution has been to put relatively high-speed, point-to-point data links (anywhere from 56 Kbps to over 1 Mbps) between pairs of buildings. Each end of the line is terminated with a multiplexer so that multiple lines in each building share the common interbuilding link. Again, this approach is inflexible. A link is needed for each possible pair of buildings that needs to communicate. Patch panels or switches are needed to activate a particular link for a particular connection.

All these difficulties provide strong motivation for the purchase of a LAN. With a LAN, you make an initial investment in wire installation. The wire is installed and used in such a way as to provide a shared transmission facility, with attachment points. When we discuss specific LAN topologies in Chapter 2, we will explain the various wiring approaches used for LANs. For now, it is sufficient to say that a building or portion of a building can be prewired for a LAN. Devices can be added at any point along the prewired installation, both when the wire is initially installed and later to accommodate expansion.

## Distributed Processing and Computer Networking

Until the early 1970s, the centralized data processing approach enjoyed near-universal use in businesses. Since that time, there has been a steady evolution to distributed data processing (DDP).

The key factor that has made DDP possible is the dramatic and continuing decrease in computer hardware costs, accompanied by an increase in computer hardware capability. Today's personal computers have speeds, instruction sets, and memory capacities comparable to those of minicomputers and even mainframes of just a few years ago. This trend has spawned a number of changes in the way information is collected, processed, and used in organizations. There is an increasing use of small, single-function systems, such as engineering workstations and small business computers, and of general-purpose microcomputers, such as personal computers and UNIX workstations. These small, dispersed systems are more accessible to the user, more responsive, and easier to use than large, central time-sharing systems.

The use of DDP implies the existence of a collection of dispersed systems throughout the organization. (If all these systems were used in a standalone fashion, no data communications requirements would exist!) Therefore, the use of DDP almost invariably means that interconnection is required.

Consider an organization that adopts a DDP strategy and begins to acquire minicomputers and personal computers. As the number of systems increases, the company wants to interconnect these systems for a variety of reasons, including:

- Sharing expensive resources
- Exchanging data between systems

Sharing expensive resources, such as bulk storage and laser printers, is an important way to contain costs. Although the cost of data processing hardware has dropped, the cost of essential electromechanical equipment remains high. Even when data can be uniquely associated with a small system, economies of scale encourage the storage of that data on a centralized server system. The cost per bit for storage on a personal computer's floppy disk is orders of magnitude higher than that for a large disk or tape on a minicomputer or mainframe.

The capability to exchange data is an equally compelling reason for interconnection. Individual users of computer systems do not work in isolation and will want some of the benefits provided by a central system, including the capability to exchange messages with other users and the capability to access data and programs from several sources in the preparation of a document or the analysis of data.

Several other benefits are worth mentioning. An interconnected distributed system is more reliable, available to the user, and able to survive failures. The loss of any one system should have minimal impact, and key systems can be made redundant so that other systems can quickly take up the load after a failure. Finally, a distributed system provides the potential to connect devices from multiple vendors, which gives the customer greater flexibility and bargaining power.

Thus, we see a need to interconnect systems in an organization to share resources and exchange data. In general, the interconnection must be flexible enough to allow data to be exchanged between any two devices. This is a major feature of a LAN.

# LAN Applications

The range of applications for local networks is wide. Table 1-1 lists some applications. We will see that not all local networks support all applications. To give some feel for the use of local networks, several different applications are presented.

**TABLE 1-1**   Local Network Applications

| | |
|---|---|
| **Data processing**<br> Data entry<br> Transaction processing<br> File transfer<br> Inquiry/response<br> Batch/RJE | **Energy management**<br> Heating<br> Ventilation<br> Air conditioning |
| **Office automation**<br> Document/word processing<br> Electronic mail<br> Intelligent copying/facsimile | **Process control**<br><br> **Fire and security**<br> Sensors/alarms<br> Cameras and monitors |
| **Factory automation**<br> CAD/CAM<br> Inventory control/order entry/<br> shipping<br> Monitor and control of factory floor<br> equipment | **Telephones**<br><br> **Teleconferencing**<br><br> **Television**<br> Off-the-air<br> Video presentations |

## Personal Computer Local Networks

We start at one extreme in terms of price: a system designed to support personal computers. With the relatively low cost of such systems, managers in organizations are independently buying personal computers for standalone applications, such as spreadsheet and project management tools. Today's personal computers put processor power, file storage, high-level languages, and problem-solving tools in an inexpensive, user-friendly package. The reasons for acquiring such a system are compelling. And, as Figure 1-6 shows, the number of personal computers in the office continues to grow.

But a collection of standalone processors will not meet all of an organization's needs; central processing facilities are still required. Some programs,

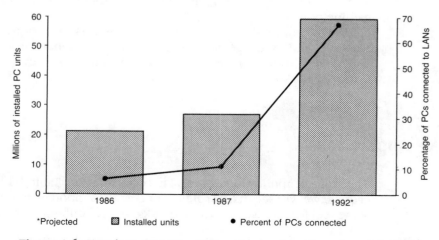

**Figure 1-6.** Trends in PC LANs. *(Source: International Data Corp., July 1988.)*

such as econometric forecasting models, are too big to run on a small computer. Corporate-wide data files, such as accounting and payroll, require a centralized facility but should be accessible to a number of users. In addition, other kinds of files, although specialized, must be shared by a number of users. Further, there are sound reasons for connecting individual intelligent workstations not only to a central facility but also to each other. Members of a project or a team need to share work and information. By far the most efficient way to do so is electronically.

Figure 1-7 is an example of a local network of personal computers for a hypothetical aerospace engineering group. The figure shows four types of users who have personal computers, each equipped with particular applications. Each type of user has electronic mail and word processing to improve the effi-

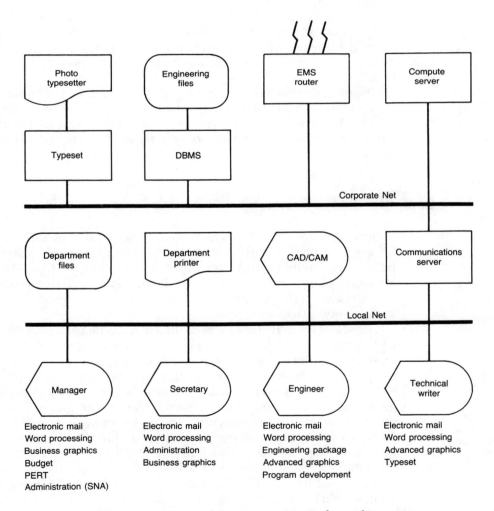

**Figure 1-7.** Personal computers in support of a working team.

ciency of creating and distributing messages, memos, and reports. Managers are also given a set of program and budget management tools. With the amount of automation that personal computers supply, the role of a secretary becomes less that of a typist and more that of an administrative assistant. Tools such as electronic calendar and graphics support become valuable for these workers. In the same fashion, engineers and technical writers can be supplied with tailored systems.

Certain expensive resources, such as a hard disk or a laser printer, can be shared by all users of the departmental local network. In addition, the network can tie into larger corporate network facilities. For example, the corporation may have a local area network in a single building and a wide-area private network. A communications server can provide controlled access to these resources.

A key requirement for the success of such a network is low cost. To attach each device to the network should cost one hundred to a few hundred dollars; otherwise, the cost of attachment will approach the cost of the attached device. Because the capacity and data rate of the network need not be high, this is a realizable goal.

Figure 1-6, which indicates the growth in the use of personal computers, also reveals the increasing interconnection of these devices on LANs. The PC LAN market is the most important segment of the overall LAN market, and we will need to examine the types of systems available to support this requirement.

## Computer Room Networks

At the other extreme from a personal computer local network is one designed for use in a computer room, containing large, expensive mainframe computers, as is typical in large data processing installations. Typically, these sites are large companies or research installations with large data processing budgets. Because of the size involved, a small difference in productivity can mean millions of dollars.

Consider a site that uses a dedicated mainframe computer. This implies a fairly large application or set of applications. As the load at the site grows, the existing mainframe may be replaced by a more powerful one, perhaps a multiprocessor system. At some sites, a single-system replacement will not be able to keep up; equipment performance growth rates will be exceeded by demand growth rates. The facility will eventually require multiple independent computers. Again, there are compelling reasons for interconnecting these systems. Because the cost of system interrupt is high, it should be possible to easily and quickly shift applications to backup systems. It must be possible to test new procedures and applications without degrading the production system. Large bulk storage files must be accessible from more than one computer. Load leveling should be possible to maximize utilization and performance.

An example of such a multiple-mainframe installation is the one at the

National Center for Atmospheric Research (NCAR), shown in Figure 1-8. The atmospheric research and analysis performed at the NCAR facility entails the storage of massive amounts of data and the use of huge number-crunching simulation and analysis programs. There is also an extensive on-site graphics facility. Initially, the NCAR facility consisted of a single mainframe run in batch mode. When it became clear that additional batch machines were needed, NCAR investigated the requirements for a new configuration that could meet their needs. The result was four objectives:

- Provide front-end processors to remove job and file preparation tasks from the batch computers
- Provide an efficient method for interactive processing
- Design a system architecture that would allow different services for special needs and purposes
- Provide a system that would allow configuration flexibility without excessive modification to existing resources

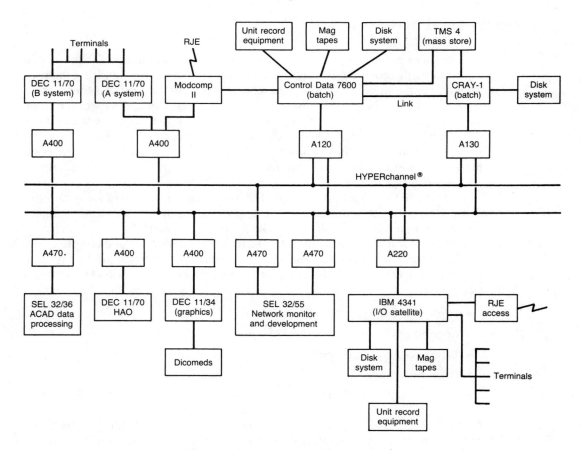

**Figure 1-8.** A computer room network.

The result of this study was a plan that called for the procurement of front-end processors, special-purpose computers, and bulk storage systems. A network was needed that met two requirements:

- Easy addition and removal of equipment
- High sustained data transfer speeds

These requirements were met with a high-speed LAN product, HYPER-channel.

Some key requirements for computer room networks are the opposite of those for personal computer local networks. High data rates are required to keep up with the work, which typically involves the transfer of large blocks of data. The electronics for achieving high speeds are expensive, costing tens of thousands of dollars per attachment. Fortunately, given the much higher cost of the attached devices, such costs are reasonable.

## Factory Local Networks

The factory environment is becoming increasingly dominated by automated equipment: programmable controllers, automated materials-handling devices, time and attendance stations, machine vision devices, and various forms of robots. To manage the production or manufacturing process, it is essential to tie this equipment together. Indeed, the very nature of the equipment facilitates this. Microprocessor devices have the potential to collect information from the shop floor and accept commands. With the proper use of information and commands, we can improve the manufacturing process and provide detailed machine control.

The more that a factory is automated, the greater is the need for communications. Only by interconnecting all the devices and by providing mechanisms for their cooperation can the automated factory be made to work effectively. The means for interconnection is the factory local network. An example of the kind of distributed environment supported by such a network can be found in Case Study 1 (at the end of this chapter). Key characteristics of a factory local network are

- High capacity
- Capability to handle a variety of data traffic
- Large geographic extent
- High reliability
- Capability to specify and control transmission delays

Factory local networks are a niche market requiring, in general, more flexible and reliable local networks than are found in the typical office environment.

## Integrated Voice and Data Local Network

In virtually all offices today, the telephone system is separate from any local network used to interconnect data processing devices. With the advent of digital voice technology, the capability now exists to integrate the telephone switching system of a building with the data processing equipment, providing a single local network for both.

Such integrated voice and data networks might simplify network management and control. They would also provide the required networking for the kinds of integrated voice and data devices expected in the future. An example is an executive voice and data workstation that provides verbal message storage, voice annotation of text, and automated dialing.

# A Local Area Network Strategy

## Information Distribution

In determining the requirements for local networking, it is important to examine expected traffic patterns. Figure 1-9 illustrates the distribution of nonvoice information that has been consistently reported in a number of studies. About half of the information generated in a small unit of an organization (such as a department) remains in that unit. Typically, only summary information or consolidated data is disseminated beyond the basic unit of an organization. Another 25 percent is normally shared with peer departments in a somewhat larger grouping (e.g., a division) and the immediate superior of the department. In a typical office layout, this would translate to a radius of about 600 feet. Another 15 percent goes elsewhere in the organization, such as to other departments in other divisions, central staff organizations, and top management. Finally, only about 10 percent of the total generated information is distributed beyond the confines of a single building or cluster of buildings. Example destinations include remote corporate headquarters, customers, suppliers, and government agencies.

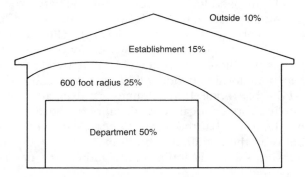

**Figure 1-9.** Information distribution.

This pattern of information communications suggests that a single LAN might not be the most cost-effective means of linking all the equipment in an organization. Before suggesting a way of designing a LAN strategy to meet these information distribution requirements, let us consider another way of looking at the requirement.

## Tiered Local Area Networks

Consider the kinds of data processing equipment supported in a typical organization. In rough terms, we can group this equipment into three categories:

- *Personal computers and terminals*: The workhorse in most office environments is the microcomputer, including personal computers and workstations. Terminals are also found when shared systems are in an organization. Most of this equipment is at the departmental level, used by individual professionals and secretarial personnel. When used for network applications, the generated load tends to be modest.
- *Minicomputers*: Minicomputers may function as servers in a department or be shared by users in a number of departments. In many organizations, a number of commonly used applications are provided on time-shared minicomputers. Because of this shared use, these machines may generate more traffic than microcomputers.
- *Mainframes*: For large database and scientific applications, the mainframe is still the machine of choice. When the machines are networked, bulk data transfers dictate the use of a high-capacity network.

The requirements indicated by this spectrum suggest that a single local network will not be the most cost-effective solution in many cases. A single network would have to be high speed to support the aggregate demand. The cost of attachment to a local network, however, tends to increase as a function of the network data rate. Accordingly, attaching low-cost personal computers to a high-speed local network would be very expensive.

An alternative approach, which is becoming increasingly common, is to use two or three tiers of local networks (Figure 1-10). Within a department, a low-cost, low-speed local network supports a cluster of microcomputers and terminals. These departmental local networks are then lashed together with a backbone local network of higher capacity. Shared systems are also supported off this backbone. If mainframes are also part of the office equipment, a separate high-speed local network supports these devices and may be linked, as a whole, to the backbone local network to support a modest amount of traffic between the mainframes and other office equipment. We will see that local network standards and products address the need for all three types of local networks.

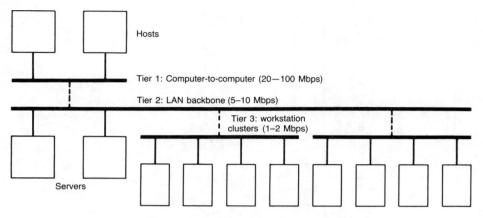

**Figure 1-10.** Tiered local networks.

## Applications and Tiers

A tiered local area network strategy fits well not only with the hardware attached to the networks but also with the applications. As the cost of an application (hardware and software) grows, we can expect that the cost of the communications facilities to support that application will also grow. However, end users are willing to pay no more than 10 to 15 percent of their system cost to obtain data communication capability; this percentage constrains the kind of local area networking solution. Fortunately, we can map application requirements into our three-tiered model easily.

Figure 1-11 shows, in general terms, the communication costs and performance requirements for various applications. At the very high end are database and scientific applications. These are generally supported on mainframes and involve the production and communication of large amounts of data. Thus, high data rates are required. Because of the cost of the system and the importance of the application, the user is willing to pay the high network costs needed to support the high data rate. Average connection costs of tens of thousands of dollars are typical for tier 1 types of LANs.

Tier 2 corresponds to resource sharing and server applications that are of general use to many users. Because of the number of users involved, moderately high data rates are needed. In addition, applications that require very expensive peripherals (for example, electrostatic plotters and large disks), need a networking solution that allows sharing of these devices at reasonable response times. Connection costs in the thousands of dollars are tolerable, and this is what is available with tier 2 types of LANs.

At the lowest end of the performance spectrum are terminal and personal computer requirements. This application category spans a wide range of performance requirements. At the low end, the data entry application can be supported effectively at very low data rates, which can be provided at low cost. At

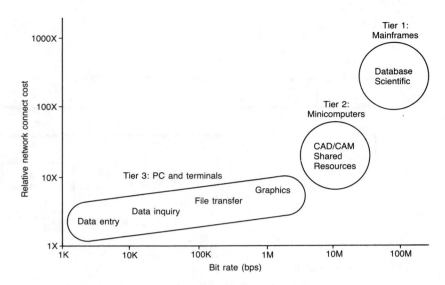

**Figure 1-11.** Office application performance spectrum.

the higher end, resource sharing and graphics requirements for personal computers require at least 1 Mbps for adequate performance. Because of the increased cost of the systems and the need for high productivity, users are willing to pay more for the increased data rate.

The wide range of personal computer and terminal data rate requirements makes the selection of tier 3 LANs challenging. You could spend too much for performance that will not be used. On the other hand, it is easy to get locked in to a LAN that cannot grow gracefully in response to increased performance requirements. We have more to say about this subject in Chapter 9, which addresses the problem of LAN selection. For now, this concept of a tiered network architecture gives us a context in which to study the various types of LAN products on the market.

## Evolution Scenario

One final aspect of tiered architecture should be mentioned: the way such a networking implementation comes about in an organization. This varies widely from one organization to the next, but two general scenarios can be defined. It is useful to be aware of these scenarios because of their implications for the selection and management of local area networks.

In the first scenario, LAN decisions are made from the bottom up, with each department making decisions in isolation. The particular application requirements of a department are well known. For example, an engineering department has very high data rate requirements to support its CAD environment, whereas the sales department has low data rate requirements for their order entry and order inquiry needs. Because the applications are well known, a decision can be made quickly on which network to purchase. Departmental budgets usually can cover the costs of these networks, so approval of a higher authority is not required. The result is that each department develops its own cluster network (tier 3). In the meantime, if this is a large organization, the central data processing organization may acquire a high-speed LAN (tier 1) to interconnect mainframes.

Over time, many departments develop their own cluster tier; each department realizes they have a need to interconnect among each other. For example, the marketing department may have to access cost information from the finance department as well as last month's order rate from sales. When cluster-to-cluster communication requirements become important, the company makes a decision to provide interconnect capability. This interconnect capability is realized through the LAN backbone (tier 2).

The advantage of this scenario is that local interconnect strategies can be responsive to the specific applications of the department and acquisition can be timely because the department manager is closest to the department's needs. But there are several disadvantages to this approach. First, there is the problem of suboptimization. If procurement is made by individual departments, rather than on a company-wide basis, the total equipment purchased might be more than is necessary to satisfy the total need. In addition, smaller-volume purchases may result in less favorable terms. Second, the company eventually will be faced with the need to interconnect all these departmental LANs. If there are a wide variety of LANs from different vendors, the interconnection problem becomes more difficult.

For these reasons, an alternative scenario is becoming increasingly common: a top-down design of a LAN strategy. In this case, the company decides to map a total local networking strategy. The decision is centralized because it impacts the entire operation or company. The advantage of this approach is built-in compatibility to interconnect the users. The difficulty with this approach is the need to be responsive and timely in meeting needs at the departmental level.

# The Growing Importance of Local Area Networks

In the previous section, we indicated that the decision-making process for buying LANs is now commonly done at a high level in the corporation to resolve compatibility and suboptimization problems. This is confirmed by a recent survey of 170 corporations and businesses (Figure 1-12). In three-quarters of the cases, the authority for LAN decisions is held at the corporate level or at least the division level. In less than a quarter of the cases, the department or work group is given the authority to procure LANs. This reflects an increasing emphasis on LANs as an organization-wide issue.

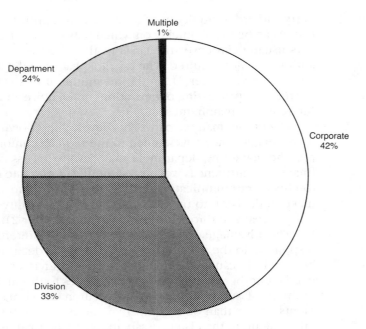

**Figure 1-12.** Authority for LAN decisions.

There are two reasons—one tangible and one intangible—for this growing awareness of LANs and the growing importance that companies place on LANs. The tangible reason is cost. As Figure 1-13 indicates, the cost of LANs has become a significant portion of the overall data communications budget. Growth in that spending is projected to be the most among users of small LANs; users of large LANs expect to keep their percentage of LAN spending steady as they increase their overall data communications budget. In any case, the budget for LANs is substantial enough to get the attention of top management.

A final chart provides a dramatic illustration of why the costs of LANs are higher than one might think and why top management is increasingly asserting its authority to plan and manage LAN strategy. Figure 1-14 shows the total life cycle cost of a low-cost personal computer LAN, the type that in former times could readily be acquired by a department manager. Notice that the actual cost of the hardware, software, and system installation is only 6% of the total cost! For effective use of the LAN, it is vital that users be trained in how to exploit the services and resources available on the LAN; such training accounts for fully 36% of the cost. If there is a unified LAN strategy so that individual departments get the same type of LAN, training can be centralized, which should reduce costs. Furthermore, when an employee moves from one department to another, retraining is not required.

Another major cost factor is the management of the system. This includes assigning user passwords, maintaining the security of the system and its resources, and making sure that the system runs properly with minimum down-

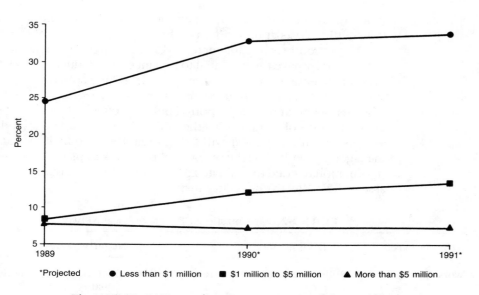

**Figure 1-13.** LAN spending as a percentage of the total data communications budget. *(Source: The Yankee Group, July 1989.)*

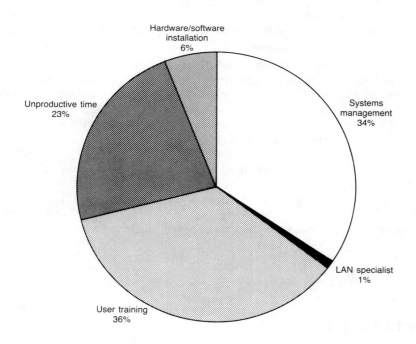

**Figure 1-14.** The real cost of installing, using, and maintaining personal computer networks. *(Source: The Ferrin Corp., January 1989.)*

time. Again, a unified LAN strategy should simplify the network management task, cutting costs and increasing effectiveness.

The second reason for increased management attention to LANs is that, although they have the potential to enhance the productivity of the work force, this enhancement is not guaranteed. Table 1-2 is a sobering report on a recent survey of LAN users. Although some noted positive effects from the installation of a LAN, a similar number reported negative effects. The conflicting and exaggerated claims of vendors plus the multiplicity of choices has led to confusion and disappointment. LANs will aid an organization only if they are chosen and managed properly. It is the purpose of this book to provide the reader with the information needed to evaluate LAN offerings before a purchase is made and to assess their effectiveness after installation.

**TABLE 1-2**   Organizational Effects of Local Networks

| Affected Area | Positive Effects | Negative Effects |
|---|---|---|
| Work quality | Wider data accessibility; fewer "lost" items | Indeterminate or mediocre data quality |
| | Wider participation in creating and reviewing work | Reduced independence and initiative |
| Productivity | Increased work load handled by more powerful office-systems equipment | Greater resources used to perform inconsequential work |
| Employee changes | Improved skill levels in current staff | Fewer jobs for marginal performers |
| | More challenging work | Less personal interaction |
| | Reduced status distinctions | Insufficient status distinctions |
| Decision-making effectiveness | Quicker availability of relevant facts | Factual component of decision making becomes too high |
| | Greater analytic capability | "Forest and trees" problem could encourage "group think" |
| | More people involved in hypothesis building and testing | |
| Organizational structure | More effective decentralization | Decentralization can get out of control |
| Costs | Overall cost reduction | Overall cost increase; soft benefits used as justification |
| Total impact | Permits the planning of new business approaches | Creates increased complexity and poorly functioning dependence relationships |

## How to Keep Up

I hope that this book will serve as both a tutorial for learning about the field of local area networks and a reference that can be returned to for help on a specific topic. With the rapid changes taking place in this field, however, no book can stand alone for very long. The reader who is truly interested in this field needs to invest time keeping up with new developments. The list of publications that could be recommended is huge, and I have resisted the temptation to overwhelm the reader with quantity. Rather, I have included a small, select list of publications that will repay the time that you devote to them.

## Business-Oriented Publications

Because of the growing importance of data communications to business, virtually all business periodicals now provide some coverage of this field. Two of the best follow.

### Forbes

*Forbes* recently inaugurated a "Computer/Communications" section that includes two or three articles plus a regular column each issue. The articles are timely, to the point, and cover a broad range. Highly recommended.

Forbes
60 Fifth Avenue
New York, NY 10011

### Business Week

*Business Week* has a regular "Information Processing" section that includes two or three articles each week. The section is oriented more toward computers than communications, but does provide coverage of the latter. In addition, the magazine sometimes has cover stories in this area that provide more in-depth discussion.

Business Week
P. O. Box 430
Hightstown, NJ 08520

## Trade and Technical Publications

The number of periodicals that cover some aspect of local networks is almost uncountable and growing. This section lists some of the most useful. With one exception, these periodicals cover data communications and networking as a whole and are not confined to LAN coverage. Nevertheless, because of the importance of LANs, the coverage provided is quite extensive even in the more general publications.

## Data Communications

If you will read only one publication in this field, make it *Data Communications*. It is by far the best. This monthly magazine provides excellent coverage of the industry, including a regular column on communication tariffs, articles on companies, statistics on communications-related stocks, and coverage of industry trends and regulatory issues. The magazine also regularly features buyers' guide articles on products and services. In addition, every month there are one or two case study articles that relate the experience of a company that has installed a distributed system or network. Usually, these articles are written by someone with the company. Finally, each month there are as many as half a dozen technical tutorial articles. These provide a discussion of a particular aspect of communications technology, standards, or applications. The articles provide considerable depth but are written in a way that is accessible to one who is not expert in the field. In summary, anyone who reads this magazine every month will soon become his or her company's resident expert.

> Data Communications
> McGraw-Hill
> 1221 Avenue of the Americas
> New York, NY 10020

## Network World

*Network World* is a weekly tabloid-size newspaper. It is an excellent source of information about the industry and communications products and services. The coverage is quite thorough and includes buyers' guides on products and services. Each week, one or more in-depth articles touch upon a single area, such as network management. The treatment is from a management rather than a technical orientation. The newspaper also provides several case studies each week. Like those of *Data Communications*, they relate the experiences of a company trying to solve a problem. They are written by reporters, and are concerned more with a management perspective than the technical details.

> Network World
> Box 9171
> 375 Cochituate Road
> Framingham, MA 01701

## LAN Magazine

*LAN Magazine,* a monthly magazine devoted to LANs, takes a practical approach to the subject. Although there are some technical articles from time to time, the magazine is more involved in explaining the features and services of various LAN products than their underlying technology. The magazine covers industry trends and provides product reviews.

LAN Magazine
P.O. Box 50047
Boulder, CO 80321

# Outline of the Book

This chapter, of course, is as an introduction to the entire book. A brief synopsis of the remaining chapters follows.

## LAN Technology

The essential technology underlying all forms of local area networks comprises topology, transmission medium, and medium access control techniques. Chapter 2 provides an overview of the first two of these elements. Three topologies are in common use: ring, bus, and tree. The most common transmission media for local networking are twisted pair (unshielded and shielded), coaxial cable (baseband and broadband), and optical fiber. These topologies and transmission media are discussed, and the most promising combinations are described. The chapter also examines the issue of wiring layout: how the cable is actually distributed in a building.

## Communications Architectures

A local area network by itself provides a means of moving data among machines, but does not provide all that is necessary for two devices to cooperate. A communications architecture that implements all the functions necessary for cooperation must be shared by the devices attached to a LAN. Chapter 3 discusses the concept of communications architecture, then examines the three that are most commonly used in LAN applications: OSI, TCP/IP, and SNA.

## LAN Standards and Configurations

The discussion of LAN technology continues in Chapter 4, which focuses on the protocols needed for stations attached to a LAN to cooperate with each other in the exchange of packets. Specifically, the chapter deals with link control and medium access control protocols. The latter include token-passing and contention-based protocols. The discussion is structured on the standards developed for LANs: IEEE 802 and FDDI. The pros and cons of the various standardized alternatives are examined.

## LAN Software

Chapter 5 looks at the most important and common types of software that provide services on a LAN. The chapter begins with a discussion of servers. The concept of server has been most commonly associated with personal computer LANs, although it can be applied to any type of LAN supporting any type of equipment. We look at the general architecture that supports the server concept, then examine some examples. Next, we look at the issue of terminal support. This is one of the more awkward problems to handle across a network, and the main approaches are examined. Finally, some distributed applications developed as part of a communications architecture are presented.

## The Internetworking Requirement: Bridges, Routers, and Gateways

The increasing use of local networks has led to an increased need to interconnect local networks with each other and with wide-area networks. Chapter 6 focuses on the three most important devices used in internetworking involving local area networks: bridges, routers, and application-level gateways. The protocols and techniques involved in each are examined in detail.

## LAN Security

The increasing reliance on communications and networks has increased the security risks. Chapter 7 examines the type of threats faced by local area network complexes. The chapter goes on to deal with tools that can enhance security. The most important of these is encryption. Next, the issue of computer and network access control is examined. Finally, the threat posed by viruses and worms is discussed.

## LAN Management

Within a given organization, the trend is toward larger, more complex LANs supporting more equipment and applications and more users. As these networks grow, two facts become painfully evident:

- The network and its associated resources and distributed applications become indispensable to the organization.

- More things can go wrong, disabling the network or a portion of the network, or degrading performance to an unacceptable level.

A large network cannot be put together and managed by human effort alone. The complexity of such a system dictates the use of automated network management tools. Chapter 8 provides an overview of a very big and complex subject: network management. Specifically, it focuses on hardware and software tools, and organized systems of such tools, that aid the human network manager in this difficult task.

## LAN Selection

The first eight chapters look at the requirements that LANs are intended to satisfy, and the various hardware and software elements available in the LAN market. The range of choices is broad, making the selection of a particular LAN or set of LANs difficult. Chapter 9 provides some guidelines to aid in the selection process. The suggestions are necessarily general because the requirements of each organization are unique. Nevertheless, it is hoped that this chapter will stimulate the decision-maker to approach the problem in a systematic and comprehensive fashion.

We begin by looking at the overall process of planning a data processing and networking installation. To make the process concrete, we concentrate on an installation whose main goal is the provision of office automation tools. The same principles should apply in other contexts. The remainder of the chapter looks at the various elements in making a selection decision.

## The Visual Revolution

In terms of requirements, technology, applications, and product implementations, the first nine chapters address what might be referred to as contemporary local area networks. Chapter 10 is oriented to future requirements for LANs, although the future has become very short-term in this context. Specifically, the technological ingredients are falling into place to allow a revolutionary shift in the form of information used by organizations. A much more substantial reliance on image (fixed) and video (moving image) forms is already taking place. By the mid-1990s, this change will transform the way information is used in organizations. This "visual revolution" has substantial implications for LANs developed in the near future.

In Chapter 10, we begin by summarizing the key technological developments that are making the visual revolution possible. We then look at image and video communications. In both cases, typical applications and the implications for communications requirements are examined. The chapter closes with some thoughts about the types of future LANs needed to support these applications.

## *Case Study 1*
## General Motors' Factory of the Future[1]

### Background: Computer-Integrated Manufacturing

As the automobile industry has become increasingly competitive, there has been an increasing use of automation. Initially, automation simply meant the replacement of human labor with machine labor for repetitive tasks. But the use of computer processors allows a far more fundamental change in the manufacturing process. Four examples follow:

- Flexible manufacturing systems
- Dynamic quality control
- Just-in-time inventory control
- Computer-aided engineering

With a *flexible manufacturing system*, the factory floor is equipped with microprocessors, programmable controllers, and robots. These not only automate much of the manufacturing and assembly process, but also permit variations in the products produced. A flexible manufacturing system allows rapid changes in production schedules, processes, and designs. When a new order arrives, it is possible to enter the order, schedule the production run, and ship the result in a short time because all the steps are automated.

*Dynamic quality control* is the control of quality through constant and automatic monitoring of the production line. Measurement and inspection are accomplished with sensors and vision systems linked to computerized monitoring equipment and machine controllers. Some faults in the production line (e.g., producing out-of-spec parts) can be analyzed and corrected automatically. Others can be signaled as an early warning to engineering or production personnel, who can diagnose the problem and communicate corrections to automated factory-floor equipment.

*Just-in-time inventory control* is used to deliver parts when they are needed and only when they are needed, thus saving on inventory costs. This approach places the burden on the manufacturing planner and scheduler at the receiving end and on the quality control and production people at the supplier end. At the receiving end, the inventory that does exist has to be tracked and correlated with production schedules. The supplier must then be told what to deliver and when to deliver it. All of this can be made more accurate and more efficient if the process relies principally on computers and communications facilities rather than on a manual approach.

As a final example, *computer-aided engineering* makes use of powerful engineering graphics workstations and specialized software. The software not

---

[1] This case study is based on material in J. Dwyer and A. Ioannou, *MAP and TOP: Advanced Manufacturing Communications*, Kogan Page Ltd., London, 1987, and M. Kaminski, "Protocols for Communicating in the Factory," *IEEE Spectrum*, April 1986.

only supports the creation of engineering design drawings, but also analyzes engineering aspects of the design, including stress tolerance and physical placement.

All of these computerized tools have contributed to increased productivity and quality in the manufacturing process. However, if each function is approached separately, resulting in so-called islands of automation, the impact is far less than it could be. In the last several years, thanks to advances in computer and communications technology, a new approach known as *computer-integrated manufacturing (CIM)* has become possible. With CIM, every aspect of the manufacturing process is affected. Engineers who produce and alter designs are linked with each other and with machines in the factory. Thus, a new design can be directly communicated from a computer-aided engineering workstation to a programmable machine tool, which automatically makes the adjustment in the production process. The ordering department is tied in so that new build orders can be sent to the shop, parts retrieved from storage, and machine tools downloaded with the proper instructions. When an order is completed, the finished products database is updated, shipping instructions are issued, inventory is updated, and parts used in the process reordered as needed.

## The DDP Structure for Computer-Integrated Manufacturing

The use of CIM in a manufacturing plant can lead to a variety of DDP structures. Figure 1-15 shows a typical layout, one that matches the approach taken by General Motors. The layout consists of a four-layer, vertically partitioned system. The top layer consists of a large computer or computer complex that controls an entire plant. This subsystem meets the needs of management and includes accounting, administration, purchasing, ordering, and general data processing. The subsystem at this level must be able to coordinate orders, inventory, and production cycles and send instructions to and receive status information from the factory-floor computers at the next lower level of the DDP structure.

At the factory-floor level are smaller computers that receive data and instructions from the plant-level computers. A factory-floor computer is responsible for coordinating events among the production cells that occupy the next lower layer. A production cell is a small area of the factory that does some well-defined portion of the manufacturing process. One computer usually has several production cells under its control.

The third level contains the cell controllers. A cell may have several types of machines, including robots and programmable controllers, that perform a task such as welding or painting. Typically, a cell is controlled by one computer that sends instructions to the factory devices and directs tools in step-by-step procedures.

Finally, the fourth level consists of the machine tools, robots, and sensors that perform the manufacturing process as directed by the controlling cell computer and report status and results to the cell computer.

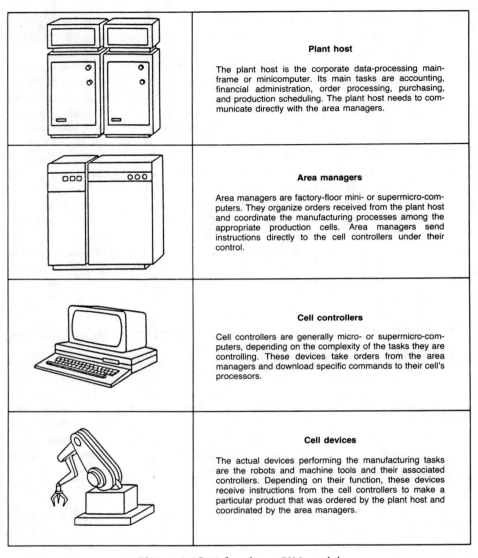

**Plant host**

The plant host is the corporate data-processing mainframe or minicomputer. Its main tasks are accounting, financial administration, order processing, purchasing, and production scheduling. The plant host needs to communicate directly with the area managers.

**Area managers**

Area managers are factory-floor mini- or supermicro-computers. They organize orders received from the plant host and coordinate the manufacturing processes among the appropriate production cells. Area managers send instructions directly to the cell controllers under their control.

**Cell controllers**

Cell controllers are generally micro- or supermicro-computers, depending on the complexity of the tasks they are controlling. These devices take orders from the area managers and download specific commands to their cell's processors.

**Cell devices**

The actual devices performing the manufacturing tasks are the robots and machine tools and their associated controllers. Depending on their function, these devices receive instructions from the cell controllers to make a particular product that was ordered by the plant host and coordinated by the area managers.

**Figure 1-15.** A four-layer CIM model.

## The Steering Gear Division Plant

General Motors (GM) has been one of the most aggressive American manufacturing companies in pursuing computer-integrated manufacturing and in defining communications standards to link computers and microprocessors from a variety of vendors. As a first step in the development of a full-blown CIM system, GM has implemented a pilot study at its Vanguard Steering Gear Division plant in Saginaw, Michigan.

The CIM implementation controls forty manufacturing cells containing sixty robots and a number of other automated machines in a 70,000-square-foot plant. The plant makes three components for a front-wheel drive axle and assembles them with about twenty components manufactured elsewhere into a finished axle. Other GM plants manufacture the same axle without benefit of CIM. Thus, GM can make direct comparisons of the cost, quality, delivery time, and reliability between products made conventionally and products made by automated manufacturing. The system is linked to production control and computer-aided design systems. The factory can make axles in a variety of sizes and with a batch size of 2. That is, the production process can be defined to fill an order of as little as two axles with no loss of productivity.

Briefly, the manufacturing process can be described as follows. In the fabrication process, robots change clamps that hold a tool or the material being worked on, or they change the end effector of a clamp. Tools are moved by automatically guided vehicles, which also remove and replace the bins that collect the shavings from the use of cutting tools. Software-driven, in-process gauging is used extensively. As a robot loads a tool into the machine, the tool is probed so that the robot knows how far to load it into the machine and the controller knows where the cutting point of the tool is. This information is used to amass cumulative information for quality control as well as to modify the controller software.

The fabricated parts plus parts supplied by other plants are assembled by robots equipped with vision systems. The parts to be assembled are all collected at one end of the assembly area and conveyed to the appropriate assembly cells by a gantry-mounted robot. The robot receives information about the locations for collection and delivery by a transponder on the pallets going through the assembly process.

## The DDP Configuration

To support the manufacturing process just described, a variety of computers and microprocessors must be interconnected in a DDP system. The overall layout is shown in Figure 1-16.

The device control systems are a variety of programmable controllers and robots from a number of different manufacturers. At the current state in the development of CIM systems, no attempt was made to define a standardized interface to these devices; rather, off-the-shelf microprocessor-based equipment was purchased. The cell control computers are from a small San Francisco-based startup called Maxitron. The Maxitron controllers are microprocessors that can be easily programmed to handle a variety of device controller interfaces and to provide a standardized interface to factory-control computers. Factory control is provided by a Stratus microcomputer, a fault-tolerant system. That is, the system is designed so that it continues to function properly despite faults and failures in

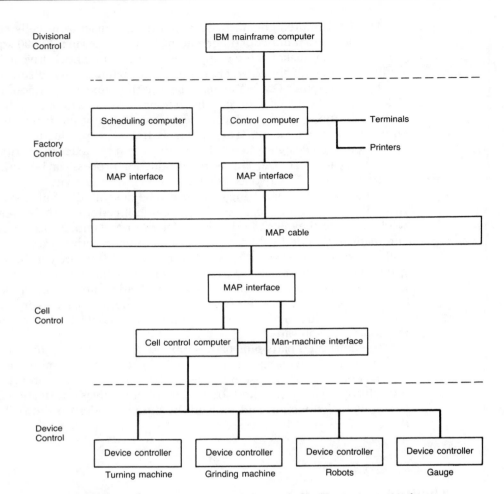

**Figure 1-16.** General Motors' Vanguard plant in Saginaw, Michigan.

some of its components[2]. The control computer is linked to another Stratus computer which runs custom materials requirements-planning software. The factory-level computers are linked to each other and to the cell control computers by a network referred to as a MAP network[3].

The top level of the DDP system is an IBM 3084 mainframe computer, which contains production planning and design data. The interaction between this computer and the factory computers is limited. But as more applications are introduced into the CIM process, the IBM machine will provide more information to and exert more control over the factory-level computers.

---

[2] The architecture of the Stratus fault-tolerant computer is described in William Stallings, *Computer Organization and Architecture, Second Edition*, Macmillan, 1990.
[3] The network is a broadband coaxial cable local area network. This type of network is ideally suited to the factory environment. Such networks are discussed in Chapter 2.

## Discussion

To achieve the desired gains in productivity and quality, GM has seen that it is not enough to automate various portions of an automotive manufacturing plant. What is required is a distributed system of computers and microprocessor-controlled devices with the communications facility needed to allow them to work together.

The DDP organization was selected based on the nature of the function to be performed. The management of a computer-integrated manufacturing installation lends itself naturally to a vertical partitioning of application processes. Each level of the DDP system is concerned with only one level of the task at hand. Thus, the factory-control computer controls the production process in terms of the movement of material and the scheduling of activities. However, it need not be concerned with the details of how individual robots and programmable controllers are directed and monitored. The application at each level is of limited scope, which makes the design, implementation, and modification of the software more manageable.

Although it is clear from Figure 1-16 that the application is vertically distributed, the data is also distributed. A partitioned, rather than replicated, database is used. Links are needed between data stored at the various levels, but by and large, data needed locally can be stored locally.

The type of communications and networking facilities that GM uses to tie together all this equipment is suggested in Figure 1-16. Between the plant and factory levels, a direct link is used between the IBM mainframe and the Stratus control computer. This limited interconnection reflects the current state of the CIM implementation. Many features that we might expect to see with CIM, such as direct ties from computer-aided engineering to factory control, have not yet been implemented in this pilot project. Going down to the next level, a more complex solution is needed. The factory-control computer must interact with the scheduling computer and with a number of cell control computers. Rather than a variety of direct links between each possible communicating device, it makes more sense to use a network to which all devices attach. The network provides the communications service of transferring data between any two attached devices on request of one of those devices.

At this point in the book, we cannot go into technical detail concerning the network used to tie together the computers for factory control and cell control. We can, however, address the issue of the networking requirements imposed by GM's configuration. A good summary of these requirements is presented in Table 1-3. This statement of requirements is from a standard called PROWAY (process data highway), which specifies a network used in the factory- and process-control environment. The standard was developed by the Instrument Society of America and is endorsed by GM. Perhaps the most important requirements from the point of view of the Saginaw application are

- *Availability*: The entire operation of the factory depends on continuous communications among the distributed systems. Loss of the communication network means that the fabrication and assembly processes must be shut down.

- *Real-time response*: Timing is critical to the correct operation of the factory. Thus, the network must have sufficient capacity to support the rapid exchange of messages and must adopt a priority policy to allow more critical messages to preempt less critical ones on the network.

- *Ruggedness*: The network must operate effectively in an environment that is electromagnetically noisy and harsh in terms of temperature, airborne dust, and other environmental stresses.

These requirements determine the networking technologies that are most appropriate for the GM Saginaw application. We will elaborate on these technologies in Chapter 2.

---

**TABLE 1-3**  Proway Requirements

**Application Characteristics**

The characteristics of the data highway should be such that they provide optimum features for use in industrial control systems and shall be applicable to both continuous and discrete processes. An industrial data highway is characterized by the following:

a. Event driven communication that allows real-time response to events.
b. Very high availability.
c. Very high data integrity.
d. Proper operation in the presence of electromagnetic interference and differences in earth potentials.
e. Dedicated intraplant transmission lines.

**Economic versus Technical Factors**

To achieve broad applicability, it is essential that industrial data highways should be economically viable in control systems under the following conditions:

a. With low or high information transfer rate requirements.
b. Within a control room and/or while exposed to the plant environment.
c. In geographically small or large process plants.

The economic and technical factors may need to be reconciled to achieve a balance of transmission line length versus data signaling rate.

---

## Future Directions

The networking facilities introduced by General Motors at Saginaw, at present, provide support for their factory CIM operations. GM plans to extend the use of the network to support additional communication functions. The Saginaw plant will serve as a pilot test for application in other GM plants. Following are some key requirements that will be addressed:

- Work force involvement has proven to be a valuable tool in GM's quality-

and cost-improvement effort. In an attempt to provide facts about the state of the business, employees will be told GM's competitive position in relation to quality and costs. This information will be communicated by video setups at numerous locations in the plant complex.

- An indirect effect on manufacturing costs has been an escalating cost of utilities. To control this area, GM will measure usage of water, gas, pressurized air, steam, electricity, and other resources using sensors that communicate with a computer facility that monitors values and makes alterations by communicating with programmable controllers and effectors.

- To protect its large investment in facilities, GM will use closed-circuit TV surveillance and computerized monitoring systems to warn of fires and other dangers.

- Accounting, personnel, material and inventory control, warranty, and other systems use large mainframe computers with remote terminals located throughout the manufacturing facility. This facility will be integrated onto the same network that supports the manufacturing operation.

# Summary

A local area network (LAN) is a communication facility that interconnects data transmitting and receiving devices in a small area, such as a single building or a cluster of buildings. The network itself is a shared transmission medium that allows any device on the LAN to transmit to any other device on the LAN. Data rates can be from 1 Mbps to 100 Mbps.

LANs meet critical communication needs in organizations. First, a LAN serves as a means of wire replacement; a maze of wire used to interconnect individual devices can be replaced with a simplified and unified wiring scheme. LANs are also needed to support distributed processing and computer networking.

# Chapter 2

# LAN Technology

T HE KEY ELEMENTS OF A LOCAL AREA NETWORK ARE

- Topology: bus or ring
- Transmission medium: twisted pair, coaxial cable, or optical fiber
- Layout: linear or star
- Medium access control technique: CSMA/CD or token-passing

Together, these elements determine not only the cost and capacity of the LAN, but also the type of data that can be transmitted, the speed and efficiency of communications, and even the kinds of applications that can be supported. Table 2-1 provides an overview of these elements.

This chapter surveys the major technologies in use in the first three categories. It will be seen that there is an interdependence among the choices in different categories. Accordingly, a discussion of pros and cons relative to specific applications is best done by looking at preferred combinations. This, in turn, is best done in the context of standards, which is a subject of Chapter 4. The final category, medium access control technique, is also briefly raised in this chapter, and pursued in greater depth in Chapter 4.

## Topologies

In the context of a communications network, the term *topology* refers to the way in which the end points, or stations, attached to the network are interconnected. The common topologies for LANs are bus, tree, and ring (Figure 2-1). The bus is a special case of the tree, with only one trunk and no branches.

**TABLE 2-1**   LAN Technology Elements

| Element | Options | Restrictions | Comments |
|---|---|---|---|
| Topology | Bus | Not with optical fiber | No active elements |
| | Ring | Not CSMA/CD or broadband | Supports fiber; high availability with star wiring |
| Transmission medium | Unshielded twisted pair | — | Inexpensive; prewired; noise vulnerability |
| | Shielded twisted pair | — | Relatively inexpensive |
| | Baseband coaxial cable | — | — |
| | Broadband coaxial cable | Not with ring | High capacity; multiple channels; rugged |
| | Optical fiber | Not with bus | Very high capacity; security |
| Layout | Linear | — | Minimal cable |
| | Star | Best limited to twisted pair | Ease of wiring; availability |
| Medium access control | CSMA/CD | Bus, not good for broadband or optical fiber | Simple |
| | Token passing | Bus or ring, best for broadband | High throughput, deterministic |

## Bus and Tree Topologies

With the *bus topology,* the communications network is simply a linear run of cable, called a bus. All stations attach directly to the bus through appropriate hardware interfacing called a tap. Full-duplex operation between the station and the tap allows data to be transmitted on the bus and received from the bus. A transmission from any station travels the length of the medium in both directions and can be received by all other stations. At each end of the bus, a terminator absorbs any signal, removing it from the bus.

Two problems present themselves in this arrangement. First, because a transmission from one station can be received by all other stations, there needs to be some way of indicating for whom the transmission is intended. Second, a mechanism is needed to regulate transmission. If two stations on the bus attempt to transmit at the same time, their signals will overlap and become gar-

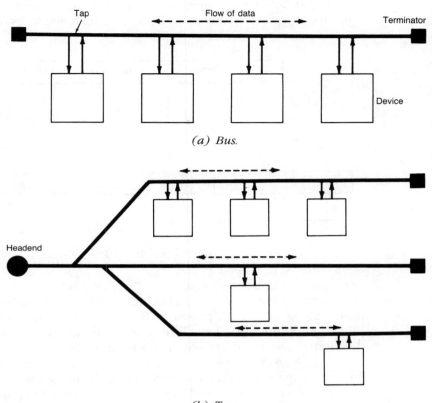

*(a) Bus.*

*(b) Tree.*

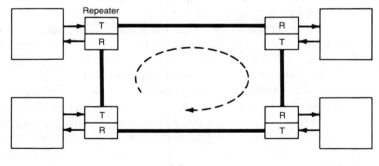

*(c) Ring.*

**Figure 2-1** LAN topologies.

bled. Or, if one station decides to transmit continuously for a long period of time, other stations cannot transmit.

To solve these problems, stations are required to transmit data in small blocks, known as *packets*. Each packet consists of a portion of the data that a station wants to transmit, plus a packet header that contains control information (Figure 2-2). Each station on the bus is assigned a unique address, or identifier; the destination address for a packet is included in its header.

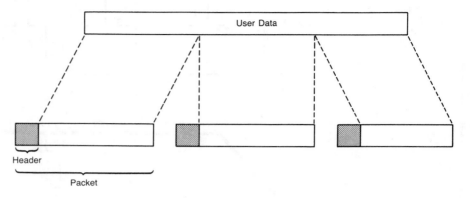

**Figure 2-2** The use of packets.

Figure 2-3 illustrates the scheme. In this example, station C wants to transmit a packet of data to A. The packet header includes A's address. As the packet travels along the bus, it passes B. B observes the address and ignores the packet. A, on the other hand, sees that the packet is addressed to itself and therefore copies the data from the packet as it goes by.

So the packet structure solves the first problem: It provides a mechanism for indicating the intended recipient of data. It also provides the basic tool for solving the second problem, the regulation of access. In particular, the station take turns sending packets in some cooperative fashion. This involves putting additional control information into the packet header. We defer a discussion of this regulation until Chapter 4.

The *tree topology* is a generalization of the bus topology. The transmission medium is a branching cable with no closed loops. The tree layout begins at a point known as the *beadend.* One or more cables start at the headend, and each of these may have branches. The branches in turn may have additional branches, resulting in complex layouts. Again, a transmission from any station travels throughout the medium and can be received by all other stations.

As with the bus, packet transmission is typically used for communication. A station wanting to transmit breaks its message into packets and sends these one at a time. For each packet that a station wants to transmit, it waits for its next turn, then transmits the packet. The intended destination station recognizes its address as the packets go by and copies them.

With the bus or tree, no special action needs to be taken to remove packets from the medium. When a signal reaches the end of the medium, it is absorbed by the terminator.

One difficulty with a bus or tree topology, but not with a ring topology, has to do with signal balancing. When two stations exchange data over a link, the signal strength of the transmitter must be adjusted to be within certain limits.

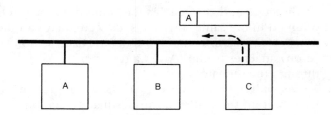

*(a) C transmits packet addressed to A.*

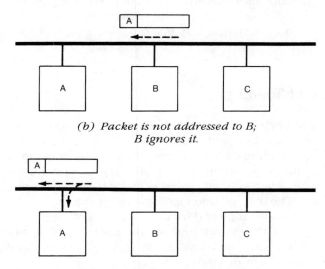

*(b) Packet is not addressed to B;
B ignores it.*

*(c) A copies packet as it goes by.*

**Figure 2-3** Packet transmission on a bus.

The signal must be strong enough so that, after attenuation across the medium, it meets the receiver's minimum signal strength requirements. It must also be strong enough to maintain an adequate signal-to-noise ratio. On the other hand, the signal must not be so strong that it overloads the circuitry of the transmitter, which distorts the signal. Although signal balancing is easily done for a point-to-point link, it is no easy task for a multipoint line. If any station can transmit to any other station, the signal balancing must be performed for all possible combinations of transmitter and receiver. This limits the size of the network.

## Ring Topology

In the *ring topology,* the LAN consists of a set of repeaters joined by point-to-point links in a closed loop. The repeater is a comparatively simple device, capable of receiving data on one link and transmitting it, bit by bit, on the other link as fast as it is received, with no buffering at the repeater. The links are unidirectional; that is, data is transmitted in one direction only and all data is oriented in the same way. Thus, data circulates around the ring in one direction (clockwise or counterclockwise). Each station (computer, terminal, and so on) attaches to the LAN at a repeater, and can transmit data onto the LAN through the repeater.

As with the bus and tree, data is transmitted in packets. As a packet circulates past all the stations, the destination station recognizes its address and copies the packet into a local buffer as it goes by. The packet continues to circulate until it returns to the source station, where it is removed (Figure 2-4).

Because multiple stations share the ring, control is needed to determine when each station may insert packets. Again, this topic is explored in Chapter 4.

## Choice of Topology

The choice of topology depends on a variety of factors, including reliability, expandability, and performance. Because this choice is part of the overall task of designing a LAN, it cannot be made in isolation, independent of the choice of transmission medium, wiring layout, and access control technique. However, a few general remarks can be made at this point.

The bus and tree topologies appear to be the most flexible. They can handle a wide range of devices, in terms of number of devices, data rates, and data types. The tree topology has the advantage that it is relatively easy to lay out, regardless of the physical configuration of the building and the location of wiring ducts or other cable pathways. Any time an intersection is reached, the cable can simply be branched in all desired directions. The ring topology is somewhat more awkward to lay out than a bus because a closed loop is required. Also, there is a concern about reliability: The failure of any one repeater disables the entire network. In later chapters, we will examine various techniques for minimizing this reliability problem.

# Transmission Media for LANs

Three forms of transmission media have been commonly used for LANs: twisted pair, coaxial cable, and optical fiber. Twisted pair uses digital signaling, and optical fiber uses analog signaling. Coaxial cable uses either digital or analog signaling; in this case, the two forms of signaling are referred to as baseband and broadband, respectively. For those unfamiliar with the various techniques used to transmit digital signals, an appendix to this chapter provides the necessary background.

In this section, we look at these three types of transmission media. The specific details of their use in LANs depends on the topology, and this topic is covered in the "LAN Configurations" section in this chapter.

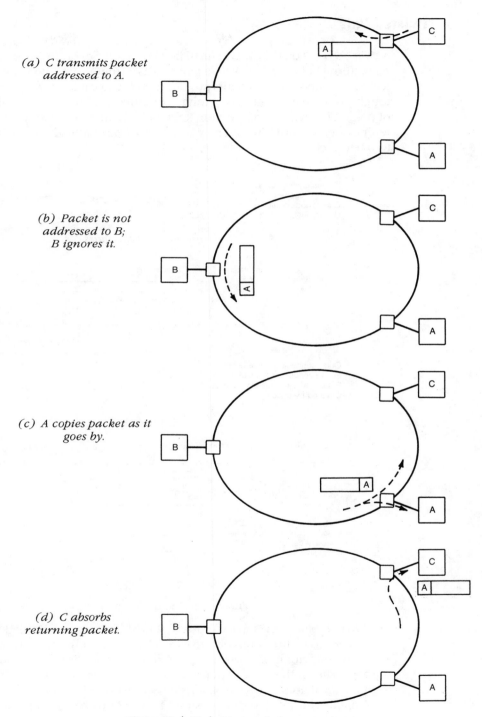

(a) C transmits packet addressed to A.

(b) Packet is not addressed to B; B ignores it.

(c) A copies packet as it goes by.

(d) C absorbs returning packet.

**Figure 2-4** Packet transmission on a ring.

# Twisted Pair

A twisted pair consists of two insulated copper wires arranged in a regular spiral pattern (Figure 2-5a). A wire pair acts as a single communications link. Typically, a number of these pairs are bundled into a cable by wrapping them in a tough protective sheath. Over longer distances, cables may contain hundreds of pairs. The twisting of the individual pairs minimizes electromagnetic interference between the parts. The wires in a pair have thicknesses of from 0.0016 to 0.036 inch.

- Separately insulated
- Twisted together
- Often bundled into cables
- Usually installed in building when built

*(a) Transmission wire pairs.*

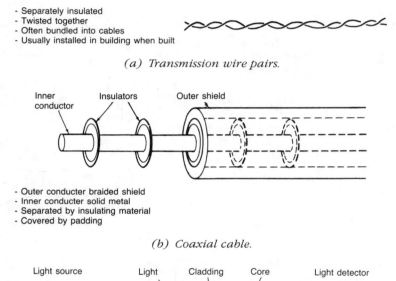

- Outer conducter braided shield
- Inner conducter solid metal
- Separated by insulating material
- Covered by padding

*(b) Coaxial cable.*

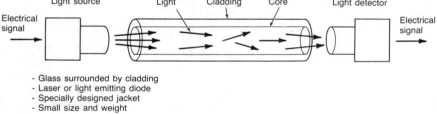

- Glass surrounded by cladding
- Laser or light emitting diode
- Specially designed jacket
- Small size and weight

*(c) Optical fiber.*

**Figure 2-5** Transmission media.

Twisted pair comes in two varieties: unshielded and shielded. *Unshielded twisted pair* is ordinary telephone wire. Office buildings, by universal practice, are prewired with more twisted pair wire than is needed for simple telephone support. This is the least expensive of all the transmission media commonly used for local area networks, and is easy to work with and easy to install.

Unshielded twisted pair is subject to external electromagnetic interference, including interference from nearby twisted pair and from noise generated in the environment. A way to improve the characteristics of this medium is to shield the twisted pair with a metallic braid or sheathing that reduces interference. This *shielded twisted pair* provides better performance at lower data rates. However, it is more expensive and more difficult to work with than unshielded twisted pair.

Digital signaling, also referred to as *baseband,* is used on both unshielded and shielded twisted pair.


## Coaxial Cable

Coaxial cable, like twisted pair, consists of two conductors, but it is constructed differently so that it can operate over a wider range of frequencies (Figure 2-5b). A hollow cylindrical conductor surrounds a single inner wire conductor, which is held in place by either regularly spaced insulating rings or a solid dielectric material. The outer conductor is covered with a jacket or shield. The diameter of a single coaxial cable is from 0.4 to about 1 inch.

For local area networks, we can classify coaxial cable into three categories, depending on the type of signaling used. A *baseband coaxial cable* uses digital signaling. The signal occupies the entire frequency spectrum of the cable; therefore, only one channel is allowed on the cable. Baseband coaxial LANs use a special-purpose 50-ohm cable, which is usually referred to as Ethernet cable because it was originally used in the Ethernet LAN.

The remaining two types of coaxial cable used for LANs are broadband and carrierband. With *broadband coaxial cable,* analog signaling is used. That is, the digital data to be transmitted on the LAN is first passed through a modem to produce an analog signal (see the appendix to this chapter). As a result, multiple signals can be on the cable at the same time, each at its own frequency band. This is the way that cable television is implemented. A single coaxial cable comes into the home of the subscriber; multiple channels, each occupying a separate frequency, are carried on the cable. The subscriber can receive any of these channels by tuning the television set attached to the cable. Similarly, with multiple data channels on a single cable, a number of devices can be attached to the cable and tuned to one of the various channels (Figure 2-6).

*Carrierband* transmission on a coaxial cable also uses a modem and analog signaling. But carrierband uses very inexpensive modems, which spill energy across the entire frequency spectrum. The result is that carrierband, like baseband, allows the use of only a single data channel on the cable.

Both broadband and carrierband use standard cable television cable. The various types of this cable are discussed later in this chapter.

Coaxial cable, like shielded twisted pair, provides good immunity from electromagnetic interference. Coaxial cable is more expensive than shielded twisted pair, but provides greater capacity.

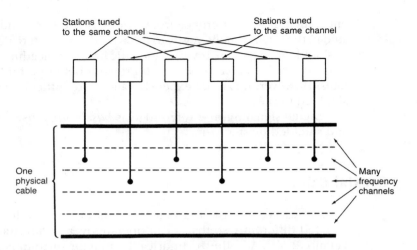

**Figure 2-6** The use of multiple data channels on a broadband LAN.

## Optical Fiber

An optical fiber is a thin (2 to 125 micrometers), flexible medium capable of conducting an optical ray. Various glasses and plastics can be used to make optical fibers. The lowest losses have been obtained using fibers of ultrapure fused silica, but ultrapure fiber is difficult to manufacture. Higher loss multicomponent glass fibers are more economical and still provide good performance. Plastic fiber is even less costly and can be used for short-haul links, for which moderately high losses are acceptable.

An optical fiber cable has a cylindrical shape and consists of three concentric sections: the core, the cladding, and the jacket (Figure 2-5c). The *core* is the innermost section and consists of one or more very thin strands, or fibers, made of glass or plastic. Each fiber is surrounded by its own *cladding*, a glass or plastic coating with optical properties different from those of the core. The outermost layer, surrounding one or a bundle of cladded fibers, is the *jacket*. The jacket is composed of plastic and other material layered to protect against moisture, abrasion, crushing, and other environmental dangers.

One of the most significant technological breakthroughs in information transmission has been the development of practical fiber optic communications systems. Optical fiber already enjoys considerable use in long-distance telecommunications, and its use in military applications is growing. The continuing improvements in performance and decline in prices, together with the inherent advantages of optical fiber, have made it increasingly attractive for local area networking. The following characteristics distinguish optical fiber from twisted pair or coaxial cable:

- *Greater capacity:* The potential bandwidth, and hence data rate, of optical fiber is immense; data rates of 2 Gbps over tens of kilometers have been demonstrated. Compare this to the practical maximum of hundreds of Mbps over about 1 kilometer for coaxial cable and just a few Mbps over 1 kilometer for twisted pair.

- *Smaller size and lighter weight:* Optical fibers are considerably thinner than coaxial cable or bundled twisted pair cable—at least an order of magnitude thinner for comparable information transmission capacity. For cramped conduits in buildings and underground along public rights-of-way, the advantage of small size is considerable. The corresponding reduction in weight reduces structural support requirements.

- *Lower attenuation:* Attenuation is significantly lower for optical fiber than for coaxial cable or twisted pair and is constant over a wide range.

- *Electromagnetic isolation:* Optical fiber systems are not affected by external electromagnetic fields. Thus, the system is not vulnerable to interference, impulse noise, or crosstalk. By the same token, fibers do not radiate energy, causing little interference with other equipment and providing a high degree of security from eavesdropping. In addition, fiber is inherently difficult to tap.

Optical fiber systems operate in the range of about $10^{14}$ to $10^{15}$ hertz; this covers portions of the infrared and visible spectrums. Figure 2-7 shows the principle of optical fiber transmission. Light from a source enters the cylindrical glass or plastic core. Rays at shallow angles are reflected and propagated along the fiber; other rays are absorbed by the surrounding material. This form of propagation is called *multimode,* which refers to the variety of angles that will reflect. When the fiber core radius is reduced, fewer angles will reflect. By reducing the radius of the core to the order of a wavelength, only a single angle, or mode, can pass: the axial ray.

*Single-mode* propagation provides superior performance for the following reason. With multimode transmission, multiple propagation paths exist, each with a different path length and hence a different time to traverse the fiber. This causes signal elements to spread in time, which limits the rate at which data can be accurately received. Because single-mode transmission has a single transmission path, such distortion cannot occur.

Finally, by varying the index of refraction of the core, a third type of transmission, known as *multimode graded index,* is possible. This type is intermediate between the other two in characteristics. The variable refraction focuses the rays more efficiently than ordinary multimode. (Multimode is also known as multimode step index.) Table 2-2 compares the three fiber transmission modes.

Two different types of light sources are used in fiber optic systems: the light-emitting diode (LED) and the injection laser diode (ILD). Both are semiconductor devices that emit a beam of light when a voltage is applied. The LED is less costly, operates over a greater temperature range, and has a longer operational life. The ILD, which operates on the laser principle, is more efficient and can sustain greater data rates.

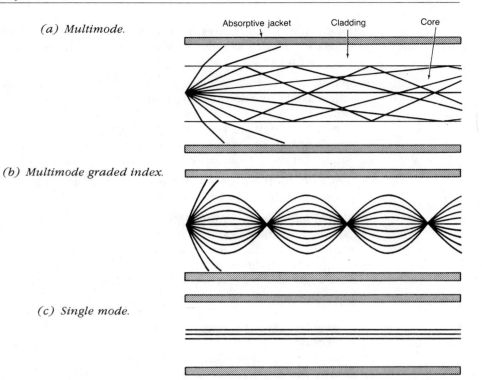

*(a) Multimode.*

Absorptive jacket    Cladding    Core

*(b) Multimode graded index.*

*(c) Single mode.*

**Figure 2-7** Optical fiber transmission.

**TABLE 2-2**    Three Types of Optical Fibers

|  | Step-Index Multimode | Graded-Index Multimode | Single Mode |
|---|---|---|---|
| Light source | LED or laser | LED or laser | Laser |
| Bandwidth | Wide (up to 200 MHz/km) | Very wide (200 MHz to 3 GHz/km) | Extremely wide (3 GHz to 50 GHz/km) |
| Splicing | Difficult | Difficult | Difficult |
| Typical application | Computer data links | Moderate-length telephone lines | Telecommunication long lines |
| Cost | Least expensive | More expensive | Most expensive |
| Core diameter (μm) | 50 to 125 | 50 to 125 | 2 to 8 |
| Cladding diameter (μm) | 125 to 440 | 125 to 440 | 15 to 60 |

There is a relationship among the wavelength used, the type of transmission, and the achievable data rate. Both single mode and multimode can support several different wavelengths of light and can use a laser or an LED light source. In optical fiber, light propagates best in three distinct wavelength "windows," centered on 850, 1300, and 1550 nanometers (nm). These are all in the infrared portion of the frequency spectrum, below the visible-light portion, which is 400 to 700 nm. Most local applications today use 850-nm LED light sources. Although this combination is relatively inexpensive, it is generally limited to data rates under 100 Mbps and distances of a few kilometers. To achieve higher data rates and longer distances, a 1300-nm LED or laser source is needed. The highest data rates and longest distances require 1500-nm laser sources.

## Choice of Transmission Medium

The choice of transmission medium is determined by a number of factors. As we shall see, it is constrained by the topology of the LAN. Other factors come into play, including:

- *Capacity:* to support the expected network traffic
- *Reliability:* to meet requirements for availability
- *Types of data supported:* tailored to the application
- *Environmental scope:* to provide service over the range of environments required

The choice is part of the overall task of designing a local network, and we will be in a better position to assess the choices in Chapter 4. In this chapter, we can make a few general observations.

Unshielded twisted pair is an inexpensive, well-understood medium. Typically, office buildings are wired to meet the anticipated telephone system demand plus a healthy margin; thus, there are no cable installation costs in the use of unshielded twisted pair. However, the data rate that can be supported is quite limited. Unshielded twisted pair is likely to be the most cost-effective for a single building, low-traffic LAN installation. An office automation system, with a preponderance of dumb terminals or intelligent workstations or both, plus a few minis, is a good example.

Shielded twisted pair and baseband coaxial cable are more expensive than unshielded twisted pair, but provide greater capacity. Broadband cable is even more expensive but provides even greater capacity. For the broad range of LAN requirements at tiers 1 and 2 (Figure 1-10), these are the media of choice. For most requirements, a system based on one of these media can meet current demand with plenty of room for expansion, at reasonable cost. Broadband coaxial cable systems excel when there are a lot of devices and a considerable amount of traffic. Examples include large data processing installations and sophisticated office automation systems, which may support facsimile machines, image-processing systems, and graphics-intensive computing.

Optical fiber has a number of attractive features—such as electromagnetic isolation, high capacity, and small size—that have attracted a great deal of interest. As yet, the market penetration of fiber LANs is low; this is primarily due to the high cost of fiber components and the lack of skilled personnel to install and maintain fiber systems.

Figure 2-8, which is based on a survey of 170 companies that currently use LANs, projects that optical fiber will rapidly become a major factor in the LAN marketplace. Fiber will have a major role in tier 1 and 2 applications, while twisted pair will provide low-cost support for tier 3 applications. The result is that the current market dominance of coaxial cable will erode.

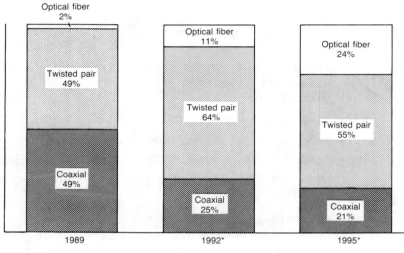

**Figure 2-8** Choice of LAN transmission medium.
*(Source: The Yankee Group, June 1989.)*

## Relationship between Medium and Topology

The choices of transmission medium and topology are not independent. Table 2-3 shows the preferred combinations. The ring topology requires point-to-point links between repeaters. Twisted-pair wire, baseband coaxial cable, and optical fiber can be used to provide the links. However, broadband coaxial cable would not work well in this topology because each repeater would have to be capable of receiving and transmitting data simultaneously on multiple channels; the expense of such devices probably could not be justified. Table 2-4 summarizes representative parameters for transmission media for commercially available ring LANs.

For the bus topology, twisted pair and both baseband and broadband coaxial cable are appropriate. At present, optical fiber cable is not feasible because

**TABLE 2-3**   Medium versus Topology for LANs

| Transmission Medium | Ring | Bus | Tree |
|---|---|---|---|
| Twisted pair | ✓ | ✓ | |
| Baseband coaxial cable | ✓ | ✓ | |
| Broadband coaxial cable | | ✓ | ✓ |
| Optical fiber | ✓ | | |

**TABLE 2-4**   Characteristics of Transmission Media for Local Networks: Ring

| Transmission Medium | Data Rate (Mbps) | Repeater Spacing (km) | Number of Repeaters |
|---|---|---|---|
| Unshielded twisted pair | 4 | 0.1 | 72 |
| Shielded twisted pair | 16 | 0.3 | 250 |
| Baseband coaxial cable | 16 | 1.0 | 250 |
| Optical fiber | 100 | 2.0 | 240 |

structing low-loss optical taps. The tree topology can be used with broadband coaxial cable because the unidirectional nature of broadband signaling allows the construction of a tree architecture. On the other hand, the bidirectional nature of baseband signaling on either twisted pair or coaxial cable is not suited to the tree topology. Again, optical fiber is presently not cost effective for the multipoint nature of the tree topology. Table 2-5 summarizes representative parameters for transmission media for commercially available bus and tree LANs.

**TABLE 2-5**   Characteristics of Transmission Media for Local Networks: Bus

| Transmission Medium | Data Rate (Mbps) | Range (km) | Number of Taps |
|---|---|---|---|
| Unshielded twisted pair | 1–2 | <2 | 10's |
| Baseband coaxial cable | 10/70 | <3/<1 | 100's/10's |
| Broadband coaxial cable | 20 per channel | <30 | 100's–1,000's |

The reader will note that the performance for a given medium is considerably better for the ring topology compared with the bus and tree topologies. In the bus and tree topologies, each station is attached to the medium by a tap, and each tap introduces attenuation and distortion to the signal as it passes by. In the ring, each station is attached to the medium by a repeater, and each repeater generates a new signal to compensate for effects of attenuation and distortion.

# Wiring Layout

One practical issue related to the selection of both medium and topology is the layout of the transmission medium in the building. To address this issue, we need to make a distinction between the abstract topology, as depicted in Figure 2-1, and the actual path that the cable follows. That path is constrained by the physical characteristics of the building. The cable must follow routes that accommodate the walls and floors of the building. Typically, predefined cable paths are used, sometimes defined by the existence of conduits. Thus, to some extent, the actual layout of the cable will be distorted relative to the intended topology.

Let us consider some requirements that dictate the layout of the installed cable. Of prime importance is the need to minimize cost while providing the required capacity. One determinant of cost, of course, is the medium itself. As mentioned, twisted pair is cheaper than coaxial cable, which is in turn cheaper than optical fiber. Often, however, installation costs, which are primarily labor costs, far exceed the cost of the materials. This is particularly true when adding new cable to existing buildings, which may present difficulties in finding pathways for new cable. In new buildings, the problems and costs can be minimized if the cable layout for a LAN can be designed ahead of time. Then the cable can be installed during construction.

A second important requirement is that the layout should accommodate equipment relocation and network growth. It is not unusual for half of the installed data terminals and personal computers in an office building to be moved each year. And, with the continuing proliferation of personal computers and other microcomputers, virtually any LAN can be expected to grow. The safest way to plan for both relocation and growth is to install a cable plant that reaches every office, or at least to install a smaller network that can be easily expanded to include additional offices with little or no disruption of the existing network. Finally, the layout should facilitate servicing and maintenance. When a fault occurs in the network, we want to locate the fault, isolate it from the rest of the network, and fix it as soon as possible.

With these requirements in mind, we can identify two general strategies for laying out the LAN transmission medium: linear and star. The *linear* strategy attempts to provide the desired topology with the minimum cable, subject to the physical constraints of the building. The medium is laid to the subscriber locations, which may be some or all offices in the building. Any of the media that have been described can be used, and bus, tree, and ring topologies can be provided.

The *star* layout strategy uses an individual cable from a concentration point to each subscriber location. This approach can be used for both the bus and ring LAN topologies, as depicted in Figure 2-9. In the bus topology, the bus is very short and resides at the concentration point; the drop cables to the attached devices are relatively long. In the ring topology, the ring is distorted so that each link of the ring loops through the concentration point. Typically, a separate layout is used on each floor of a building. The concentration point is referred to as a wiring closet; some or all offices on the floor are connected to the closet on that floor. Connections between floors are provided by linking the closets. This type of layout is invariably used to support telephones in an office building and is becoming increasingly popular for LANs.

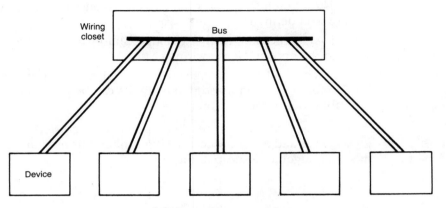

*(a) Bus using star wiring.*

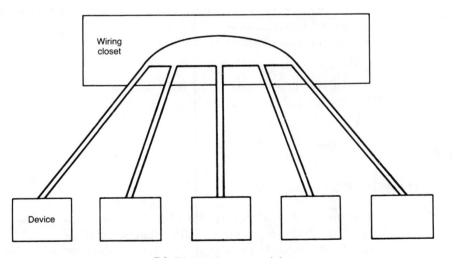

*(b) Ring using star wiring.*

**Figure 2-9** Bus and ring topologies using star wiring.

The main disadvantage of the star strategy is that it requires more cable than the linear strategy, increasing cost and cable congestion. For this reason, the star strategy is rarely used for coaxial cable and, up until recently, was also not used for expensive optical fiber. However, the star approach is well suited to twisted pair LANs, where the cost penalty is lower. Some of the advantages of the star strategy follow:

- It lends itself to prewiring of the building. The layout is a regular one and conforms to normal installation practice for telephone support in office buildings. Furthermore, most existing buildings are prewired with excess unshielded twisted pair. Thus, for LANs that use unshielded twisted pair, it may be possible to use existing wiring. Even in the case of shielded twisted pair, installation will be easier because the paths for the new cable are well defined.
- The system can be easily expanded, simply by patching additional cables into the network at the wiring closet.
- Servicing and maintenance are easier. Diagnosis of problems can be performed from centralized points. Faults can be easily isolated by patching cables out of the network.

The star strategy is increasingly popular for twisted pair LANs. With the growing use and dropping cost of optical fiber, this medium is also being used in star arrangements, despite the cost.

# LAN Configurations

Now that we have reviewed the alternatives for topologies and transmission media, we can discuss specific configurations in greater detail. The following are the most common arrangements:

- Coaxial baseband bus
- Twisted pair baseband star layout
- Broadband bus and tree
- Twisted pair ring
- Optical fiber ring

## Coaxial Baseband Bus

The principal characteristics of a baseband bus LAN are listed in Table 2-6. A baseband bus uses digital signaling; that is, the binary data to be transmitted is put on the cable as a sequence of voltage pulses, usually using Manchester or Differential Manchester encoding (see Figure 2-19). The nature of digital signals is such that the entire frequency spectrum of the cable is used. Hence, it is not possible to have multiple channels (frequency-division multiplexing) on the cable. Transmission is bidirectional; that is, a signal inserted at any point on the medium travels in both directions to the ends, where it is absorbed (Figure 2-10a).

Digital signaling requires a bus topology because digital signals, unlike analog signals, cannot be easily propagated through the branching points required for a tree topology. Baseband bus LAN systems can extend only a lim-

**TABLE 2-6**   Bus/Tree Transmission Techniques

| Baseband | Broadband |
|---|---|
| Digital signaling | Analog signaling (requires RF modem) |
| Entire bandwidth consumed by signal—no FDM | FDM possible—multiple data channels, video, audio |
| Bidirectional | Unidirectional |
| Bus topology | Bus or tree topology |
| Distance: up to a few kilometers | Distance: up to tens of kilometers |

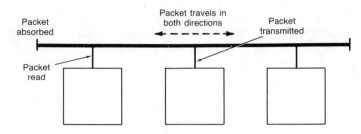

*(a) Bidirectional (baseband, single-channel broadband).*

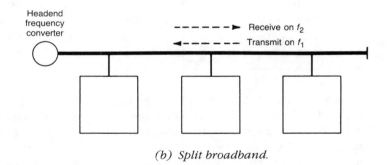

*(b) Split broadband.*

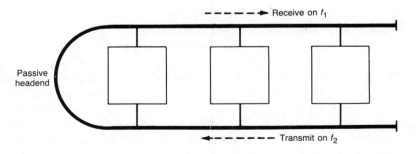

*(c) Dual cable broadband.*

**Figure 2-10** Baseband and broadband transmission techniques.

ited distance, about 1 km at most, because the attenuation of the signal, which is most pronounced at higher frequencies, blurs the pulses and weakens the signal to the extent that communication over larger distances is impractical.

The original use of baseband coaxial cable for a bus LAN was the Ethernet system, which operates at 10 Mbps. Later, a less expensive version, dubbed Cheapernet, was introduced. Table 2-7 compares some of the parameters of the two systems. As with any transmission system, there are engineering trade-offs involving data rate, cable length, number of taps, and the diameter of the cable. For example, the lower the data rate, the longer the cable can be. That statement is true for the following reason: When a signal is propagated along a transmission medium, the integrity of the signal suffers due to attenuation, noise, and other impairments. The longer the length of propagation, the greater the effect, increasing the probability of error. However, at a lower data rate, the individual pulses of a digital signal last longer and can be recovered in the presence of impairments more easily than higher rate, shorter pulses.

**TABLE 2-7**   A Comparison of Ethernet and Cheapernet

|  | **Ethernet** | **Cheapernet** |
|---|---|---|
| Data rate | 10 Mbps | 10 Mbps |
| Maximum segment length | 500 m | 200 m |
| Network span | 2500 m | 1000 m |
| Nodes per segment | 100 | 30 |
| Cable diameter | 0.4 in | 0.25 in |

In the case of Ethernet versus Cheapernet, the data rate is the same. Here the trade-off is on the basis of cable diameter. Cheapernet uses a smaller diameter cable that is lower in cost and flexible, making it easier to work with and install. On the other hand, the thinner cable suffers greater attenuation and lower noise resistance than the thicker cable. Thus, it supports fewer taps over a shorter distance.

To extend the length of the network, repeaters can be used. This device works in a somewhat different fashion than the repeater on the ring. The bus repeater is not used as a device attachment point, and it can transmit in both directions. A repeater joins two segments of cable and passes digital signals in both directions between the two segments. A repeater is transparent to the rest of the system; because it does no buffering, it does not logically isolate one segment from another. So, for example, if two stations on different segments attempt to transmit at the same time, their packets will interfere with each other (collide). To avoid multipath interference, only one path of segments and repeaters is allowed between any two stations. Figure 2-11 illustrates a multiple-segment baseband bus LAN.

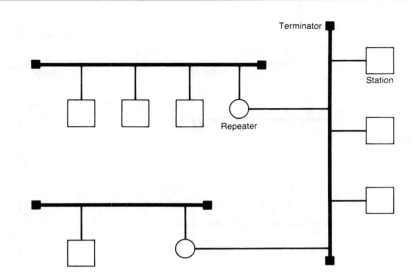

**Figure 2-11** Baseband configuration.

In the Ethernet scheme, and subsequently in the similar IEEE 802.3 standard discussed in Chapter 4, two types of repeaters are specified (Figure 2-12):

- A single repeater that directly connects two cables
- Two repeaters connected by a point-to-point inter-repeater link

On one or both sides, depending on the configuration, a repeater attaches to an Ethernet or Cheapernet coaxial cable. This attachment is the same as with an ordinary station. That is, the repeater attachment obeys the Ethernet or Cheapernet specification.

The basic function of the repeater is to accept a frame transmitted on one cable and to repeat it, bit by bit, on the other cable. If a collision is detected on either of its ports, the repeater will transmit a brief jamming signal on the other port. The jamming signal can be any pattern, beginning with 62 bits of alternating ones and zeros.

So far, the only inter-repeater link that has been specified is a fiber optic link operating at 10 Mbps. The link consists of two optical fibers, one for transmission in each direction. The characteristics of the link are as follows:

- Maximum length: 1000 meters
- Center wavelength: 790 to 860 nanometers
- Optical modulation: amplitude-shift keying

For modulation, the Manchester signal from the cable is fed directly into the optical transmitter. A high voltage is transmitted as a pulse of light; a low voltage is transmitted as the absence of light.

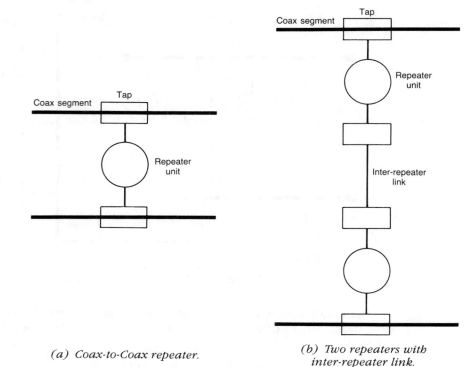

(a) Coax-to-Coax repeater.

(b) Two repeaters with
inter-repeater link.

**Figure 2-12** Repeater configurations.

## Twisted Pair Baseband Star Layout

In recent years, there has been increasing interest in the use of twisted pair as a transmission medium for LANs. From the earliest days of commercial LAN availability, twisted pair bus LANs have been popular. However, such LANs suffer in comparison with a coaxial cable LAN. First, the apparent cost advantage of twisted pair is not as great as it might seem when a linear bus layout is used. True, twisted pair cable is less expensive than coaxial cable. On the other hand, much of the cost of LAN wiring is the labor cost of installing the cable, which is no greater for coaxial cable than for twisted pair. Second, coaxial cable provides superior signal quality, and therefore can support more devices over longer distances at higher data rates than twisted pair.

The renewed interest in twisted pair, at least in the context of bus and tree type LANs, is in the use of unshielded twisted pair in a star wiring arrangement (see the discussion in "Wiring Layout"). The reason for the interest is that unshielded twisted pair is simply telephone wire, and virtually all office buildings are equipped with spare twisted pairs running from wiring closets to each office. This yields several benefits when using a LAN:

- There is essentially no installation cost with unshielded twisted pair because the wire is already there. Coaxial cable has to be pulled. In older buildings, this may be difficult because existing conduits may be crowded.

- In most office building, it is impossible to anticipate all the locations where network access will be needed. Because it is extravagantly expensive to run coaxial cable to every office, a coaxial cable based LAN will typically cover only a portion of a building. If equipment subsequently has to be moved to an office not covered by the LAN, a significant expense is involved in extending the LAN coverage. With telephone wire, this problem does not arise because all offices are covered.

The most popular approach to the use of unshielded twisted pair for a LAN is therefore a star wiring approach. In Figure 2-9, we indicated how a star wiring approach was compatible with a bus topology. In general, however, the products on the market use a scheme suggested by Figure 2-13, in which the central element of the star is an active element, referred to as the hub. Each station is connected to the hub by two twisted pairs (transmit and receive). The hub acts as a repeater: When a single station transmits, the hub repeats the signal on the outgoing line to each station.

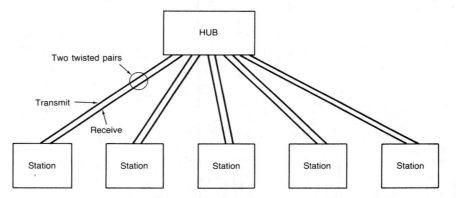

**Figure 2-13** Twisted pair, star wiring, logical bus arrangement.

Note that although this scheme is physically a star, it is logically a bus: A transmission from any one station is received by all other stations, and if two stations transmit at the same time there will be a collision.

Multiple levels of hubs can be cascaded in a hierarchical configuration. Figure 2-14 illustrates a two-level configuration. There is one *header hub* (HHUB) and one or more *intermediate hubs* (IHUB). Each hub may have a mixture of stations and other hubs attached to it from below. This layout fits well with building wiring practices. Typically, there is a wiring closet on each floor of an office building, and a hub can be placed in each one. Each hub could service the stations on its floor.

Figure 2-15 shows an abstract representation of the intermediate and header hubs. The header hub performs all the functions described previously for a single-hub configuration. In the case of an intermediate hub, any incoming signal from below is repeated upward to the next higher level. Any signal

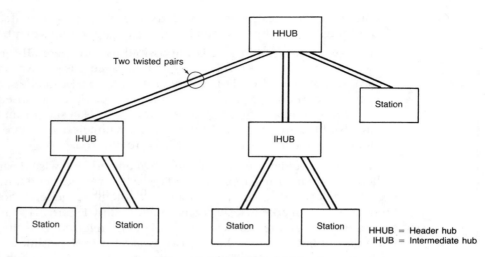

**Figure 2-14** Two-level hierarchy.

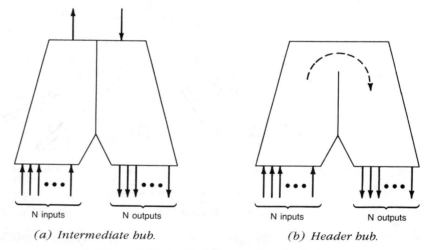

(a) Intermediate hub.    (b) Header hub.

**Figure 2-15** Intermediate and header hubs.

from above is repeated on all lower-level outgoing lines. Thus, the logical bus characteristic is retained: A transmission from any one station is received by all other stations, and if two stations transmit at the same time there will be a collision.

The initial version of this scheme used a data rate of 1 Mbps, and was dubbed StarLAN. Recently, products operating at 10 Mbps have appeared. These are compatible with the 10-Mbps baseband coaxial cable bus systems, requiring only a change of transceiver. Although there is now a fair amount of practical experience with these higher speed systems, there remains a controversy about their practicality due to several reasons:

• Existing telephone wire in buildings can be inadequate for data transmission. Problems include twisted pair that isn't twisted, splicing and other connections, and other faults that are not noticeable for voice transmission but produce very high error rates at 10 Mbps.

- Twisted pair cables are tightly packed in conduits. The mutual capacitance from adjacent pairs adversely affects attenuation, crosstalk, and velocity of propagation. The effects on data transmission may not be noticeable at 1 Mbps, but become a problem at 10 Mbps.

To some extent, these problems can be overcome by the use of signal processing techniques and by careful design of the transceiver. However, just as we saw with the 10-Mbps coaxial cable bus, there are trade-offs. In this case, both products and standards use a maximum distance between station and hub of 250 meters at 1 Mbps and 100 meters at 10 Mbps.

## Broadband Bus and Tree

Table 2-6 summarizes the key characteristics of broadband LANs. As mentioned, broadband implies the use of analog signaling. Thus, frequency-division multiplexing is possible; the frequency spectrum of the cable can be divided into channels or sections of bandwidth. Separate channels can support separate and independent data traffic, television, and radio signals. Broadband components allow splitting and joining operations; hence, both bus and tree topologies are possible. Compared to baseband, broadband can support much greater distances—tens of kilometers—because the analog signals that carry the digital data can propagate greater distances before noise and attenuation damage the data.

Unlike baseband, broadband is inherently a unidirectional signaling technique; signals on the medium can propagate in only one direction. The primary reason for this is that it is unfeasible to build amplifiers that will pass signals of one frequency in both directions. This unidirectional property means that only those stations "downstream" from a transmitting station can receive its signals. How, then, can full connectivity be achieved?

Clearly, two data paths are needed. These paths are joined at the headend (Figure 2-1b). For the bus topology, the headend is simply one end of the bus. For the tree topology, the headend is the root of a branching tree. All stations transmit on one path toward the headend (inbound). Signals arriving at the headend are then propagated along a second data path away from the headend (outbound). All stations receive on the outbound path.

Physically, two alternative configurations are used to implement the inbound and outbound paths (Figure 2-10b and c). In a *dual-cable* configuration, the inbound and outbound paths are separate cables, with the headend simply a passive connector between the two. Stations send and receive on the same frequency. In a *split* configuration, the inbound and outbound paths are different frequencies on the same cable. Bidirectional amplifiers pass lower frequencies inbound and higher frequencies outbound. The headend contains a device, known as a frequency converter, for translating inbound frequencies to outbound frequencies.

Split systems are categorized by the frequency allocation of the two paths, as shown in Table 2-8. *Subsplit,* commonly used by the cable television industry, was designed for metropolitan television distribution, with limited subscriber-to-central-office communication. It provides the easiest way to upgrade an existing one-way cable system to two-way operation. Subsplit has limited usefulness for local area networking because a bandwidth of only 25 MHz is available for two-way communication. *Midsplit* is more suitable for LANs because it provides a more equitable distribution of bandwidth. However, midsplit was developed when the practical spectrum of a CATV cable was 300 MHz, whereas a spectrum of around 400 MHz is now common. Accordingly, a *highsplit* specification has been developed to provide the maximum two-way bandwidth for a split cable configuration.

**TABLE 2-8**    Common Broadband Frequency Splits

| Format | Inbound Frequency Band | Outbound Frequency Band | Maximum Two-Way Bandwidth |
|---|---|---|---|
| Subsplit | 5 to 30 MHz | 54 to 400 MHz | 25 MHz |
| Midsplit | 5 to 115 MHz | 168 to 400 MHz | 111 MHz |
| Highsplit | 5 to 174 MHz | 232 to 400 MHz | 168 MHz |
| Dual cable | 40 to 400 MHz | 40 to 400 MHz | 360 MHz |

The differences between split and dual systems are minor. The split system is useful when a single cable plant is already installed in a building. Also, the split system is about 10 to 15 percent less expensive than a dual-cable system. On the other hand, a dual cable has over twice the capacity of a split cable, and it does not require the frequency translator at the headend.

The key components of broadband bus systems are more complex than those of baseband bus systems. These are

- Cable
- Amplifiers
- Directional couplers

Three types of cables are used in broadband networks. *Trunk cable* forms the spine of a large LAN system. Trunk cables use a semirigid construction. As the name implies, semirigid cable is not flexible. The outer portion of the cable is made of solid aluminum. The cable can be bent, but not too many times and not very easily. Trunk lines come in six sizes, ranging form 0.412 to 1 inch in diameter. The greater the diameter of the cable, the lower the attenuation. Semirigid cable has excellent noise rejection characteristics and can be used indoors and outdoors. Typically, a trunk cable will extend from a few kilometers to tens of kilometers.

*Distribution cables,* or *feeder cables,* are used for shorter distances and for branch cables. They may be semirigid or flexible, and are typically 0.4 to 0.5 inch in diameter. Whereas trunk cables may be used indoors or outdoors, feeder cables are generally limited to indoor use. The choice of cable depends on a number of criteria:

- The physical constraints of the route: smaller diameter cables are easier to install.
- The required signal level for the distribution network: larger diameter cables have less signal loss.
- Local and national building codes.

The flexible cable most commonly used for feeder cable has the designation RG-11. With a diameter of 0.405 inch, and with poorer noise resistance than semirigid cable, distance is limited to about 800 meters.

*Drop cables* connect outlets and stations to distribution cables. These are short (10 to 50 feet) and therefore need not be very large in diameter; although attenuation per unit length is greater for narrower cable, the short distance means that the total attenuation will be small even with a narrow cable. The cables are flexible and include RG-59 (0.242 inch diameter), RG-6 (0.332 inch), and RG-11 (0.405 inch) cables.

*Amplifiers* may be used on trunk and distribution cables to compensate for cable attenuation. As Figure 2-16 indicates, attenuation on a cable is an increasing function of frequency. Therefore, amplifiers must account for the variability of attenuation. For split systems, amplifiers must be bidirectional, passing and amplifying lower frequencies in one direction and higher frequencies in the other.

Directional couplers provide a means for dividing one input into two outputs and combining two inputs into one output. *Splitters,* used to branch the cable, provide roughly equal attenuation along the split branches. *Taps,* used to connect the drop cable and hence used to connect the station to the LAN, provide more attenuation to the drop cable.

## Ring LANs

For a ring to function properly, three functions are required: data insertion, data reception, and data removal. Each repeater, in addition to serving as an active element of the ring, serves as a station attachment point to perform these three functions. Corresponding to these two repeater roles are two states: the listen state and the transmit state. See Figure 2-17. In the *listen state,* each bit that is received is retransmitted with a small delay, required so that the repeater can perform necessary functions. Ideally, the delay should be on the order of one bit time. (One bit time is the time it takes for a repeater to transmit one complete bit onto the outgoing line; for example, at a data rate of 1 Mbps, the repeater delay should be about 1 microsecond.) The repeater performs the following functions:

- Scan passing bit stream for pertinent patterns. Chief among these is the address or addresses of attached stations. Another pattern, used in the token-passing control strategy explained in Chapter 4, indicates permission to transmit. Note that to perform the scanning function, the repeater must have some knowledge of packet format.

- Copy each incoming bit and send it to the attached station, while continuing to retransmit each bit. This is done for each bit of each packet addressed to this station.

- Modify a bit as it passes by. In certain control strategies, bits may be modified as part of the access control process.

When a repeater's station has data to send and when the repeater, based on the access control strategy, has permission to send, the repeater enters the *transmit state*. In this state, the repeater receives bits from the station and retransmits them on its outgoing link. During the transmission, bits may appear on the incoming ring link. Typically, these are the wrapped-around bits from the packet currently being transmitted. The repeater passes the bits back to the station. This absorption of bits continues until the entire transmitted packet is removed from the ring.

These two states, listen and transmit, are sufficient for proper ring operation. A third state, the *bypass state,* is also useful. In this state, a bypass relay is activated so that signals propagate past the repeater with no delay other than medium propagation.

Four types of media have been commonly used for ring LANs: unshielded twisted pair, shielded twisted pair, baseband coaxial, and optical fiber. As Ta-

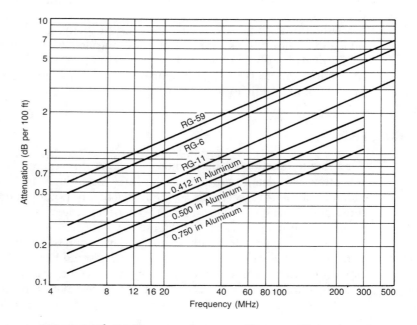

**Figure 2-16** Cable attenuation versus frequency for various sizes of coaxial cable.

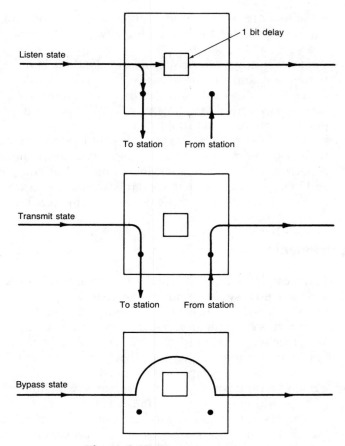

**Figure 2-17** Ring repeater states.

ble 2-4 indicates, these support increasing numbers of devices at increasing data rates, over increasing distances. Of course, the cost increases as well.

# Case Study 2
# Alcoa Technical Center[1]

## Background

Alcoa Technical Center is a research laboratory specializing in materials production, materials processing, materials science, and product development. It

---

[1] This case study is based on material in J. Jalan, "Laboratory LAN: A Network Makes Alcoa's Research Easier," *LAN Magazine,* August 1988.

is the research and development arm for the Aluminum Company of America, and is responsible for developing new technology to yield improvements in processes and materials.

Metallurgists, physicists, chemists, and mathematicians at Alcoa use computers to manipulate quantitative models that directly and indirectly suggest the processes that will yield certain desired properties. In addition, computers support applications ranging from CAD/CAM design and artificial intelligence to electronic mail and sophisticated technical library retrieval.

Engineers require access to data and video resources across a five-building, 2300-acre campus. The laboratory uses a combination of minicomputers, superminis, and mainframes, including Digital Equipment Corporation VAXs and PDP/11s and Hewlett-Packard systems. There are over 600 asynchronous terminals and about as many personal computers located at the facility.

## Requirements

In the early 1980s, the Research Center was using a mixture of hardwired lines, a digital PBX system, and multiplexers from clusters of terminals to computers. With the increased use of terminals and the increasing number of terminals, this configuration was having a negative effect on productivity. A user at a given terminal could generally access only one computer or a small number of computers. To access other computers, another terminal would be needed. When an employee changed offices (a common occurrence), that person's terminal would have to be moved with him or her. This often required tedious and expensive rewiring. Furthermore, a large number of personal computers were beginning to be acquired, and there was no clear strategy for integrating these into the existing data processing suite. Finally, there was a recognition that there would be an increasing need for the use of video.

The Research Center decided to develop a master plan for future communications support. The following key requirements were defined:

- Efficient local communications in a multivendor environment
- The capability to support a large number of users and rapid growth
- The flexibility to allow a user to disconnect at one location and plug into another location
- Enough connectivity to allow any system to talk to any other system and any terminal to talk with multiple computers or other terminals
- The capability to transmit video signals across the campus

## The Solution

The Research Center considered four alternatives:

- Digital PBX

- Baseband bus LAN
- Broadband tree LAN
- Fiber ring LAN

The digital PBX approach would provide connectivity, but the connections would be limited in speed and in the types of devices that could be hooked up. Baseband was ruled out because it couldn't support video. Fiber optics was ruled out because it could not support the approximately 1200 drops needed. Thus, early on, it was decided that a broadband LAN would best serve the center's needs.

Alcoa looked at three broadband vendors: 3M, Sytek, and TRW Information Networks Division. Because the product line of 3M emphasized factory systems rather than office systems, the Research Center thought that the 3M product line might not develop to meet evolving office needs. The Sytek product used a single-cable split system, which cut the amount of available bandwidth on the cable in half. Because the Research Center anticipated heavy video requirements, a solution that offered comparatively limited bandwidth was thought to be risky. TRW offered a dual-cable design and was thus the front-runner.

In addition to providing the necessary bandwidth, the TRW product had features that were attractive to the Research Center. TRW provided interface units, called Intelligent Connector Units (ICUs), for hooking up terminals, personal computers, and other computers. These interface units had some excellent network management tools. For example, a network manager could easily change the parameters on an interface unit from a remote location. In addition, the terminal user interface was powerful and easy to use.

Figure 2-18 shows the installed network. With broadband, it is possible to divide the total cable bandwidth into a number of independent 6-MHz channels. Currently, ten channels on the LAN are devoted to data and eight are reserved for video. The data channels are used for different functions, such as office automation and modeling. Terminal users can access any channel through the ICU to which the terminal is attached.

One video channel is used as a company billboard and six channels serve as delivery vehicles for instructional television via satellite. In addition, Alcoa uses its satellite earth stations to host technical video conferences.

## Benefits

Alcoa estimates that the LAN has saved them at least $500,000 in systems costs in fewer terminals and computers needed to service the existing user population. Also, users now enjoy a consistent interface for access to any multivendor computers located throughout the facility. Moving terminals from place to place has also become easier and more cost-effective. Now that the buildings are wired, adding more terminals or computers is a simple matter.

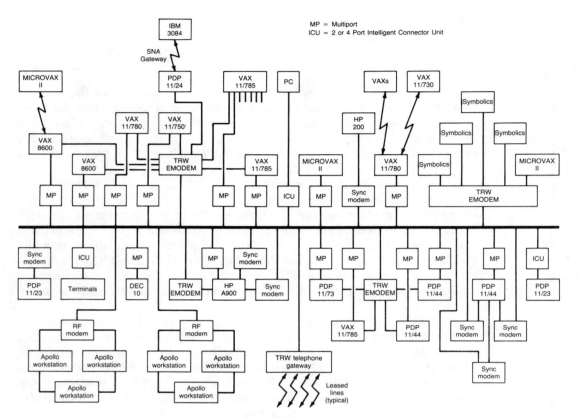

**Figure 2-18** The Alcoa LAN.

# Summary

The key elements of a local area network are topology, transmission medium, layout, and medium access control technique. This chapter has introduced the first three. The concept of medium access control and an overall assessment of various LAN configurations are presented in Chapter 4.

The topology of a network refers to the way in which the stations attached to the network are interconnected. The most popular alternatives for LANs are bus, tree, and ring. The bus topology consists of a linear run of cable to which all stations attach. A transmission from any one station can be received by all the others. To regulate this transmission, data is transmitted in packets; this same scheme is also used in tree and ring topologies. The tree topology consists of a branching cable, emanating from a headend, with no closed loops. As with the bus, a transmission from any one station is heard by all other stations. Finally, the ring topology consists of a closed loop of repeaters joined by point-to-point links. A transmission from any one station circulates around the ring; it may be read by any other station that it passes, and is removed from the ring by the sender after a complete circulation.

A number of transmission media have become popular for LANs. Unshielded twisted pair is the cheapest and has the advantage that excess cable is usually preinstalled in an office building and available for use. However, it is especially vulnerable to external electromagnetic interference, which limits the data rate that can be achieved. Shielded twisted pair provides better performance, at increased cost. Even greater capacity is available with coaxial cable. Baseband coaxial cable uses digital signaling, which allows one data channel on the cable. Broadband coaxial cable uses analog signaling, which allows multiple data channels on the cable at the same time. Finally, optical fiber is the most attractive of the transmission media for LANs. It provides excellent electromagnetic isolation, small size, and great capacity. Its introduction has been delayed primarily by its high cost, but with costs now dropping, it is rapidly becoming popular.

The layout of the transmission medium in the building is also an issue of concern. In general, two approaches are possible. The linear strategy attempts to minimize cable length by routing the cable along the shortest possible path consistent with LAN topology and the physical constraints of the building. The star strategy makes use of one or more concentration points with cable emanating to individual offices.

# Appendix 2A Digital and Analog Signaling

The principal function of local networks is the transmission of digital data. As has been discussed in this chapter, there are two general techniques for this:

- *Digital:* The digital data is transmitted as digital signals, consisting of a sequence of constant-voltage pulses. This technique is sometimes referred to as baseband, especially if the transmission medium is coaxial cable.

- *Analog:* The digital data is transmitted as an analog signal, which is a continuously varying electromagnetic wave. In the case of coaxial cable, if multiple channels are permitted, the technique is referred to as broadband; if a single channel is possible, it is referred to as carrierband.

In both these cases, some form of encoding is required. That is, the digital data (binary 1s and 0s) must be represented by signal elements that are suitable for transmission over the given medium and can be recognized by the receiver and decoded to reproduce the transmitted data. Typically, the form of the encoding is chosen to optimize the transmission in terms of cost, performance, reliability, or a combination of these. Following is a brief survey of some of the more common encoding techniques.

## Digital Signaling

The most common and easiest way to transmit digital signals is to use two different voltage levels for the two binary digits. Typically, a negative voltage is used to represent binary one and a positive voltage is used to represent binary zero (Figure 2-19a). This code is known as nonreturn-to-zero-level (NRZ-L), which means the signal never returns to zero voltage and the value during a bit time is a level voltage.

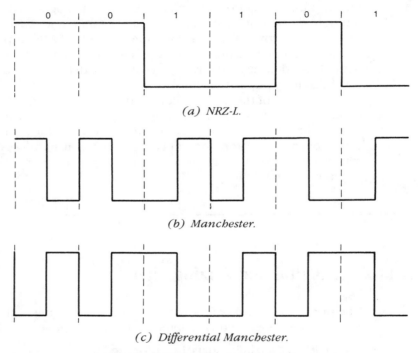

*(a) NRZ-L.*

*(b) Manchester.*

*(c) Differential Manchester.*

**Figure 2-19** Digital signal encoding.

A significant disadvantage of NRZ-L transmission is that it is difficult to determine where one bit ends and another begins. To picture the problem, consider that with a long string of ones or zeros for NRZ-L, the output is a constant voltage over a long period of time. Any drift between the timing of the transmitter and the receiver will result in the loss of synchronization between the two.

A set of alternative coding techniques, grouped under the term *biphase,* overcomes this problem. Two of these techniques, Manchester and Differential Manchester, are in common use. All biphase techniques require at least one transition per bit time and may have as many as two transitions. Thus, the maximum modulation rate is twice that for NRZ-L; this means that the required bandwidth is correspondingly greater. To compensate for this, the biphase schemes have several advantages:

- *Synchronization:* Because there is a predictable transition during each bit time, the receiver can synchronize on that transition. For this reason, the biphase codes are known as self-clocking codes.
- *Error detection:* The absence of an expected transition can be used to detect errors. Noise on the line would have to invert both the signal before and the signal after the expected transition to cause an undetected error.

In the *Manchester* code, there is a transition at the middle of each bit period. The mid-bit transition serves as a clocking mechanism and also as data. A high-to-low transition represents a 0, and a low-to-high transition represents a 1. In *Differential Manchester,* the mid-bit transition is used only to provide clocking. The encoding of a 0 is represented by the presence of a transition at the beginning of a bit period, and a 1 is represented by the absence of a transition at the beginning of a bit period.

Differential Manchester has the added advantage of using differential encoding. In differential encoding, the signal is decoded by comparing the polarity of adjacent signal elements rather than determining the absolute value of a signal element. One benefit of this scheme is that it may be more reliable to detect a transition in the presence of noise than to compare a value to a threshold. Another benefit is that with a complex transmission layout, it is easy to lose the sense of the polarity of the signal. For example, on a multipoint twisted pair line, if the leads from an attached device to the twisted pair are accidentally inverted, all ones and zeros for NRZ-L will be inverted. This cannot happen with differential encoding.

## Analog Signaling

The basis for analog encoding is a continuous constant-frequency signal known as the *carrier signal.* Digital information is encoded by means of a modem that modulates one or some combination of the three characteristics of the carrier: amplitude, frequency, or phase. Figure 2-20 illustrates the three basic forms of modulation of analog signals for digital data:

- Amplitude-shift keying
- Frequency-shift keying
- Phase-shift keying

In all these cases, the resulting signal contains a range of frequencies on both sides of the carrier frequency. This is the bandwidth of the signal.

In *amplitude-shift keying (ASK),* the two binary values are represented by two different amplitudes of the carrier frequency. In some cases, one of the amplitudes is zero. That is, one binary digit is represented by the presence, at constant amplitude, of the carrier; the other is represented by the absence of the carrier. Amplitude-shift keying is susceptible to sudden gain changes and is a rather inefficient modulation technique.

The amplitude-shift keying technique is commonly used to transmit digi-

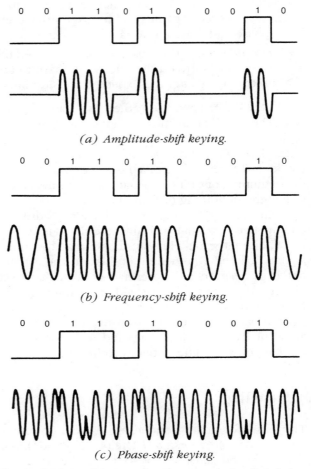

(a) Amplitude-shift keying.

(b) Frequency-shift keying.

(c) Phase-shift keying.

**Figure 2-20** Modulation of analog signals for digital data.

tal data over optical fiber. For LED transmitters, binary one is represented by a short pulse of light and binary zero by the absence of light. Laser transmitters normally have a fixed bias current that causes the device to emit a low light level. This low level represents binary zero; a higher amplitude lightwave represents another signal element.

In *frequency-shift keying (FSK),* the two binary values are represented by two different frequencies near the carrier frequency. This scheme is less susceptible to error than amplitude-shift keying. It is commonly used for high-frequency (4 to 30 MHz) radio transmission.

In *phase-shift keying,* the phase of the carrier signal is shifted to encode data. Figure 2-20c is an example of a two-phase system. In this system, a 0 is represented by sending a signal burst of the same phase as the previous signal burst sent. A 1 is represented by sending a signal burst of opposite phase to the previous one. Phase-shift keying can use more then two phase shifts. A four-phase system would encode two bits with each signal burst. The phase-shift keying technique is more noise resistant and efficient than frequency-shift keying.

Finally, the techniques just discussed may be combined. A common combination is phase-shift keying and amplitude-shift keying, where some or all of the phase shifts may occur at one or two amplitudes. These techniques are referred to as *multilevel* signaling because each signal element represents multiple bits. Note that four-phase phase-shift keying is also in this category. With multilevel signaling, we must distinguish between the data rate (the rate in bits per second that bits are transmitted) and the modulation rate, or signaling rate (the rate at which signal elements are transmitted). This latter rate is expressed in *bauds,* or signal elements per second.

# Commu...
## Archit...

$B$EFORE WE LOOK AT MEDIUM ACCESS CONTROL TECHNIQUES and LAN standards, it will be useful to place these concepts into the context of a communications architecture. It is important to note that a LAN, by itself, does not provide the capability for attached devices to cooperate. Rather, it simply provides a means for moving bits from one device to another. For two devices to cooperate, they must be using the same data formats, and their respective applications must be able to communicate. For example, it is generally not possible to transfer a word processing file from one vendor's machine to another vendor's machine and then edit the file, unless the two machines share a common communications architecture, with common protocols.

We begin this chapter by introducing a simple communications architecture consisting of just three modules, or layers. This will allow us to present the key characteristics and design features of a communications architecture without getting bogged down in details. With this background, we will be ready to examine the three most important architectures: the open systems interconnection (OSI) architecture, the TCP/IP protocol suite, and the systems network architecture (SNA). Virtually all local area network installations use one of these three architectures to integrate their various systems.

# A Simple Communications Architecture

## The Need for a Communications Architecture

When computers, terminals, and other data processing devices exchange data, the procedures involved can be complex. Consider, for example, the transfer of a file between two computers attached to a network. These are some of the typical tasks to be performed:

1. The source system must inform the network of the identity of the desired destination system.
2. The source system must determine that the destination system is prepared to receive data.
3. The file transfer application on the source system must determine that the file management program on the destination system is prepared to accept and store the file from this particular user.
4. If the file formats used on the two systems are incompatible, one of the two systems must perform a format translation function.

There must be a high degree of cooperation between the two computers. Instead of implementing the logic for this as a single module, the task is broken up into subtasks, each implemented separately. Figure 3-1 suggests a way to implement a file transfer facility. Three modules are used. A file transfer module performs tasks 3 and 4 in the preceding list. The modules on the two systems exchange files and commands. The communications service module, however, deals with the details of actually transferring data and commands. This module makes sure that the file transfer commands and data are reliably exchanged between systems. Among other things, this module would perform task 2. Now the exchange between systems is independent of the network that interconnects them. Therefore, rather than building details of the network interface into the communications service module, it makes sense to have a third module, the network access module, that performs task 1 by interacting with the network.

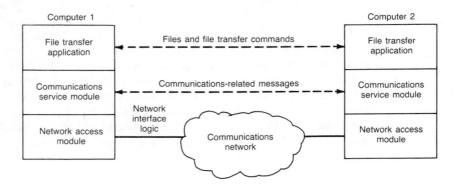

**Figure 3-1** A simplified architecture for file transfer.

Let us summarize the motivation for the three modules in Figure 3-1. The file transfer module contains all the logic that is unique to the file transfer application, such as transmitting passwords, file commands, and file records. These files and commands need to be transmitted reliably. However, the same sorts of reliability requirements are relevant to a variety of applications (e.g., electronic mail and document transfer). Therefore, these requirements are met by a separate communications service module that can be used by different applications. The communications service module makes sure that the two computer systems are active and ready for data transfer and keeps track of the data that is being exchanged to assure delivery. However, because these tasks are independent of the type of network used, the logic for actually dealing with the network is separated into a network access module. That way, if the network is changed, only the network access module is affected.

Thus, instead of a single module for performing communications, a structured set of modules implements the communications function. That structure is referred to as a *communications architecture*. In the remainder of this section, we generalize the preceding example to present a simplified communications architecture. Then we look at three more complex, real-world examples.

## A Three-Layer Model

In general terms, communication involves three agents: applications, computers, and networks. Examples of applications include file transfer and electronic mail. The applications that we are concerned with here are distributed applications involving the exchange of data between two computer systems. These applications, and others, execute on computers that can often support multiple simultaneous applications. Computers are connected to networks, and the data to be exchanged is transferred by the network from one computer to another. Thus, the transfer of data from one application to another involves getting the data to the computer in which the application resides, then getting it to the intended application in the computer.

With these concepts in mind, it appears natural to organize the communication task into three relatively independent layers:

- Network access layer
- Transport layer
- Application layer

The *network access layer* is concerned with the exchange of data between a computer and the network to which it is attached. The sending computer must provide the network with the address of the destination computer, so that the network can route the data to the appropriate destination. The sending computer may want to invoke certain services that might be provided by the network, such as priority. The software used at this layer depends on the type of network; different standards have been developed for circuit-switching, packet-switching, and local area networks, as well as others. Thus, it makes sense to separate functions having to do with network access into a separate layer. By doing this, the remainder of the communications software, above the network access layer, need not be concerned about the specifics of the network used. The same higher-layer software should function properly regardless of the particular network to which the computer is attached.

There is usually a requirement that data be exchanged reliably. We want to be assured that all the data arrives at the destination application and that the data arrives in the same order in which it was sent. As we shall see, the mechanisms for providing reliability are essentially independent of the nature of the applications. Thus, it makes sense to collect those mechanisms in a common layer shared by all applications; this is referred to as the *transport layer.*

Finally, the *application layer* contains the logic to support the various user applications. For each different type of application, such as file transfer, we need a separate, unique module.

Figures 3-2 and 3-3 illustrate this simple architecture. Figure 3-2 shows three computers connected to a network. Each computer contains software at the network access and transport layers, and software at the application layer for one or more applications. For successful communication, every entity in the overall system must have a unique address. Actually, two levels of addressing are needed. Each computer on the network must have a unique network address; this allows the network to deliver data to the proper computer. Each application on a computer must have an address that is unique within that computer; this allows the transport layer to deliver data to the proper application. These latter addresses are known as *service access points (SAPs),* connoting that each application is individually accessing the services of the transport layer.

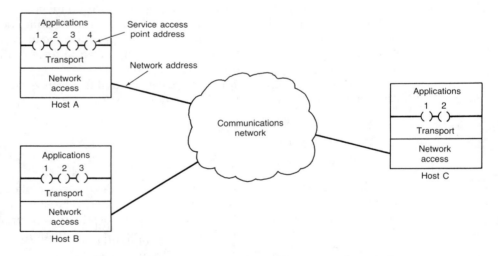

**Figure 3-2** Communications architectures and networks.

Figure 3-3 indicates the way in which modules at the same level on different computers communicate with each other: by a protocol. A protocol is the set of rules or conventions governing the way two entities cooperate to exchange data. A protocol specification details the control functions that may be performed, the formats and control codes used to communicate those functions, and the procedures that the two entities must follow.

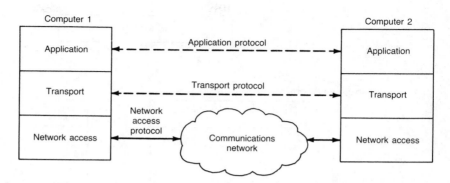

**Figure 3-3** Protocols in a simplified architecture.

Let us trace a simple operation. Suppose that an application, associated with SAP 1 at computer A, wants to send a message to another application, associated with SAP 2 at computer B. The application at A hands the message to its transport layer with instructions to send it to SAP 2 on computer B. The transport layer hands the message to the network access layer, which instructs the network to send the message to computer B. Note that the network need not be told the identity of the destination service access point. All that it needs to know is that the data is intended for computer B.

To control this operation, control information (as well as user data) must be transmitted, as suggested in Figure 3-4. Let us say that the sending application generates a block of data and passes this to the transport layer. The transport layer may break this block into two smaller pieces to make it more manageable. To each of these pieces the transport layer appends a transport header, containing protocol control information. The combination of data from the next higher layer and control information is known as a protocol data unit (PDU); in this case, it is referred to as a transport protocol data unit. The header in each transport PDU contains control information to be used by the peer transport protocol at computer B. Examples of items that may be stored in this header include:

- *Destination SAP:* When the destination transport layer receives the transport protocol data unit, it must know to whom the data will be delivered.

- *Sequence number:* Because the transport protocol sends a sequence of protocol data units, it numbers them sequentially. Then, if they arrive out of order, the destination transport entity can reorder them.

- *Error-detection code:* The sending transport entity may calculate and insert an error-detection code so that the receiver can determine if an error has occurred and discard the protocol data unit.

The next step is for the transport layer to hand each protocol data unit to the network layer, with instructions to transmit it to the destination computer. The network access protocol must present the data to the network with a request for transmission. As before, this operation requires the use of control

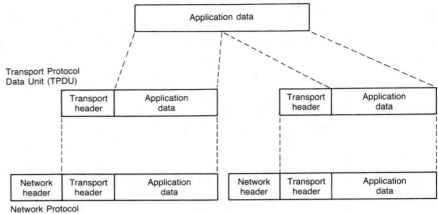

**Figure 3-4** Protocol data units.

information. In this case, the network access protocol appends a network access header to the data it receives from the transport layer, creating a network access PDU. Examples of the items that may be stored in the header include:

- *Destination computer address:* The network must know to which computer on the network the data will be delivered.
- *Facilities requests:* The network access protocol might want the network to make use of certain facilities, such as priority.

Figure 3-5 puts all these concepts together, showing the interaction between modules to transfer one block of data. Let us say that the file transfer module in computer X is transferring a file one record at a time to computer Y. Each record is handed to the transport layer module. We can picture this action as being in the form of a command or procedure call, A-SEND (application-send). The arguments of this procedure call are the destination computer address, destination service access point, and record. The transport layer appends the destination service access point and other control information to the record to create a transport PDU. This is handed down to the network access layer in a T-SEND command. In this case, the arguments for the command are the destination computer address and the transport protocol data unit. The network access layer uses this information to construct a network PDU (packet).

The network accepts the data packet from X and delivers it to Y. The network access module in Y receives the packet, strips the packet header, and transfers the enclosed transport protocol data unit to X's transport layer module. The transport layer examines the transport protocol data unit header and, on the basis of the SAP field in the header, delivers the enclosed record to the appropriate application, in this case the file transfer module in Y.

This example will repay close study. In the remainder of this chapter, we

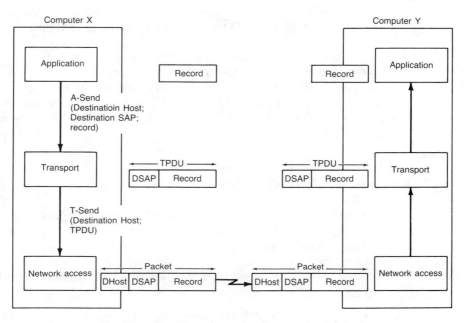

**Figure 3-5** Operation of a communications architecture.

will be looking at more complex communications architectures. However, these architectures are based on the same principles and mechanisms as those shown in this simple example.

# The OSI Architecture

## Motivation

When communication is desired among computers from different vendors, the software development effort can be a nightmare. Different vendors use different data formats and data exchange protocols. Even within one vendor's product line, different model computers may communicate in unique ways.

As the use of computer communications and computer networking proliferates, a one-at-a-time, special-purpose approach to communications software development is too costly. The only alternative is for computer vendors to adopt and implement a common set of conventions. For this to happen, international standards are needed. Such standards would have two benefits:

- Vendors would feel encouraged to implement the standards because of an expectation that the wide usage of the standards would make their products less marketable without them.

- Customers are in a position to require that the standards be implemented by any vendor wanting to propose equipment to them.

This line of reasoning led the International Standards Organization (ISO) to develop a communications architecture known as the *Open Systems Interconnection (OSI)* model. The model is a framework for defining standards for linking heterogeneous computers. The term *open* denotes the capability of any two systems that conform to the architecture and associated standards to communicate.

## The Concept of Open Systems

Open Systems Interconnection is based on the concept of cooperating distributed applications. In the OSI model, a system consists of a computer, all its software, and any peripheral devices attached to it, including terminals. A distributed application is any activity that involves the exchange of information between two open systems. Examples of such activities include the following:

- A user at a terminal on one computer is logged onto an application such as transaction processing on another computer.
- A file management program on one computer transfers a file to a file management program on another computer.
- A user sends an electronic mail message to a user on another computer.
- A process-control program sends a control signal to a robot.

OSI is concerned with the exchange of information between a pair of open systems and not with the internal functioning of each individual system. Specifically, it is concerned with the capability of systems to cooperate in the exchange of information and in the accomplishment of tasks.

The objective of the OSI effort is to define a set of standards that will enable open systems anywhere in the world to cooperate by being interconnected through some standardized communications facility and by executing standardized OSI protocols.

An open system may be implemented in any way if it conforms to a minimal set of standards that allows communication with other open systems. An open system consists of a number of applications, an operating system, and system software such as a database management system and a terminal-handling package. It also includes the communications software that turns a closed system into an open system. Different manufacturers implement open systems in different ways to achieve a product identity that will increase their market share or create a new market. To provide their customers with the ability to communicate with other open systems, however, virtually all manufacturers are now committed to providing communications software that conforms with OSI.

# The Model

A widely accepted structuring technique, and the one chosen by ISO, is layering. The communications functions are partitioned into a hierarchical set of layers. Each layer performs a related subset of the functions required to communicate with another system. It relies on the next lower layer to perform more primitive functions and to conceal the details of those functions. It provides services to the next higher layer. Ideally, the layers should be defined so that changes in one layer do not require changes in the other layers. Thus, we divide one problem into more manageable subproblems.

The task of ISO was to define a set of layers and the services performed by each layer. The partitioning should group functions logically. It also should have enough layers to make each layer manageably small, but not so many layers that the processing overhead is burdensome. The resulting OSI architecture has seven layers, which are listed with a brief definition in Table 3-1.

**TABLE 3-1** The OSI Layers

| Layer | Definition |
|---|---|
| 1 Physical | Concerned with transmission of unstructured bit stream over physical link; involves such parameters as signal voltage swing and bit duration; deals with the mechanical, electrical, and procedural characteristics to establish, maintain, and deactivate the physical link. |
| 2 Data link | Provides for the reliable transfer of data across the physical link; sends blocks of data (frames) with the necessary synchronization, error control, and flow control. |
| 3 Network | Provides upper layers with independence from the data transmission and switching technologies used to connect systems; responsible for establishing, maintaining, and terminating connections. |
| 4 Transport | Provides reliable, transparent transfer of data between end points; provides end-to-end error recovery and flow control. |
| 5 Session | Provides the control structure for communication between applications; establishes, manages, and terminates connections (sessions) between cooperating applications. |
| 6 Presentation | Performs generally useful transformations on data to provide a standardized application interface and to provide common communications services; examples: encryption, text compression, and reformatting. |
| 7 Application | Provides services to the users of the OSI environment; examples: transaction server, file transfer protocol, and network management. |

Figure 3-6 illustrates the OSI architecture. Each computer contains the seven ISO layers. Communication is between applications in the two computers, labeled application X and application Y in the figure. If application X wants to send a message to application Y, it invokes the application layer (layer

7). Layer 7 establishes a peer relationship with layer 7 of the target computer, using a layer-7 protocol (application protocol). This protocol requires services from layer 6, so the two layer-6 entities use their own protocol, and so on down to the physical layer, which actually transmits bits over a transmission medium.

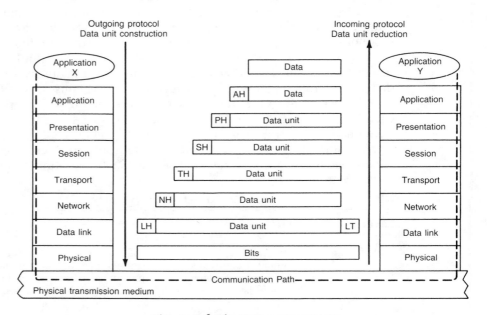

**Figure 3-6** The OSI environment.

The figure also illustrates the way protocols at each layer pass information. When application X has a message to send to application Y, it transfers the data to an application layer module. That module appends an application header to the data; the header contains the control information needed by the peer layer on the other side. The original data plus the header, referred to as an application PDU, is passed as a unit to layer 6, the presentation layer. The presentation module treats the whole unit as data and appends its own header. This process continues down through layer 2, which generally adds both a header and a trailer. This layer-2 protocol data unit, usually called a *frame,* is then transmitted by the physical layer on the transmission medium. When the frame is received by the target computer, the reverse process occurs. As we ascend the layers, each layer strips the outermost header (layer 2 strips both the header and the trailer), acts on the protocol information contained therein, and passes the remainder up to the next layer.

## The OSI Layers

The principal motivation for the development of the OSI model was to provide a framework for standardization. Within the model, one or more protocol standards can be developed at each layer. The model defines in general terms the functions to be performed at that layer and facilitates the standards-making process in two ways:

- Because the functions of each layer are well defined, standards can be developed independently and simultaneously for each layer. This speeds the standards-making process.

- Because the boundaries between layers are well defined, changes in standards in one layer need not affect existing software in another layer. This makes it easier to introduce new standards.

We now turn to a brief description of each layer and discuss some of the standards that have been developed for each layer.

## Physical Layer

The physical layer covers the physical interface between a data transmission device and a transmission medium and the rules by which bits are passed from one to another. A well-known physical layer standard is RS-232C. In Chapter 4, we will examine physical layer standards for LANs.

## Data Link Layer

The physical layer provides only a raw bit stream service. The data link layer attempts to make the physical link reliable and provides the means to activate, maintain, and deactivate the link. The principal service provided by the data link layer to higher layers is error detection and control. Thus, with a fully functional data link layer protocol, the next higher layer may assume that there is error-free transmission over the link.

A well-known data link layer standard is HDLC. In Chapter 4, we will examine data link layer standards for LANs.

## Network Layer

The network layer transfers information between computers across some sort of communications network. It relieves higher layers of the need to know anything about the underlying data transmission and switching technologies used to connect systems. The network service is responsible for establishing, maintaining, and terminating connections across the intervening network. At this layer, the computer system engages in a dialogue with the network to specify the destination address and to request certain network facilities, such as priority.

There is a spectrum of possibilities for intervening communications facilities to be managed by the network layer. At one extreme is the direct point-to-point link between stations. In this case, there may be no need for a network layer because the data link layer can perform the necessary function of managing the link.

Next, the systems could be connected across a single network, such as a circuit-switching or packet-switching network. Figure 3-7 shows how the presence of a network affects the OSI architecture. The lower three layers are concerned with attaching to and communicating with the network; a well-known example of a standard for these three layers is the X.25 standard. The packets created by the end system pass through one or more network nodes. These nodes act as relays between the two end systems and implement layers 1 through 3 of the architecture. In the figure, two end systems are connected through a single network node, referred to in the figure as a relay system. Layer 3 in the node performs a switching and routing function. Within the node, there are two data link layers and two physical layers, corresponding to the links to the two end systems. Each data link (and physical) layer operates independently to provide service to the network layer over its respective link. The upper four layers are "end-to-end" protocols between the attached computers.

At the other extreme, two stations might want to communicate but are not even connected to the same network. Rather, they are connected to networks that are connected—directly or indirectly—to each other. This case requires the use of some sort of internetworking technique; we explore this approach in Chapter 6.

## Transport Layer

The transport layer provides a reliable mechanism for the exchange of data between computers. It ensures that data is delivered error-free, in sequence, with no losses or duplications. The transport layer may also optimize the use of network services and provide a requested quality of service. For example, the session layer may specify acceptable error rates, maximum delay, priority, and security features.

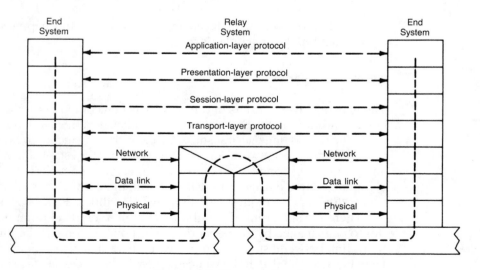

**Figure 3-7** The use of a relay.

The mechanisms used by the transport protocol to provide reliability are very similar to those used by data link control protocols such as HDLC: the use of sequence numbers, error-detection codes, and retransmission after timeout. The reason for this apparent duplication of effort is that the data link layer deals with only a single, direct link, whereas the transport layer deals with a chain of network nodes and links. Although each link in that chain is reliable because of the use of HDLC, a node along that chain may fail at a critical time. Such a failure affects data delivery, and it is the transport protocol that addresses this problem.

The size and complexity of a transport protocol depend on the reliability of the underlying network and network layer services. Accordingly, ISO has developed a family of five transport protocol standards, each tailored to a different level of reliability of the network layer software and the network itself.

## Session Layer

The session layer controls the dialogue between the two end systems. In many cases, there is little or no need for session-layer services, but some applications use such services. The key services provided by the session layer are

- *Dialogue discipline:* This can be two-way simultaneous (full duplex) or two-way alternate (half duplex).
- *Grouping:* The flow of data can be marked to define groups of data. For example, if a retail store is transmitting sales data to a regional office, the data can be marked to indicate the end of the sales data for each department. This would signal the host computer to finalize running totals for that department and start new running counts for the next department.
- *Recovery:* The session layer can provide a checkpoint mechanism, so that if a failure occurs between checkpoints, the session entity can retransmit all data since the last checkpoint.

ISO has issued a standard for the session layer that includes as options services such as those just described.

## Presentation Layer

The presentation layer defines the format of the data to be exchanged between applications and offers application programs a set of data transformation services. For example, data compression or data encryption could occur at this level.

## Application Layer

The application layer provides a means for application programs to access the OSI environment. This layer contains management functions and generally useful mechanisms to support distributed applications. In addition, general-purpose applications such as file transfer, electronic mail, and terminal access to remote computers reside at this layer.

## Operation of an OSI Architecture

Figure 3-8 outlines typical steps in the transfer of a message from a terminal of one host computer, through a network, and ultimately to an application in another host computer. In this example, the message passes through just one network node, as in Figure 3-7. Before data can be transmitted, each OSI layer in the sending host computer establishes with the corresponding layer in the receiving host the applicable ground rules for a communication session. These include the character code to be used and the error-checking method. The protocol at each layer is used for this purpose and then is used in the transmission of the message.

## Perspectives on the OSI Model

Figure 3-9 provides a useful perspective on the OSI architecture. The annotation suggests viewing the seven layers in three parts. The lower three layers contain the logic for a computer to interact with a network. The host is attached physically to the network, uses a data link protocol to reliably communicate with the network, and uses a network protocol to request an exchange of data with another device on the network and to request network services. The X.25 standard for packet-switching networks encompasses these three layers. Continuing from this perspective, the transport layer provides a reliable end-to-end service regardless of the intervening network facility; in effect, it is the user's liaison to the communications facility. Finally, the upper three layers, taken together, are involved in the exchange of data between end users, making use of a transport service for reliable data transfer. This perspective corresponds to the simple three-layer architecture used previously in the chapter.

Another way of thinking about the OSI architecture is in terms of how a computer system is configured as an open system in a network of computers. This is suggested in Figure 3-10. In any given computer system, there is typically a connection to a single network facility. This might be a local area network, a wide-area X.25 network, or an ISDN (integrated services digital network). The logic for this connection is provided in the lowest three layers of the architecture. If the computer is connected to a single network, only a single protocol is needed at each of the lower three layers. Which specific protocols are used will depend on which network is present. For the transport layer, one of five classes of transport protocol will be used, depending on the reliability of the network. A single session layer protocol is used. Finally, a variety of applications may all be included in the computer. For example, users of the system may wish to have file transfer, electronic mail, and document

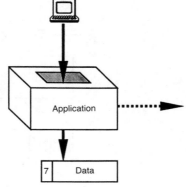

**1. Coding the message.** The application layer converts input from a terminal into bits and organizes them into a block of user data.

**2. The application-layer header.** A header is affixed that identifies the sender's terminal and the receiver's application, as agreed upon earlier during the peer-to-peer dialogue.

● **Peer-to-peer dialogue.** Before a message is transmitted, the sending and receiving hosts's application layers agree on a label that identifies this communication and its originator and recipient.

**3. Using a common language.** If the two hosts use different character codes, the presentation layer translates the code from the originator's code to the recipient's.

**4. Shrinking the data.** The presentation layer may compress the data to reduce storage and transmission costs.

**5. Ensuring privacy.** To keep information confidential, the data may be encrypted.

**6. The presentation-layer header.** This header indicates any encoding, compression, or encryption that has been performed.

● **Peer-to-peer dialogue.** The sending and receiving presentation layers agree on an encoding for transmission (e.g., ASCII). Schemes for compression and encryption may also be agreed.

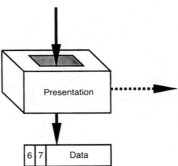

**7. The boundaries of the message.** A message may be transmitted as a sequence of blocks. The session layer marks the beginning and ending of the sequence.

**8. Taking turns.** If a half-duplex discipline is observed, the session layer will include a marker with the last block of data that it sends before giving the turn to the other side.

**9. The session-layer header.** This header contains any markers that accompany this block of data.

● **Peer-to-peer dialogue.** The originating host's session layer opens a session with the receiving host's session layer. The dialogue is used to agree on the conditions of the communication, such as full-duplex versus half-duplex.

*(a) Establishing a Connection and initiating a message transfer.*

**Figure 3-8** Operation of an OSI architecture.

transfer facilities all available. Each of these facilities corresponds to the upper two layers of the architecture.

**10. Subdividing the message.** The transport layer may break a message into a number of segments, keeping track of their sequence. The lead segment contains all presentation and application headers.

**11. The transport-layer header.** To each segment, a header is added which includes a sequence number and a frame check sequence for error detection. This forms a transport protocol data unit (TPDU).

**12. Duplicating TPDUs.** A copy is made of each TPDU, in case the loss or damage of a TPDU necessitates retransmission. When an acknowledgment is received from the other transport layer, a TPDU is erased.

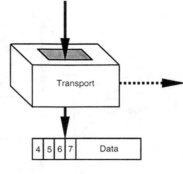

● **Peer-to-peer dialogue.** The two transport layers agree to open a connection. Details such as the maximum size of a TPDU are agreed.

**13. Subdividing the TPDUs.** The network layer may break a TPDU into several pieces to meet size requirements of the communications network.

**14. The network-layer header.** This header includes a sequence number and a destination address. This forms a network protocol data unit, or packet.

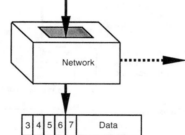

● **Peer-to-peer dialogue.** The network layers of the two hosts initiate, maintain, and terminate a network-level connection. For example, across a packet-switching network, this is a virtual circuit.

**15. Framing the packets.** A header and trailer is added to each packet, forming a frame. The header includes a sequence number for the link control protocol. The trailer includes a frame check sequence for error detection and control.

**16. Duplicating frames.** A copy is made of each frame, in case the link control protocol requires that it be retransmitted because of a lost or damaged frame.

**17. Transmission.** Each frame is transmitted over the medium as a sequence of bits.

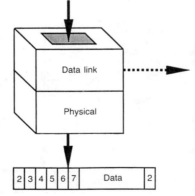

● **Peer-to-peer dialogue.** A link control protocol, such as HDLC, is exercised between the host and the network node to which it is attached.

*(b) Accessing the network.*

**Figure 3-8** (Cont.)

# Indications of Success: MAP, TOP, COS, and GOSIP

The OSI architecture and the accompanying standards at each layer provide unarguable benefits to customers. Because customers can acquire new hardware and software from a variety of vendors, they can take advantage of competition. New services, such as document transfer, can readily be fit into the existing communications architecture.

However, there are obstacles to the introduction of OSI. Historically, each computer vendor has developed its own proprietary architecture and protocols; these differing schemes do not work together. For example, you cannot take a document prepared with a Wang word processing package, transfer it to an IBM mainframe, and use the IBM word processor to edit the document.

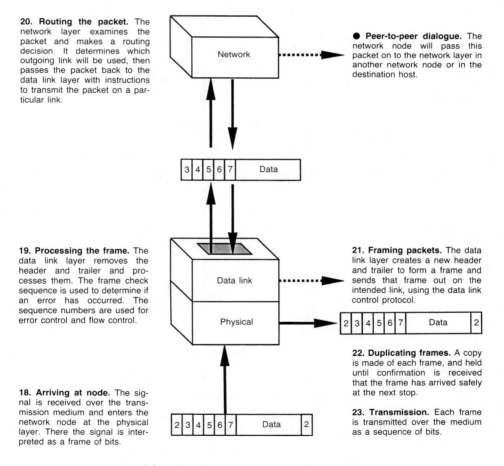

**20. Routing the packet.** The network layer examines the packet and makes a routing decision. It determines which outgoing link will be used, then passes the packet back to the data link layer with instructions to transmit the packet on a particular link.

● **Peer-to-peer dialogue.** The network node will pass this packet on to the network layer in another network node or in the destination host.

**19. Processing the frame.** The data link layer removes the header and trailer and processes them. The frame check sequence is used to determine if an error has occurred. The sequence numbers are used for error control and flow control.

**21. Framing packets.** The data link layer creates a new header and trailer to form a frame and sends that frame out on the intended link, using the data link control protocol.

**22. Duplicating frames.** A copy is made of each frame, and held until confirmation is received that the frame has arrived safely at the next stop.

**18. Arriving at node.** The signal is received over the transmission medium and enters the network node at the physical layer. There the signal is interpreted as a frame of bits.

**23. Transmission.** Each frame is transmitted over the medium as a sequence of bits.

*(c) Relay through an intermediate node.*

**Figure 3-8** (Cont.)

After a customer has installed a set of equipment using the proprietary software, the migration to an OSI-based set of software is expensive, resource-consuming, and time-consuming.

**29. Reassembling the message.** If a message was broken into a number of TPDUs, the transport layer waits until all of those arrive, reassembles the message based on the sequence numbers in the header, and passes it up to the session layer.

**28. Examining the header.** The transport layer removes and examines the header. It recalculates the frame check sequence and compares it with the original. If they match, an acknowledgment is returned to the originating host. Otherwise, the TPDU is discarded and the originating host will have to retransmit it.

**27. Reassembling TPDUs.** If a transport protocol data unit (TPDU) was broken into a number of packets, the network layer waits until all of those packets arrives, reassembles the TPDU, and passes it up to the transport layer.

**26. Examining the header.** The network layer removes and examines the header to verify the destination address and proper sequence number.

**25. Processing the frame.** The data link layer removes the header and trailer and processes them. The frame check sequence is used to determine if an error has occurred. The sequence numbers are used for error control and flow control.

**24. Arriving at node.** The signal is received over the transmission medium and enters the network node at the physical layer. There the signal is interpreted as a frame of bits.

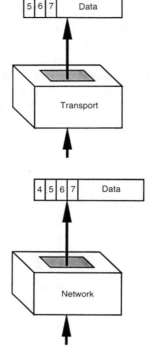
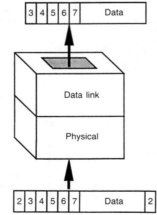

*(d) Entering the destination host.*

**Figure 3-8** (Cont.)

Thus, the success of standards related to OSI depends not only on the development of timely, useful standards, but also on their acceptance by the vendors who supply equipment that conforms to the standards and the customers

**36. Delivering the message.** The application layer converts the bits into readable characters and directs the data to the application program for which it is intended.

**35. Examining the header.** The application layer examines and removes the header. It determines to whom the message will be delivered.

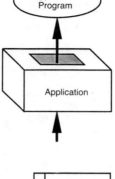

**34. Expanding the data.** If the data was compressed by the originating host (step 4), the presentation layer expands the data back into its original form.

**33. Decrypting the message.** If the data was encrypted by the originating host (step 5), the presentation layer deciphers it according to the rules agreed at the start of the communication.

**32. Examining the header.** The presentation layer examines and removes the header. It determines if any encryption or data compression techniques have been used.

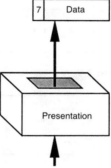

**31. Awaiting complete data.** The session layer holds the message until the arrival of the closing bracket signals that the message is complete. At that point, the session layer passes the message to the presentation layer.

**30. Examining the header.** The session layer examines and removes the session-layer header. It notes any markers in the header.

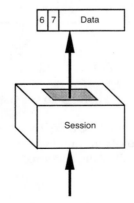

*(e) Completion of journey.*

**Figure 3-8** (Cont.)

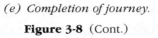

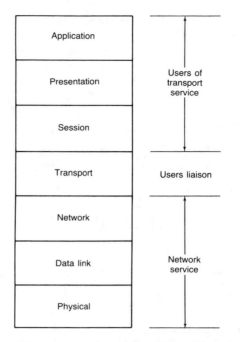

**Figure 3-9** A perspective on the OSI architecture.

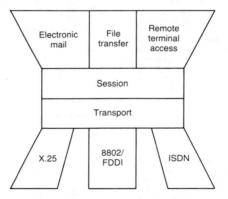

**Figure 3-10** An OSI configuration.

who buy such equipment. One of the most promising developments in recent years is the creation of a number of organizations whose goal is to ensure that acceptance. In the following sections, we briefly describe the four most important ones.

## Manufacturing Automation Protocol (MAP)

MAP is an effort begun by General Motors in 1982 and since transferred to the Society of Manufacturing Engineers (SME). The objective of MAP is to define a local area network and associated communications architecture for terminals, computing resources, programmable devices, and robots in a plant or a complex. It sets standards for procurement and provides a specification for use by vendors who want to build networking products for factory use that are acceptable to MAP participants. The strategy has three parts:

1. When international standards exist, select those alternatives and options that best suit the needs of the MAP participants.
2. For standards currently under development, participate in the standards-making process to represent the requirements of the MAP participants.
3. When no appropriate standard exists, recommend interim standards until the international standards are developed.

Thus, MAP is intended to specify, at each layer of the OSI architecture, the standards and options within standards appropriate for the factory environment. This guarantees a large market for products that conform to those standards. To date, hundreds of companies have participated in the MAP effort.

## Technical and Office Protocols (TOP)

A similar effort, TOP, addresses the needs of the office and engineering environments. Like MAP, TOP specifies standards and options within standards, and has received widespread support. TOP was begun by Boeing and is now under the management of SME. There is considerable overlap between the MAP and TOP specifications. Differences are mainly in the details of the local area networks and the range of applications supported.

## Corporation for Open Systems (COS)

An equally important development is the creation, in early 1986, of the Corporation for Open Systems. COS is a nonprofit joint venture of more than 60 of the major suppliers of data processing and data communication equipment. Its purpose is "to provide a vehicle for acceleration of the introduction of interoperable, multivendor products and services operating under agreed-to OSI, ISDN, and related international standards to assure widespread customer acceptance on an open network architecture in world markets." COS is involved in a number of standards-related activities. Its most important activity is the development of a single, consistent set of test methods, test facilities, and certification procedures. This will allow vendors to certify that their products meet the international standards and will work with equipment from other vendors.

## Government OSI Users Committee

A final significant development is the creation in September of 1986 of the U.S. Government OSI Users Committee. The U.S. government is the world's largest user of computers and thus has a profound impact on the product plans of many vendors. The key objective of the committee is to facilitate the migration of government computer users to OSI-based products. The outcome of this effort has been the government OSI procurement (GOSIP) specification, which is now a federal standard. Like MAP and TOP, GOSIP specifies standards and options within the context of the OSI architecture. GOSIP is now mandatory for use on federal procurements: Unless some compelling need for a waiver can be demonstrated, all federal procurements of communications software and hardware must conform to OSI-based standards. In addition, existing non-OSI equipment will be phased out and replaced with OSI-based products as soon as practical. Thus, the federal government has become a powerful force in promoting the development of OSI-based products by the vendors.

All these organizations represent forces that virtually guarantee the widespread development and use of products that conform to the OSI-related standards.

# The TCP/IP Protocol Suite

Based on protocol research and development conducted on its experimental packet-switched network, ARPANET, the U.S. Department of Defense (DOD) has issued a set of military standards for computer communications protocols. Although there are five of these protocols (Table 3-2), the entire set is known by the names of two of them: Transmission Control Protocol (TCP) and Internet Protocol (IP). These protocols are in widespread use in the U.S. defense community. But what is more interesting is that they have been quietly building up a following in the commercial arena during a time when much attention has been focused on the international standards based on the Open Systems

**TABLE 3-2**   The TCP/IP Protocol Suite

| Protocol | Definition |
| --- | --- |
| MIL-STD-1777 Internet Protocol (IP) | Provides a connectionless service for end systems to communicate across one or more networks. Does not assume the network to be reliable. |
| MIL-STD-1778 Transmission Control Protocol (TCP) | A reliable end-to-end data transfer service. Equivalent to OSI transport protocol. |
| MIL-STD-1780 File Transfer Protocol (FTP) | A simple application for transfer of ASCII, EBCDIC, and binary files. |
| MIL-STD-1781 Simple Mail Transfer Protocol (SMTP) | A simple electronic mail facility. |
| MIL-STD-1782 TELNET | Provides a remote logon facility for simple scroll-mode terminals. |

Interconnection (OSI) model. Currently, there are over 200 vendors that provide TCP/IP products, and these are the most widely available and most widely used set of standardized computer communications protocols.

The TCP/IP architecture (like the OSI model) is layered. Four layers are involved: network access, internet, transport, and application. The TCP/IP architecture is compared with that of OSI and SNA in Figure 3-11. The network access layer contains the protocols that provide access to a communications network, such as a local area network. Protocols at this layer are between a communications node and an attached host. The TCP/IP suite does not include any unique protocols at this layer. Rather, the protocol appropriate for a particular network (e.g., Ethernet, IEEE 802, or X.25) is used.

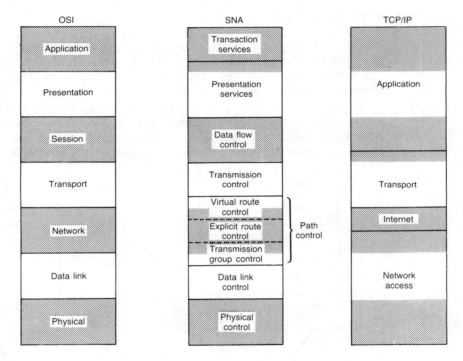

**Figure 3-11** Three communications architectures.

The internet layer consists of the procedures required to allow data to traverse multiple networks between hosts. Thus, it must provide a routing function. This protocol is implemented within hosts and routers. A router is a processor connecting two networks; its primary function is to relay data between networks using an internetwork protocol. The protocol at this layer is the *internet protocol (IP)*. A typical use of IP is to connect multiple LANs in the same building or to connect LANs at different sites through a wide-area packet-switching network.

The transport layer provides the logic for assuring that data exchanged between hosts is reliably delivered. It also is responsible for directing incoming data to the intended application. The protocol at this layer is the *transmission control protocol (TCP)*.

Finally, the application layer contains protocols for specific user applications. For each different type of application, such as file transfer, a protocol is needed that supports that application. Three such protocols are in the TCP/IP protocol suite: SMTP, FTP, and TELNET.

Note that this architecture is similar to the simple communications architecture introduced in the section titled "A Simple Communications Architecture." The only difference is the introduction of an internet layer to handle connections across multiple networks.

## Operation of TCP and IP

Figure 3-12 indicates how these protocols are configured for communications. Some sort of network access protocol, such as the Ethernet logic, connects a computer to a network. This protocol enables the host to send data across the network to another host or, in the case of a host on another network, to a router. IP is implemented in all the end systems and routers. It acts as a relay to move a block of data from one host, through one or more routers, to another host. TCP is implemented only in the end systems; it keeps track of the blocks of data to assure that all are delivered reliably to the appropriate application.

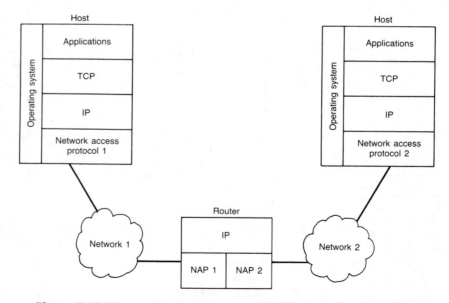

**Figure 3-12** Communications using the TCP/IP protocol architecture.

For successful communication, every entity in the overall system must have a unique address. Actually, two levels of addressing are needed. Each host on a network must have a unique global internet address; this allows the data to be delivered to the proper host. In addition, each process with a host must have an address that is unique within the host; this allows the host-to-host protocol (TCP) to deliver data to the proper process. The latter addresses are known as ports.

Let us trace a simple operation. Suppose that a process, associated with port 1 at host A, wishes to send a message to another process, associated with port 2 at host B. The process at A hands the message down to TCP with instructions to send it to host B, port 2. TCP hands the message down to IP with instructions to send it to host B. Note that IP need not be told the identity of the destination port; all that it needs to know is that the data is intended for host B. Next, IP hands the message down to the network access layer (e.g., Ethernet logic) with instructions to send it to gateway X (the first hop on the way to B).

To control this operation, control information as well as user data must be transmitted, as suggested in Figure 3-13. When TCP receives a block of data from a process, it appends control information as the TCP header, forming a TCP segment. The control information will be used by the peer TCP protocol entity at host B. Examples of items included in this header follow:

- *Destination port:* When the TCP entity at B receives the segment, it must know to whom the data will be delivered.

- *Sequence number:* TCP numbers the segments that it sends to a destination port sequentially. Then, if the segments arrive out of order, the TCP entity at B can reorder them.

- *Checksum:* The sending TCP includes a code that is a function of the contents of the remainder of the segment. The receiving TCP performs the same calculation and compares the result with the incoming code. A discrepancy results if there has been some error in transmission.

Next, TCP hands each segment over to IP, with instructions to transmit it to B. These segments must be transmitted across one or more networks and relayed through one or more intermediate routers. Thus, IP appends a header of control information to each segment to form an IP datagram. An example of an item stored in the IP header is the destination host address (in this example, B).

Finally, each IP datagram is presented to the network layer for transmission across the first network in its journey to the destination. The network access layer appends its own header, creating a packet, or frame. The packet is transmitted across the network to router X. The packet header contains the information that the network needs to transfer the data across the network, such as the destination address.

At router X, the packet header is stripped and the IP header examined. On the basis of the address information in the header, the IP module in the router directs the datagram out across network 2 to B. To do this, the datagram is again augmented with a network access header.

When the data is received at B, the reverse process occurs. At each layer, the corresponding header is removed, and the remainder is passed to the next higher layer, until the original user data is delivered to the destination process.

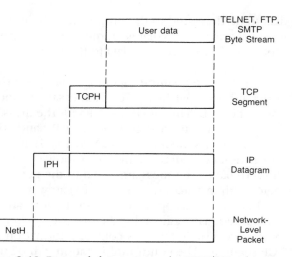

**Figure 3-13** Protocol data units in the TCP/IP architecture.

## The Applications

The *simple mail transfer protocol (SMTP)* provides a basic electronic mail facility. It provides a mechanism for transferring messages among separate hosts. Features of SMTP include mailing lists, return receipts, and forwarding. The SMTP protocol does not specify the way in which messages are created; a local editing or native electronic mail facility is required. After a message is created, SMTP accepts the message, then uses TCP to send it to an SMTP module on another host. The target SMTP module uses a local electronic mail package to store the incoming message in a user's mailbox.

The *file transfer protocol (FTP)* is used to send files from one system to another under user command. Both text and binary files are accommodated, and the protocol provides features for controlling user access. When a user wants to transfer a file, FTP sets up a TCP connection to the target system for the exchange of control messages. These control messages allow a user ID and password to be transmitted, and allow the user to specify the file and file actions desired. After a file transfer is approved, a second TCP connection is set up for the data transfer. The file is transferred over the data connection, without the overhead of any headers or control information at the application level. When the transfer is complete, the control connection is used to signal completion and to accept new file transfer commands.

*TELNET* provides a remote logon capability, which lets a user at a terminal or personal computer log on to a remote computer and function as if directly connected to that computer. The protocol was designed to work with simple scroll-mode terminals. TELNET is actually implemented in two modules. User TELNET interacts with the terminal I/O module to communicate with a local terminal. It converts the characteristics of real terminals to the network standard and vice versa. Server TELNET interacts with an application, acting as a surrogate terminal handler so that remote terminals appear as local terminals to the application. Terminal traffic between User and Server TELNET is carried on a TCP connection.

# IBM's SNA Architecture

The era of true communications architecture began with the announcement in 1974 by IBM of its systems network architecture (SNA). SNA was developed by IBM to protect its customer base and allow its customers to take advantage of new IBM offerings. A proliferation of communications protocols and user access methods on IBM machines had created a problem. Customers developed complex applications and were unable to easily incorporate new computers into their operation. Many of the communications techniques were inefficient, and a flourishing business in communications processors designed to support IBM users developed among minicomputer and communication vendors. These factors led to the development of an architecture that would provide efficient user access to a network of computers and terminals.

Even today with the success of OSI and TCP/IP, SNA is the dominant networking and communications architecture, used on virtually all IBM installations and on most so-called plug-compatible machines. As with OSI, SNA's communications architecture is defined in terms of a set of layers, each of which performs part of the communications function. Table 3-3 lists the seven SNA layers. A brief description of each follows.

**TABLE 3-3**  The SNA Layers

| Layer | Definition |
| --- | --- |
| 1 Physical control | Specifies the physical interface between nodes; may be serial or parallel interface. |
| 2 Data link control | Manages the transmission of data over a single link between adjacent nodes. |
| 3 Path control | Creates a logical channel between two endpoints (NAUs); determines route that messages will follow. |
| 4 Transmission control | Regulates session data flow; performs error control. |
| 5 Data flow control | Controls dialogue between two interacting endpoints, including full versus half duplex and session pause. |
| 6 Presentation services | Provides data transformation and formatting services. |
| 7 Transaction services | Provides network management services and an end-user logical interface into distributed services environment. |

## Physical Control

The physical control layer specifies the physical interface between nodes, which may be serial or parallel. A serial interface is a communication link of the type discussed throughout this book. The term *serial* refers to the fact that bits are transmitted one at a time. A parallel interface, on the other hand, provides multiple transmission paths, and a number of bits (usually 8, 16, or 32) are transmitted in parallel. The parallel interface is typical of I/O channel connections between mainframes and front-end processors.

## Data Link Control

The data link control layer provides the reliable transfer of data across a physical link. The protocol specified for serial communication links is synchronous data link control (SDLC). SDLC is basically a subset of HDLC.

## Path Control

The path control layer creates logical connections between network addressable units (NAUs). The path control layer is divided into three sublayers that perform different functions related to the setup and use of a logical connection:

- *Transmission group control:* Between any pair of connected nodes in a network, there may be one or more physical links. If there are multiple links, they are treated as a transmission group, and an outgoing block of data can be transmitted on any link of the group. This provides increased reliability and load balancing to improve throughput.
- *Explicit route control:* This is the routing function. A route from the source node to the destination node through zero or more intermediate nodes is established.
- *Virtual route control:* When data is exchanged between end nodes across an explicit route, a logical connection, called a virtual route, is established. This is similar to a virtual circuit and includes a flow control capability.

## Transmission Control

The transmission control layer is responsible for establishing, maintaining, and terminating SNA sessions. A session is a logical relationship between endpoints (NAUs). This layer guarantees the reliable delivery of data and corresponds to the OSI transport layer.

## Data Flow Control

The data flow control layer provides session-related services that are visible and of interest to end-user processes and terminals. The principal functions are in the following categories:

- *Send/receive mode:* Full duplex or half duplex may be specified.
- *Chaining:* This is, in effect, a checkpoint mechanism that supports recovery.
- *Bracketing:* Whereas chaining is used to delimit a sequence of data units transmitted in one direction, bracketing deals with a sequence of exchanges and supports recovery in transaction-oriented applications.
- *Response options:* Three acknowledgments may be specified. For each block of data, (1) do not send an acknowledgment, (2) send an acknowledgment only in case of an exception, and (3) always send an acknowledgment.
- *Quiesce/shutdown:* A temporary or permanent halt in the flow of data may be requested.

## Presentation Services

The presentation services layer includes the following functions:

- *Format translation:* This service allows each endpoint to have a different view of the exchanged data and provides the necessary translation or reformatting functions.
- *Compression:* Data can be compressed at the bit or byte level using specified procedures to reduce transmission volume.
- *Transaction program support:* This service controls conversation-level communication between transaction programs by (1) loading and invoking transaction programs, (2) maintaining send and receive mode protocols, and (3) enforcing correct parameter usage and sequencing restrictions.

## Transaction Services

The transaction services layer is primarily intended to provide the following network management services:

- *Configuration services:* Allow an operator to start or reconfigure a network by activating and deactivating links.
- *Network operator services:* Include such nonconfiguration operator functions as the collection and display of network statistics and the communication of data from users and processes to the network operator.

- *Session services:* Support the activation of a session on the behalf of end users and applications. In effect, this is the user interface to the transmission control layer.
- *Maintenance and management services:* Provide for the testing of network facilities and assist in fault isolation and identification.

# Choosing an Architecture

The focus of this book is the set of decisions that surround the selection, use, and management of a local area network. Although the issue of which overall communications architecture to use is beyond the scope of this book, it is worthwhile to make a few comments.

Any of the three most popular architectures (OSI, TCP/IP, and SNA) could be used on top of any LAN. The choice of architecture must be a balance between short-term need and long-term goals. As we discussed previously, a remarkable progress has been made in the acceptance of OSI as the architecture for interconnecting diverse equipment. All vendors have announced support for OSI. In addition, a tremendous amount of work is ongoing to define new applications, expand existing applications, and define a network management scheme, all within the context of OSI. Accordingly, it makes sense to set OSI as the long-range goal of an organization.

Nevertheless, the short term must be dealt with honestly. However compelling the long-range benefits of OSI, the transition to OSI from an existing architecture must be planned carefully. In general, any such transition is likely to be costly and disruptive. The more gradual the transition, the less the disruption. Therefore, if the user has an existing installation built around TCP/IP or SNA, it would be wise to consider going very slowly into the OSI world. A number of vendors offer gateway products that allow coexistence between OSI equipment and TCP/IP or SNA equipment. Such gateways are a worthwhile investment as part of an overall transition plan.

For a user lucky enough to have a blank slate, the advantages of OSI are even stronger. Even in this case, however, the user must consider short-term needs. Both the TCP/IP and the SNA architectures have been in use longer and have a greater product base. Based solely on immediate needs, a user might find one of these architectures more cost-effective than OSI. It is then necessary to project future requirements and factor in the cost of eventually converting to OSI. This is especially true for the user considering TCP/IP. Although there is a case to be made that SNA will never go away because of the tremendous installed base and IBM's aggressive program of enhancing the architecture, virtually no serious observer expects TCP/IP to survive in the face of growing OSI acceptance. Deadlines for its death vary widely—from a few years to as much as fifteen years.

The decision of which architecture to use is essentially independent of which LAN to choose. For the remainder of this book, we will concentrate on issues relating to the latter.

# Summary

A local area network is a communications facility that can transfer data from one attached device to another. For cooperative processing among the devices attached to the network, more is needed than this simple data-transfer service. We need a communications architecture to dictate a set of protocols that allows two devices to interact cooperatively to perform some application. Three architectures dominate the marketplace: OSI, TCP/IP, and SNA. Each of these architectures can be implemented on top of any LAN.

The communication functionality required for distributed applications is quite complex. This functionality is generally implemented as a structured set of modules. The modules are arranged in a vertical, layered fashion; each layer provides a portion of the functions and relies on the next lower layer for more primitive functions. Such a structure is referred to as a communications architecture.

One motivation for the use of this type of structure is that it eases the task of design and implementation. It is standard practice for any large software package to divide functions into modules that can be designed and implemented separately. After each individual module is designed and implemented, it can be tested. Then the modules can be combined and tested together. This motivation has led computer vendors to develop proprietary layered communications architectures. An example of this is the systems network architecture (SNA) of IBM.

A layered architecture can be used to also construct a standardized set of communication protocols. The advantages of modular design remain. In addition, a layered architecture is particularly well suited to the development of standards. Standards can be developed simultaneously for protocols at each layer of the architecture. This breaks down the work to make it more manageable and speeds the standards-development process. The open systems interconnection (OSI) architecture is the standard architecture used for this purpose.

The OSI architecture contains seven layers. Each layer provides a portion of the total communications function required for distributed applications. Standards have been developed for each of the layers. Development work still continues, particularly at the top (application) layer, where new distributed applications are still being defined.

Finally, an architecture that grew out of the needs of the U.S. military is the TCP/IP protocol suite. This set of protocols is currently the most popular non-proprietary communications architecture in the marketplace. Although we can expect it to eventually be replaced by OSI, it will remain a major factor for a number of years.

# Chapter 4

# LAN Standards and Configurations

For THE SYSTEM OR NETWORK MANAGER seeking to acquire a local area network (LAN), there is a wide variety of products and possible configurations. The manager first needs to choose between a single- or multiple-LAN solution. In the former case, a single, relatively high-capacity LAN supports the direct connection of all computers, workstations, and terminals at the site. In the latter case, a tiered solution (such as the one in Figure 1-10) is employed. Low-cost, low-capacity LANs are used at the departmental level to interconnect PCs and multiuser workstations. A more expensive, higher-capacity LAN serves as a backbone system, interconnecting the departmental LANs and directly supporting corporate-wide resources, such as mainframes and superminis. And a very high speed LAN may be used in large organizations to interconnect multiple mainframes.

A second choice facing the manager is between a multiple-vendor LAN or an integrated, single-vendor LAN. The multiple-vendor LAN may be procured from a LAN vendor who supplies not only the cable, but also network interface units (NIUs) that provide standardized interfaces for a variety of devices from many vendors. In the case of integrated, single-vendor LANs, a computer vendor supplies not only the computer equipment, but also the LAN, with the interface provided by communication boards that integrate with the vendor's computer equipment.

Finally, the manager is faced with choices among a number of topologies (bus, tree, or ring), transmission media (shielded or unshielded twisted pair, baseband or broadband coaxial cable, or optical fiber), and medium access control techniques.

Certainly, these choices are difficult ones. Several factors, however, make the task more palatable:

- LAN products have matured, and much LAN logic is now available on chips, resulting in reduced cost.
- LAN standards have stabilized and have been widely accepted.

International standards have been issued for LANs, and key standards-related organizations, including the MAP and TOP user's groups, the Government OSI User's Committee, and the Corporation for Open Systems, have adopted these standards.

Despite the existence of standards, the manager is still faced with a number of options in configuring a LAN solution. This chapter presents the ingredients involved in developing a complete solution, so that the reader can understand what alternatives are available.

We begin with a look at medium access control techniques, which are the basis for distinguishing among the various standards. The remainder of the chapter is devoted to an examination of the various standards and the relative pros and cons of each. Although some proprietary, nonstandard LANs are still on the market, these are becoming increasingly irrelevant. Most LAN vendors and most potential LAN customers are committed to standards. This is the direction in which the industry is going, and the customer chooses a nonstandard LAN at his or her peril.

# Medium Access Control Techniques

A LAN is a collection of stations that must share the network's transmission capacity. Some means of controlling access to the transmission medium is needed; this is known as medium access control (MAC). Three techniques enjoy widespread acceptance and are described in this section: CSMA/CD and token bus, which are used on bus and tree topologies, and token ring, used on the ring topology.

## CSMA/CD

The simplest form of medium access control for a bus or tree is carrier sense multiple access with collision detection (CSMA/CD). The original baseband version of this technique was developed by Xerox as part of the Ethernet LAN. The original broadband version was developed by MITRE as part of its MITRE-net LAN.

With CSMA/CD, a station wanting to transmit first listens to the medium to determine if another transmission is in progress (carrier sense). If the medium is idle, the station may transmit. If two or more stations attempt to transmit at about the same time, there will be a collision; the data from both transmissions will be garbled and not received successfully. Thus, a procedure is needed that specifies what a station should do if the medium is found busy and what it should do if a collision occurs:

1. If the medium is idle, transmit.
2. If the medium is busy, continue to listen until the channel is idle, then transmit immediately.

3. If a collision is detected during transmission, immediately cease transmitting.

4. After a collision, wait a random amount of time, then attempt to transmit again (repeat from step 1).

Figure 4-1 illustrates the technique. At time $t_0$, station A begins transmitting a packet addressed to D. At $t_1$, both B and C are ready to transmit. B senses a transmission and so defers. C, however, is still unaware of A's transmission and begins its own transmission. When A's transmission reaches C, at $t_2$, C detects the collision and ceases transmission. The effect of the collision propagates back to A, where it is detected some time later, $t_3$, at which time A ceases transmission.

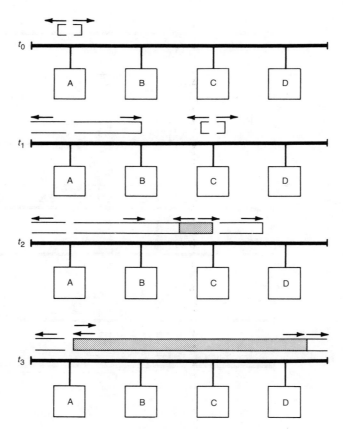

**Figure 4-1** CSMA/CD operation.

The sequence of events is somewhat different for a broadband bus or tree, as illustrated in Figure 4-2. The figure shows a dual-cable bus, but the effect would be essentially the same for split cable and for a tree topology. In this example station A begins transmitting a packet at $t_0$, on the inbound cable. At $t_1$,

C is unaware that A is transmitting, even though the leading edge of A's packet has passed C. The reason is that A's packet has begun to pass C on the inbound cable, but C is only "listening" to the network on the outbound cable. At $t_2$, C is still unaware that A is transmitting and begins to transmit itself. This creates a collision, but C is not immediately aware of the collision because it is not listening to the inbound cable. It is only at $t_3$ that C becomes aware of the collision and ceases transmitting.

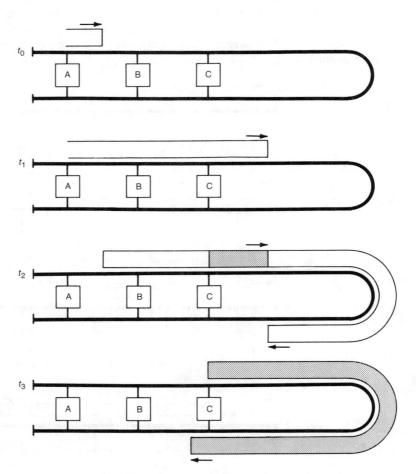

**Figure 4-2** CSMA/CD operation on a broadband cable.

## Token Bus

In a token bus, the stations on the bus or tree form a logical ring; that is, the stations are assigned logical positions in an ordered sequence, with the last member of the sequence followed by the first. Each station knows the identity of the station preceding and following it. The physical ordering of the stations on the bus is irrelevant and independent of the logical ordering.

A control packet known as the *token* regulates the right of access. The token contains a destination address. The station possessing the token is granted control of the medium for a specified time. The station may transmit one or more packets and may poll stations and receive responses. When the station is finished, or the time has expired, it passes the token to the next station in the logical sequence. This station now has permission to transmit. Hence, normal operation consists of alternating data transfer and token transfer phases. In addition, stations not using the token are allowed on the bus, but these stations can only respond to polls or requests for acknowledgment.

Figure 4-3 gives an example. At any given time, a certain number of stations are active on the network and may receive packets. A certain number of these stations are part of the logical ring. In this example, stations 60, 50, 30, and 10, in that order, are part of the logical ring. Station 60 will pass the token to station 50, which passes it to station 30, which passes it to station 10, which passes the token to station 60.

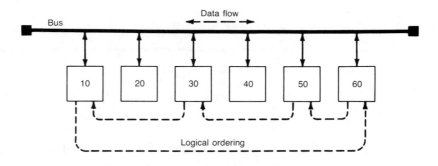

**Figure 4-3** Token bus.

Figure 4-4 shows a portion of the operation of this configuration. At $t_0$, station 10 passes the token. Because the current ordering dictates that the next station in the logical sequence is station 60, the destination address portion of the token transmitted by station 10 is 60. The token is seen by all the other stations on the LAN, but it is ignored by all but station 60, whose address matches that in the token ($t_1$). After station 60 receives the token, it is free to transmit a data packet. In this example, it transmits a data packet addressed to station 20 ($t_2$). Note that station 20 need not be part of the logical ring to receive packets; however, it cannot initiate any transmissions. After station 60 has completed its data transmission, it issues a token addressed to the next station on the logical ring, in this case station 50 ($t_3$).

This scheme requires considerable maintenance. At a minimum, the following functions must be performed by one or more stations:

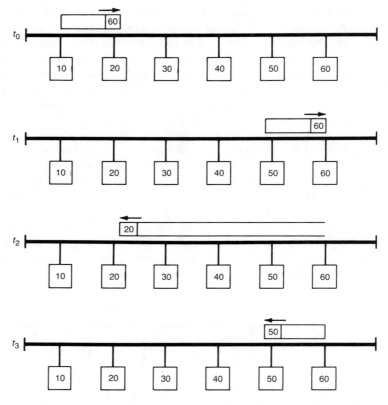

**Figure 4-4** Token bus operation.

- *Ring initialization:* When the network is started, some cooperative procedure is needed to sort who goes first, who goes second, and so on.
- *Addition to ring:* Periodically, nonparticipating stations must be granted the opportunity to join the logical ring.
- *Deletion from ring:* A station can remove itself from the logical ring.
- *Recovery:* If the token is lost, due to a transmission error or station failure, some means of recovery is needed.

All of these requirements add complexity to the scheme.

## Token Ring

The token ring technique is based on the use of a token packet that circulates when all stations are idle. A station wanting to transmit must wait until it detects a token passing by. It then seizes the token by changing one bit in the token, which transforms it from a token to a start-of-packet sequence for a data packet. The station then appends and transmits the remainder of the fields (for example, the destination address) needed to construct a data packet.

Because there is now no token on the ring, other stations wanting to transmit must wait. The packet on the ring makes a round trip and is purged by the transmitting station. The transmitting station inserts a new token on the ring after it has completed transmission of its packet. Now that the new token has been inserted on the ring, the next station downstream with data to send will be able to seize the token and transmit. Figure 4-5 illustrates the technique. In the example, A sends a packet to C, which receives it and then sends its own packets to A and D. As with the token bus technique, procedures are needed to cope with various errors and other contingencies.

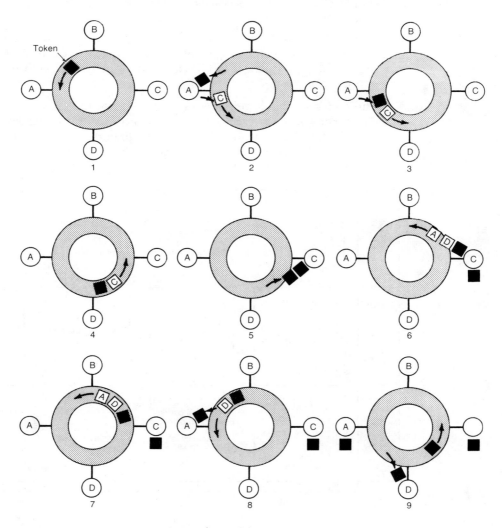

**Figure 4-5** Token ring operation.

# LAN Standards

Having surveyed the various elements of a LAN, we will look at combinations of options and analyze these from the point of view of requirements. This is best done in the context of standards for LANs. It is advisable for the manager to limit consideration to LANs that conform to standards. The reasons for this are compelling:

1. The published standards are the product of a broad-based effort involving highly knowledgeable individuals from a wide spectrum of vendor and customer organizations. Thus, the specified combinations chosen for standardization reflect a consensus as to which combinations meet typical requirements.

2. The LAN standards have achieved widespread and rapid acceptance both by vendors and customers. Thus, the customer benefits from the cost savings of mass production and has a broad range of compatible products to choose from.

The standards that have been issued are shown in Figure 4-6. Most of the standards were developed by a committee known as IEEE 802, sponsored by the Institute for Electrical and Electronics Engineers; one of the standards was developed by the American National Standards Institute (ANSI). All of these

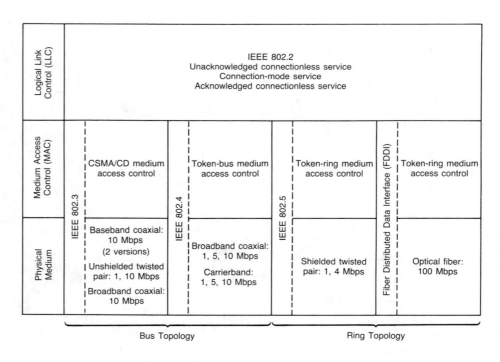

**Figure 4-6** Local area network standards.

standards have subsequently been adopted as international standards by the International Standards Organization (ISO).

The standards are organized as a three-layer protocol hierarchy. Logical link control (LLC) is responsible for addressing and data link control. It is independent of the topology, transmission medium, and medium access control technique chosen, and was issued as a separate standard. Below logical link control are the medium access control (MAC) and physical layers. Because of the interdependence between medium access control, medium, and topology, these layers were organized into standards based on the medium access control algorithm, with the physical layer specified as part of the medium access control standard.

## Overview

The key to the development of the LAN market is the availability of a low-cost interface. The cost to connect equipment to a LAN must be much less than the cost of the equipment alone. This requirement, plus the complexity of the LAN logic, dictates a solution based on the use of chips and very large scale integration (VLSI). However, chip manufacturers will be reluctant to commit the necessary resources unless there is a high-volume market. A widely accepted LAN standard assures that volume and also allows equipment from a variety of manufacturers to communicate. This is the rationale of the IEEE 802 committee.

The committee issued a set of four standards, which were subsequently adopted in 1985 by the American National Standards Institute (ANSI) as American National Standards. These standards were subsequently revised and reissued as international standards by the International Standards Organization (ISO) in 1987, with the designation ISO 8802.

The committee characterized its work in this way:

> The LANs described herein are distinguished from other types of data networks in that they are optimized for a moderate size geographic area such as a single office building, a warehouse, or a campus. The IEEE 802 LAN is a shared medium peer-to-peer communications network that broadcasts information for all stations to receive. As a consequence, it does not inherently provide privacy. The local area network enables stations to communicate directly using a common physical medium on a point-to-point basis without any intermediate switching node being required. There is always need for an access sublayer in order to arbitrate the access to the shared medium. The network is generally owned, used, and operated by a single organization. This is in contrast to Wide area networks (WANs) that interconnect communication facilities in different parts of a country or are used as a public utility. These LANs are also different from networks, such as backplane buses, that are optimized for the interconnection of devices on a desk top or components within a single piece of equipment.

Two conclusions were quickly reached. First, the task of communication across the local network is sufficiently complex that it needs to be broken up into more manageable subtasks. Second, no single technical approach will satisfy all requirements.

The second conclusion was reluctantly reached when it became apparent that no single standard would satisfy all committee participants. There was support for both ring and bus topologies. With the bus topology, there was support for two access methods (CSMA/CD and token bus) and two media (baseband and broadband). The response of the committee was to standardize all serious proposals rather than to attempt to settle on just one. Figure 4-6 illustrates the results.

## The LAN Protocol Architecture

Figure 4-7 relates the LAN standards to the OSI architecture. The work on LAN standards has resulted, in effect, in a communications architecture for LAN communication. Fortunately, this architecture was designed to be a subset of the OSI architecture. This makes it easy to see that any set of higher-layer protocols, such as TCP/IP, SNA, and the OSI-related standards, can be used with the various LAN protocols.

Note that the physical layer of the various LAN standards corresponds to the physical layer of the OSI model, as we might expect. The MAC and LLC

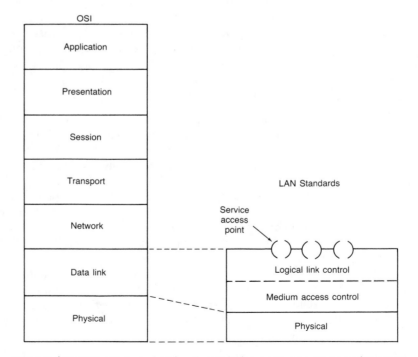

**Figure 4-7** OSI compared to local network communications architecture.

layers are both encompassed by the data link layer of OSI. There is a subdivision in the LAN architecture because a number of common link control functions can apply to any LAN, but the medium access control technique differs for the various standards.

## Logical Link Control (IEEE 802.2)

Logical link control (LLC) specifies the mechanisms for addressing stations across the medium and for controlling the exchange of data between two users. The operation and format of this standard is based on HDLC. Three alternative services are provided for attached devices using logical link control:

- *Unacknowledged connectionless service:* This service is a datagram-style service. It is a very simple service that does not involve any flow- and error-control mechanisms. Thus, the delivery of data is not guaranteed. In most devices, however, some higher layer of software deals with reliability issues.

- *Connection-mode service:* This service is similar to that offered by HDLC. A logical connection is set up between two users exchanging data, and flow control and error control are provided.

- *Acknowledged connectionless service:* This is a cross between the previous two services. Datagrams are acknowledged, but no prior logical connection is set up.

Typically, a vendor provides these services as options that the customer can select when purchasing the equipment. Or the customer can purchase equipment that provides two or all three services and select a specific service based on the application.

The *unacknowledged connectionless service* requires minimum logic and is useful in two contexts. First, higher layers of software often provide the necessary reliability and flow-control mechanisms, and it is efficient to avoid duplicating them. For example, either TCP or the ISO transport protocol standard would provide the mechanisms needed to ensure that data is delivered reliably. Second, sometimes the overhead of connection establishment and maintenance is unjustified or even counterproductive. An example is data collection activities that involve the periodic sampling of data sources, such as sensors and automatic self-test reports from security equipment or network components. In a monitoring application, the loss of an occasional data unit would not cause distress because the next report should arrive shortly. Thus, in most cases, the unacknowledged connectionless service is the preferred option.

The *connection-mode service* could be used in very simple devices that have little software operating above this level (for example, terminal controllers). It would provide the flow control and reliability mechanisms normally implemented at higher layers of the communications software.

The *acknowledged connectionless service* is useful in several contexts. With the connection-mode service, the logical link control software must maintain some sort of table for each active connection, to keep track of the status of that connection. If the user needs guaranteed delivery, but there are a large number of destinations for data, the connection-mode service may be impractical because of the large number of tables required. An example is a process control or automated factory environment where a central site may need to communicate with a large number of processors and programmable controllers. Another use of this is the handling of important and time-critical alarm or emergency control signals in a factory. Because of their importance, an acknowledgment is needed so that the sender can be assured that the signal got through. Because of the urgency of the signal, the user might not want to take the time to first establish a logical connection and then send the data.

## CSMA/CD (IEEE 802.3)

The IEEE 802.3 standard specifies the use of CSMA/CD over a bus or tree topology.

### Medium Options

The IEEE 802.3 committee has been the most active in defining alternative physical configurations. This is both good and bad. On the good side, the standard has been responsive to evolving technology. On the bad side, the customer, not to mention the potential vendor, is faced with a bewildering array of options. The committee has been careful to insure that the various options can be easily integrated into a configuration that satisfies a variety of needs. Thus, the user with a complex set of requirements may find the flexibility and variety of the 802.3 standard to be an asset.

To distinguish the various implementations that are available, the committee has developed a concise notation:

<data rate in Mbps> <signaling method>

<maximum segment length in hundreds of meters>

The defined alternatives, which are summarized in Table 4-1, are

10BASE5

10BASE2

1BASE5

10BASET

10BROAD36

The 10BASE5 specification is the original 802.3 standard; it specifies a 10-Mbps baseband coaxial cable LAN using standard baseband coaxial cable. The maximum length of a segment of cable is 500 meters, with a maximum of 100 taps per segment allowed. The length of the network can be extended using repeaters (see Figure 2-11). The standard allows a maximum of four repeaters

**Table 4-1**   IEEE 802.3 Physical Layer Medium Alternatives

| Parameter | 10BASE5 | 10BASE2 | 1BASE5 | 10BASET | 10BR OAD36 |
|---|---|---|---|---|---|
| Transmission medium | Coaxial cable (50 ohm) | Coaxial cable (50 ohm) | Unshielded twisted pair | Unshielded twisted pair | Coaxial cable (75 ohm) |
| Signaling technique | Baseband (Manchester) | Baseband (Manchester) | Baseband (Manchester) | Baseband (Manchester) | Broadband (DPSK) |
| Data rate (Mbps) | 10 | 10 | 1 | 10 | 10 |
| Maximum segment length (m) | 500 | 185 | 500 | 100 | 1800 |
| Network span (m) | 2500 | 925 | 2500 | 500 | 3600 |
| Nodes per segment | 100 | 30 | — | — | — |
| Cable diameter (mm) | 10 | 5 | 0.4–0.6 | 0.4–0.6 | 0.4–1.0 |

in the path between any two stations, extending the effective length of the network to 2.5 km.

This original version, issued in 1985, was soon followed by a new option, 10BASE2, sometimes called Cheapernet. This provides for the use of a thinner coaxial cable at the same data rate. The thinner cable results in significantly cheaper electronics, at the penalty of fewer stations and shorter length. Segment length is reduced to 185 meters with a maximum of 30 taps per segment. It is targeted to lower-cost devices, such as UNIX workstations and personal computers.

Another option, known as StarLAN, specifies an unshielded twisted pair version operating at 1 Mbps. As the name suggests, the layout of StarLAN uses star wiring. In particular, it uses the hub arrangement described in Chapter 2 (Figures 2-12 through 2-14). This option costs substantially less than either of the coaxial cable options and is targeted at personal computer installations that do not require high capacity. This option could be appropriate for a departmental-level LAN.

The attraction of the 1BASE5 specification is that it allows the use of inexpensive unshielded twisted pair wire, which is ordinary telephone wire. Such wire is often prewired in office buildings as excess telephone cable, and can be used for LANs. The disadvantage of this specification is the rather low data rate of 1 Mbps. By sacrificing some distance, it is possible to develop a 10-Mbps LAN using the unshielded twisted pair medium. Such an approach is specified in the latest physical medium addition to the 802.3 family, the 10BASET specification.

As with the 1BASE5 specification, the 10BASET specification defines a star-shaped topology. The details of this topology differ slightly from those of 1BASE5. In both cases, a simple system consists of a number of stations connected to a central point. In both cases, stations are connected to the central point with two twisted pairs. The central point accepts input on any one line and repeats it on all the other lines. In the case of the 10BASET specification, the central point is referred to as a *multiport repeater*.

Stations attach to the multiport repeater by a point-to-point link. Ordinarily, the link consists of two unshielded twisted pairs. The data rate is 10 Mbps using Manchester encoding. Because of the high data rate and the poor transmission qualities of unshielded twisted pair, the length of a link is limited to 100 meters. As an alternative, an optical fiber link may be used. In this case, the maximum length is 500 meters.

The distinction between a 1BASE5 hub and a 10BASET multiport repeater becomes clear when we consider a multi-star arrangement. Figure 4-8 shows a sample configuration for 10BASET. The medium access unit (MAU) denotes the logic required for interfacing a device to the LAN. Note that the connection between one repeater and the next is a link that appears the same as an ordinary station link. In fact, the repeater makes no distinction between a station and another repeater. Recall that in the 1BASE5 system, there is a distinction between intermediate hubs and the header hub. In the 10BASET system, all multiport repeaters function in the same manner, and indeed function in the same manner as an ordinary repeater on a 10BASE5 or 10BASE2 system:

- A valid signal appearing on any input is repeated on all other links.
- If two inputs occur, causing a collision, a collision enforcement signal is transmitted on all links.
- If a collision enforcement signal is detected on any input, it is repeated on all other links.

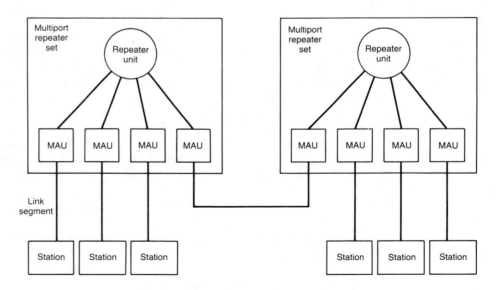

**Figure 4-8** A simple 10BASET configuration.

One advantage of the use of repeaters and the use of a data rate of 10 Mbps is that the 10BASET system can be mixed with 10BASE2 and 10BASE5 systems. The only requirement is that the medium access unit (MAU) conform to the appropriate specification. Figure 4-9 shows a configuration that contains four 10BASET systems and one 10BASE5 system.

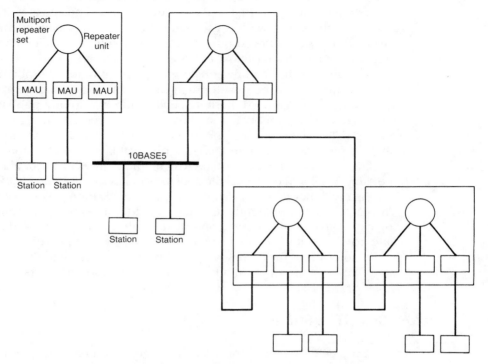

**Figure 4-9** A mixed 10BASET and 10BASE5 configuration.

Table 4-2 summarizes the allowable connections. The maximum transmission path permitted between any two stations is five segments and four repeater sets. A segment is a point-to-point link, coaxial cable 10BASE5 or coaxial cable 10BASE2 segment. The maximum number of coaxial cable segments in a path is three.

Finally, a 10-Mbps broadband option, called 10BROAD36, has been added. This supports more stations over greater distances than the baseband versions, at greater cost.

**TABLE 4-2** Allowable Connections to a 10BASET Multiport Repeater

| Transmission Medium | Number of Attached Devices | Maximum Length (m) |
|---|---|---|
| Two unshielded twisted pairs | 2 | 100 |
| Two optical fiber cables | 2 | 500 |
| Coaxial cable (10BASE2) | 30 | 185 |
| Coaxial cable (10BASE5) | 100 | 500 |

## Ethernet

The original 10-Mbps IEEE 802.3 standard was based on and is quite similar to Ethernet. Ethernet is a widely used type of LAN developed in the mid-1970s by Xerox. Xerox's announced purpose for this system was to develop a de facto industry standard for LANs and to license the technology to other vendors. Xerox strengthened its hand by enlisting Digital Equipment Corporation and Intel to participate in the development of specifications and components. In 1980, version 1.0 of the Ethernet specification was jointly published by the three participants. In 1982, a slightly revised specification, version 2.0, was released. This later version incorporates changes and enhancements at the physical layer to conform to the IEEE physical layer specification.

Ethernet uses the same CSMA/CD medium access control algorithm and the same baseband coaxial cable specification as the IEEE 802.3 standard. Unfortunately, Ethernet differs from the IEEE specification in some of the details. The packet format is slightly different. In addition, Ethernet encompasses the logic of both medium access control and logical link control, and restricts the latter to an unacknowledged connectionless service. However, it requires only minor software or firmware changes to convert from one to the other. A number of vendors offer both Ethernet and the corresponding version of 802.3.

## Token Bus (IEEE 802.4)

The IEEE 802.4 standard specifies the use of token passing over a bus or tree topology. The token bus standard specifies three physical layer options (Table 4-3). The first is a broadband system, which supports data channels at 1, 5, and 10 Mbps with bandwidths of 1.5, 6, and 12 MHz, respectively. The standard recommends the use of a single-cable split system with a headend frequency translator. The dual cable configuration is also allowed.

The second is a scheme known as *carrierband,* or single-channel broadband. Recall that carrierband signaling means that the entire spectrum of the cable is devoted to a single transmission path for analog signals. Because carrierband is dedicated to a single data channel, modem output does not need to be confined to a narrow bandwidth. Energy can spread over the cable's spectrum. As a result, the electronics are simple and inexpensive compared with those for broadband. Carrierband data rates of 1, 5, and 10 Mbps are specified.

The most recent addition to the IEEE 802.4 physical layer standard is an optical fiber specification. Three data rates are specified: 5, 10, and 20 Mbps. In keeping with standard practice for optical fiber systems, the bandwidth and carrier are specified in terms of wavelength instead of frequency. For all three data rates, the bandwidth is 270 nanometers and the center wavelength is between 800 and 910 nanometers.

The 802.4 optical fiber specification can be used with any topology that is logically a bus. That is, a transmission from any one station is received by all other stations, and if two stations transmit at the same time, a collision occurs.

**TABLE 4-3**   IEEE 802.4 Physical Layer Medium Alternatives

| Parameter | Phase Continuous Carrierband | Phase Coherent Carrierband | | Broadband | | | Optical Fiber |
|---|---|---|---|---|---|---|---|
| Data rate (Mbps) | 1 | 5 | 10 | 1 | 5 | 10 | 10 |
| Bandwidth | N.A. | N.A. | N.A. | 1.5 MHz | 6 MHz | 12 MHz | 270 nm |
| Center Frequency | 5 MHz | 7.5 MHz | 15 MHz | * | * | * | 800–910 nm |
| Modulation | Manchester/ phase continuous FSK | Phase coherent FSK | | Multilevel duobinary AM/PSK | | | Manchester/ On-off |
| Topology | Omnidirectional bus | Omnidirectional bus | | Directional bus (tree) | | | Active or passive star |
| Transmission Medium | Coaxial cable (75 ohm) | Coaxial cable (75 ohm) | | Coaxial cable (75 ohm) | | | Optical fiber |
| Scrambling | No | No | | Yes | | | No |

\* = depends on channel
N.A. = not applicable

Presently, a simple bus system is impractical because low-loss optical taps are expensive. Instead, the standard recommends the use of active or passive stars.

For both the active and passive stars, each station attaches to a central node through two optical fibers, one for transmission in each direction. The active star operates in the same fashion as the star topologies used for 802.3. That is, a transmission on any one input fiber to the central node is retransmitted on all output fibers.

The passive star system is based on the use of a passive star coupler. Such schemes have been in use for 10-Mbps CSMA/CD systems for some time. The passive star coupler is fabricated by fusing together a number of optical fibers. The transmit fibers from all the stations enter the coupler on one side, and all receive fibers exit on the other side. Any light input to one of the fibers on one side of the coupler will be equally divided among and output through all the fibers on the other side (Figure 4-10).

Two methods of constructing the star coupler have been pursued: the biconic fused coupler and the mixing rod coupler. In the biconic fused coupler, the fibers are bundled together, then heated with an oxyhydrogen flame and pulled into a biconical tapered shape. That is, the rods come together into a fused mass that tapers into a conical shape and then expands out again. The mixing rod approach begins in the same fashion. Then, the biconical taper is cut at the waist and a cylindrical rod is inserted between the tapers and fused to the two cut ends. This latter technique allows the use of a less narrow waist and is easier to make. The current 802.4 specification does not dictate which sort of coupler to use.

Commercially available passive star couplers can support a few tens of stations at a radial distance of up to a kilometer or more. Figure 4-11 shows the

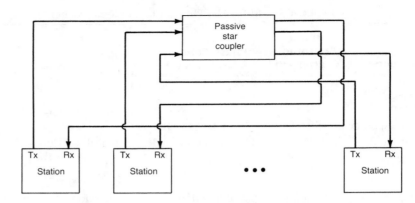

**Figure 4-10** Optical fiber passive star configuration.

operating range of the two types of couplers. The limitations on number of stations and distances are imposed by the losses in the network. With today's equipment, the optical power loss between transmitter and receiver that can be tolerated is on the order of 25 to 30 dB. In the figure, the outer edge of each region is defined by a maximum end-to-end attenuation of 30 dB.

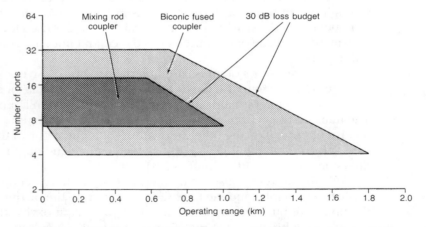

**Figure 4-11** Operating range for an optical fiber passive star LAN.

## Token Ring (IEEE 802.5)

The IEEE 802.5 standard specifies the use of token passing over a ring topology. Only a single medium option is specified in 802.5: shielded twisted pair at 1 and 4 Mbps (Table 4-4).

**TABLE 4-4** Physical Layer Alternatives for Ring LAN Standards

|  | Token Ring (IEEE 802.5) | Fiber Distributed Data Interface (FDDI) |
|---|---|---|
| Transmission medium | Shielded twisted pair | Optical fiber |
| Data rate | 1 or 4 Mbps | 100 Mbps |
| Maximum number of repeaters | 250 | 1000 |
| Maximum length between repeaters | Not specified | 2000 m |

This standard is supported by IBM, and a large number of other vendors also have 802.5 products. In addition to providing a shielded twisted pair product to conform to the IEEE standard, IBM (and other vendors) also offers unshielded twisted pair at 1 and 4 Mbps and shielded twisted pair at 16 Mbps. The IBM product is intended to be configured in a star layout (Figure 2-9b) for easy installation and maintenance.

## Fiber Distributed Data Interface (FDDI)

The newest LAN standard is the fiber distributed data interface (FDDI), developed by the American National Standards Institute. The topology of FDDI is a ring. The medium access control technique is token ring, with only minor differences from the IEEE token ring specification. The medium specified is 100-Mbps optical fiber. The medium specification incorporates guidelines designed to ensure high availability.

The FDDI standard addresses three general areas of application: backend LANs, high-speed office LANs, and backbone LANs. A *backend LAN* is used in a computer room environment to interconnect mainframe computers and mass storage devices. The key requirement here is for bulk data transfer among a limited number of devices in a small area; high reliability is also a requirement. A *high-speed office LAN* is one that can meet the high data rate requirements of today's office applications, including distributed database applications, facsimile, mixed text and facsimile terminals, and various graphics terminals and applications. This application is relatively new, and there is little experience with such networks. As with backend networks, there is a requirement here for high capacity and reliability. Finally, the *backbone LAN* interconnects other LANs and standalone equipment on a large site. The backbone LAN gives the network manager greater flexibility to tailor networking facilities to networking needs. For example, a number of low-capacity, low-cost, departmental-level LANs can be interconnected by a backbone LAN. Again, high capacity and reliability are key requirements.

# LAN Configurations

Having listed all the standardized options, we are now in a position to offer some comparisons.

## 802.3 versus 802.4

To discuss the relative merits of the two bus standards, we first need to compare baseband with broadband and to compare the two medium access control algorithms.

### Baseband versus Broadband

Baseband has the advantage of simplicity and, in principle, lower cost. The layout of a baseband cable plant is simple: A building electrician should be able to do the job. Baseband's potential disadvantages include limitations in capacity, number of stations, and distance—but these are disadvantages only if your requirements exceed those limits.

Broadband's strength is its tremendous capacity. Broadband can carry a wide variety of traffic on a number of channels and, with the use of active amplifiers, can achieve very wide coverage. Also, the system is based on mature CATV technology, with reliable and readily available components. A disadvantage of broadband systems is that they are more complex than baseband to install and maintain, requiring an experienced radio-frequency engineer. Also, because all transmissions must travel two paths (inbound and outbound) on broadband, the average propagation delay between stations is twice that for a comparable baseband system. This reduces the efficiency and performance of the system. Finally, a broadband system requires the use of modems, which are more expensive than the digital transceivers of a baseband system.

### CSMA/CD versus Token Bus

Perhaps the most significant difference between CSMA/CD and token bus is in performance. Under heavy loads, CSMA/CD performs poorly because of an increase in collisions. The problem becomes worse with an increase in data rate or an increase in the physical length of the bus. In contrast, token bus performs well under heavy loads and is less affected by data rate and bus length.

Token bus has a number of other advantages over CSMA/CD. First, it is easy to regulate the traffic in a token bus system; different stations can be allowed to hold the token for differing amounts of time. Thus, the network configuration manager can assign higher priority to some stations. Second, the requirement for listening to the bus for a collision while transmitting imposes physical and electrical constraints on the CSMA/CD system that do not appear in a token bus system. Third, token bus is deterministic; that is, there is a known upper bound to the amount of time any station must wait before transmitting. This upper bound is known because each station in the logical ring can hold the token only for a specified amount of time. In contrast, the delay time in CSMA/CD can be expressed only statistically. In addition, because every attempt to transmit under CSMA/CD can, in principle, produce a collision, there is a possibility that a station could be shut out indefinitely. For process control and other real-time applications, this nondeterministic behavior is undesirable.

The principal disadvantage of token bus is its complexity: The logic at each station far exceeds that required for CSMA/CD. However, this is a relatively minor problem. Token bus products on chips have appeared on the market, bringing the price down to the range of CSMA/CD chips.

## Application of 802.3 and 802.4

When selecting a bus or tree topology LAN that conforms to a standard, the choices are baseband or broadband with CSMA/CD (802.3), or broadband or carrierband with token bus (802.4). Optical fiber is not yet an attractive option because of the cost and technical problems of using that medium for multipoint transmission. Its use in a star configuration limits the number of devices that can be supported.

Token bus was linked with broadband in the standard due to performance. Broadband systems can cover very large areas with the use of amplifiers, and CSMA/CD performs poorly when the bus is long. CSMA/CD was linked with baseband for historical reasons. With the standards in place, that linkage is a given; that is, if the choice is baseband, the 802.3 standard must be used.

For a very large site, such as a large office building or a cluster of buildings, the CSMA/CD standard by itself is not appropriate. Broadband is more suited to supporting the long distances involved and the potentially harsher outdoor or underground environment in a multiple-building situation. However, referring back to our discussion of tiered local networks, it might be reasonable to use a token bus broadband system as a backbone and one or more of the CSMA/CD baseband options to support smaller units within the organization, with the CSMA/CD LANs interconnected through the token bus broadband backbone. The carrierband version of token bus could also be used for this purpose, but this is unlikely to be as inexpensive as a comparable CSMA/CD baseband product.

In the factory environment, the token bus standard is preferred. Indeed, the standard was developed with that application in mind. The broadband and carrierband media are well suited to the potentially harsh or electromagnetically noisy factory environment, and the token bus medium access control scheme provides the determinism needed for critical control signals and alarms.

One additional application worth considering is video support. At present, the only type of LAN that can support this requirement is a broadband LAN.

## 802.3 versus 802.5

The twisted pair token ring (802.5) is not a competitor to token bus for large-area coverage or for factory applications. However, it can be considered an alternative to CSMA/CD baseband bus (802.3) for many office applications.

Token ring has several advantages over CSMA/CD. First, as with token bus, the token ring medium access control algorithm exhibits superior performance to CSMA/CD. A 4-Mbps token ring should provide about the same effective throughput as a 10-Mbps CSMA/CD bus. Second, twisted pair is easier to work with than coaxial cable. Costs of the two systems are comparable.

## 802.4 versus FDDI

Until the use of image-processing systems is substantially increased, the high data rate of FDDI is probably more than will be required for most intrabuilding networks, with the exception of computer-room networks. The 100-Mbps fiber ring, however, would make an excellent backbone communications network. In this role, FDDI competes with token bus broadband (802.4). Factors that could influence the decision are cost, vendor reputation, and whether video support is required.

# *Case Study 3*
# Boeing Computer Services, Inc.[1]

Boeing Computer Services, Inc. (BCS) is a subsidiary of Boeing Corporation that provides computer consulting, data processing consulting, and software development services to the rest of Boeing and also to many outside clients. BCS decided to develop a data wiring plan for all of Boeing. Because BCS was in the process of moving into several new office buildings, the plan was to be tested in the new buildings. Based on this experience, a master plan for all current and new buildings for BCS and Boeing as a whole would be developed, with wiring to be retrofitted to existing buildings.

Boeing has a pressing need for a consistent single-medium solution to its data communications needs. A typical Boeing employee changes locations every nine to twelve months, and along with the employee goes his or her terminal. Looked at another way, it is not unusual for 50 percent of the installed data terminals to be moved each year. Because a variety of cable types are used to support the current data terminal inventory, this presents a cabling nightmare for the wire maintenance crew. Furthermore, it is difficult to troubleshoot cable problems in existing buildings because of the different types of cable in

---

[1] This case study is based on material in J. Kelley, "Can One Cable Type Handle All Network Needs?," *Data Communications,* September 1987.

cable trays. A lot of computer downtime at Boeing has been attributed to locating the correct cable. Installing and maintaining a separate type of wire for every different type of terminal is costly and time-consuming. The impact of moves, additions, changes, and cable faults can be minimized by prewiring new and existing buildings with a single type of cable.

In addition, Boeing needed to prepare for the introduction of local area networks. Although some terminals and computers would be wired together directly or through patch panels, Boeing expects virtually all of its interconnection needs to be met with LANs, specifically, a combination of 802.3 and 802.5 LANs using twisted pair wiring in both cases.

BCS's solution was to choose shielded 22-gauge twisted-pair cable containing four solid copper conductors that will support data speeds up to 16 Mbps in both directions (one twisted pair of copper conductors for each direction). This cable was introduced in 1984 by IBM as part of its recommended cabling system for buildings. Known as IBM Type 1 data cable, it is designed to let users permanently wire buildings in a systematic way. On each floor of a building, a twisted pair is installed between a wiring closet (usually the telephone closet) and each office. By appropriate patching in the wire closet and by the use of interconnections between closets on different floors, any form of wire interconnection can be implemented. When the wiring is completed, from 80 to 90 percent of Boeing's terminals and computers will run on this type of cable. Some specialized graphics workstations, however, will not work on Type 1 because they use more than four conductors.

The wiring scheme was first tested in a new building at Two Renton Place (2RP) in Renton, Washington. Occupancy of 2RP was set for July 1986. Two teams were put together in January 1986. The first team, called the Implementation Committee, was responsible for overseeing the process of installing the cable. The second team, called the BCS Committee, was responsible for assuring that the wiring satisfied user requirements and that data processing equipment was properly installed. Each of the two groups met every week from late January 1986 until completion of the building in July 1986. The BCS committee met every week after completion of the building to make sure all computing equipment went in without a problem. The equipment was installed every weekend from the first of July until the end of August.

Figure 4-12 is the cable layout plan for 2RP. Figure 4-12a shows the distribution rack on all seven floors. In b, 32 cables run between data closets on each floor. In c, 6 patch panels are installed above the false ceiling on the cable tray. Figure 4-12d shows how each patch panel is mounted on the cable tray.

The results from 2RP were highly satisfactory. All terminals came up immediately without any downtime. Detailed cable records and cable labeling allows BCS to relocate devices, make alterations easily, and isolate any faults quickly. The shielded twisted pair cable provides excellent performance (few errors) even at very high data rates.

Since the success at 2RP, the Type 1 cable has been designated the standard for all Boeing technical and office buildings in the Puget Sound area, and installation is proceeding.

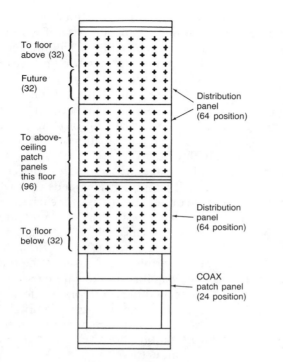

To floor above (32)

Future (32)

To above-ceiling patch panels this floor (96)

To floor below (32)

Distribution panel (64 position)

Distribution panel (64 position)

COAX patch panel (24 position)

*(a) Distribution rack (typical floors 2 through 7).*

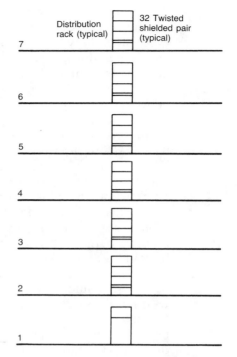

Distribution rack (typical)

32 Twisted shielded pair (typical)

7

6

5

4

3

2

1

*(b) Cables run between data closets on each floor.*

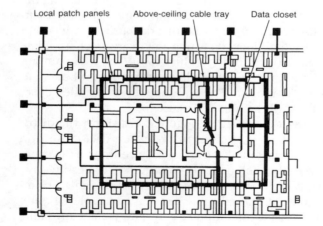

Local patch panels    Above-ceiling cable tray    Data closet

*(c) Patch panels installed in false ceiling on the cable tray.*

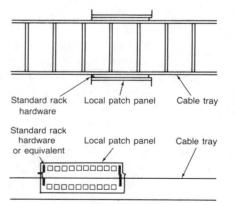

Standard rack hardware    Local patch panel    Cable tray

Standard rack hardware or equivalent    Local patch panel    Cable tray

*(d) How patch panels are mounted on cable tray.*

**Figure 4-12** 2RP layout.

# Summary

The LAN marketplace exhibits wide variety, making the job of selection difficult. Fortunately, there is a way to structure the various options so that an intelligent strategy can be developed: the standards for LANs. Although a number of proprietary and nonstandard products remain on the market, there has been an overwhelming acceptance of standards by both vendors and customers. In addition, the standards are rich enough to allow the selection of a LAN or a number of LANs tailored to the specific requirements of the customer's organization.

LAN standards are organized on the basis of logical link control, medium access control, and physical specifications. Logical link control specifies the mechanisms for addressing stations across the medium and for controlling the exchange of data between two users. Three alternatives services are provided for attached devices using logical link control: unacknowledged connectionless service, connection-mode service, and acknowledged connectionless service.

The medium access control specification depends on the topology chosen. For bus and tree topologies, the alternatives are CSMA/CD and token bus. The CSMA/CD technique was originally used on Ethernet and is perhaps the most common access technique in use. Token bus was intended for factory applications, although it can be used also in the office environment. For the ring topology, the token ring technique is used.

Four families of standards have been developed for LANs based on the medium access control technique and the physical LAN involved. The IEEE 802.3 standards employ CSMA/CD, and are used on baseband bus, broadband bus, broadband tree, and unshielded twisted pair. In the latter case, the configuration is physically a star but logically a bus. The IEEE 802.4 standard employs token bus, and is used on broadband and carrierband bus systems and broadband and carrierband tree systems. An optical fiber option has been specified, but no products are yet available. IEEE 802.5 is the well-known IBM token ring, standardized by the IEEE 802 committee. The IEEE standard is limited to shielded twisted pair; IBM offers both shielded and unshielded twisted pair versions. Finally, the FDDI standard specifies the use of optical fiber in a ring topology.

# Chapter 5

# LAN Software

U P UNTIL NOW, we have considered a local area network as a means of transferring bits from one station attached to a LAN to another station. This is the fundamental function of a LAN. For stations to take advantage of the connectivity provided by the LAN, however, logic is needed above the MAC and LLC layers. Thus, software is needed so that devices can function cooperatively on the LAN.

The scope of software that provides some sort of cooperation is immense. In this chapter, we confine the discussion to the most important and common types. The chapter begins with a discussion of servers. The concept of a server has been most commonly associated with personal computer LANs, but it can be applied to any type of LAN supporting any type of equipment. We look at the architecture to support the server concept, then examine some examples. Next, the issue of terminal support—one of the more awkward problems to handle across a network—is explored. Finally, some distributed applications developed as part of a communications architecture are presented.

# Servers

One of the key benefits of a LAN is the ability to share expensive resources, such as secondary storage devices and high-quality printers. A common way in which this is done is to provide one or more servers on the LAN. Figure 5-1 illustrates the concept in a personal computer LAN. On the LAN are a number of personal computers, not necessarily of the same type and not necessarily using the same operating system. In addition, for each shared resource, there are one or more servers. Personal computer users have access to the shared resource by means of special software in the personal computer. In this section, we discuss the design of the software needed to support servers, then look at several examples.

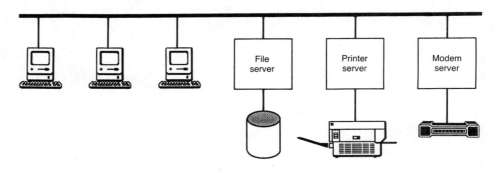

**Figure 5-1** LAN servers.

## Server Software Architecture

A LAN server provides shared access to a resource, such as a disk or printer. The various user stations (for example, personal computers or UNIX workstations) on the LAN can access this resource across the LAN.

Figure 5-2 suggests the typical architecture for a server. The server is typically a dedicated microcomputer that controls one or more resources. As with other stations on the LAN, it includes a network interface module. This module contains the hardware and software for interacting with the LAN. Typically, it includes the logic up through at least the LLC layer (Figure 4-7).

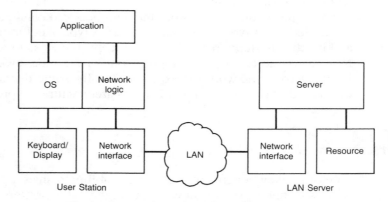

**Figure 5-2.** Architecture of a workstation server.

The user station has a network interface also. In addition, it has network logic that allows it to communicate with the server. This logic is accessed by an application. For example, to write a file to the server disk, the application issues a write command to the network logic module. This module in turn prepares and sends the appropriate messages to the server.

This architecture is both powerful and flexible. The power of this approach is that it can be used to control virtually any kind of resource. New servers can be added to a LAN at any time (with the appropriate network software added to each user station). The flexibility of this approach is that it does not depend on a particular type of computer. Thus, the network logic can be tailored for any type of personal computer or workstation.

An important characteristic of a server's capability is the degree to which it is transparent. In the ideal case, a user or an application can use the same commands and parameters to access a resource that is locally attached to the user station or remotely attached to a server. For example, the user or application should be able to read a file from or write a file to a disk using the same commands for a local disk as for the remote server disk. In some cases, the user or application will have to explicitly select either the local or remote resource, after which the commands and parameters are identical. In other cases, the decision of whether to use a local or remote resource is made by the network software on the basis of file name or another implicit designator.

## Disk and File Servers

The growth in the use of LANs and in the number of personal computers and workstations on LANs has fueled the growth in interest in file servers. As we have pointed out, there is a need for these systems to share and exchange data and files. Although each computer on the LAN could create and control its own files and make those files available to others, it is preferable to provide a centralized storage and management facility for files that will be shared by a substantial portion of the community. The individual personal computers and workstations, being controlled by their users, cannot be guaranteed to be always available and reliable. The solution is to use a file server machine to administer shared resources and support applications running on the workstations.

A file server is a separate computer (or collection of computers) attached to the LAN that provides a common service to all other systems on the LAN. Typically, the file server is a microcomputer or, occasionally, a minicomputer. The primary service of the file server is to provide a shared storage space for files. In addition, the server can provide other valuable services:

- *Automatic backup and recovery:* Backup is the function of periodically copying the contents of a file system onto a backup disk or tape. This is a defense against storage media failure and user error. Backups must be performed regularly, and the recovery procedure must be available for use. The average user of a personal computer or workstation should not be burdened with this responsibility.

- *User mobility:* A user should be able to use different computers at different times for several reasons. One, a computer may fail. Second, some people need or want to work at more than one physical location. Third, workstations are sometimes managed as a common pool. A file server makes it feasible to provide a working environment independent of the workstation used without physically transporting the file storage media (disk or tape).

- *Links to other file servers:* An organization may have a number of LANs in one or more locations, each with a file server. A file transfer facility can be implemented in each file server to allow users to access files on other LANs We will discuss this concept later in this chapter.

The term *file server* has unfortunately been used for devices covering a broad range of capabilities. Two extremes can be identified: shared storage and shared file management systems.

Many file servers simply provide a centralized disk facility that can be used as an extension of local storage by personal computer users. Such systems are sometimes referred to as *disk servers.* The user simply perceives a much larger disk space than before and may use this disk space to store and retrieve files. There is no file sharing. To send files between users, each user must employ a separate program called a file transfer facility. The disk server may provide automatic backup and user mobility. In addition, these systems may provide a cost savings: In general, the larger a storage system, the lower the cost per bit of storage. Thus centralized shared storage, which is relatively cheap, allows the use of personal computers with very little or no disk storage.

At the other extreme is a file server that provides all the file management capabilities found on a time-sharing system. Thus, in addition to providing storage space, the file server allows multiple users to have access to files. The server controls concurrent access to files, enforces access rights and restrictions, and provides directory structures that recognize file names and support the grouping of files.

## Printer Servers

A printer server (Figure 5-3) can handle the printing requirements of a number of user workstations. This not only saves money on printing, but also can make printing easier and faster.

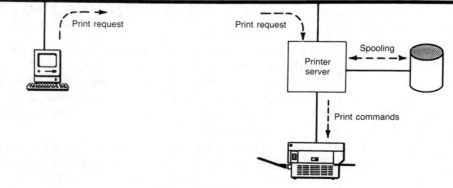

**Figure 5-3** Printer server.

The printer server uses one of the oldest of operating system techniques, known as spooling. A spool (simultaneous peripheral operation on line) is a combination of hardware and software that redirects I/O requests from the relatively slow printer to a fast disk. As print requests come in, each document or file is first spooled out onto the disk. The files are organized as a first-in, first-out queue. The server retrieves files from the disk one at a time and prints them. This spooling facility overcomes two problems relating to the use of the printer.

The first problem is when the document to be printed next is larger than the available space in main memory. With a server, the document can be stored on disk and read in a block at a time and printed. The second problem occurs when one or more users issue a print request while the printer is printing a file. These requests are queued so that users can continue their work, without waiting for the printer to become available.

## Modem Server

A simple but useful capability to add to a LAN is a modem server. We will see in the next chapter that the desire to interconnect LANs with each other and with wide-area networks leads to the use of specialized devices called bridges and routers. Sometimes, however, simple modem access is required. For example, to access an information retrieval and electronic mail system, such as CompuServe, the user needs a modem to connect to an outside telephone line and to dial into the desired system. As with other hardware resources, modems are relatively expensive and should be shared. Typically, only a small fraction of the number of users will need modem access at any one time. Thus, a server with one or a few attached modems and as many telephone lines as modems can support the LAN user community.

The user requests access to a modem and provides a phone number. The server activates the modem, dials the number, and reports the result. If the call is successfully placed, the user is provided with a connection. After the user has a connection, data can be sent and received as if the user were using the modem directly. The only difference that the user may perceive has to do with the fact that when the data arrives at the server over the modem, the data is buffered and sent to the user in packets. Thus, the user may perceive a bursty flow of characters onto the screen.

## Server Software

As mentioned, the implementation of a server requires the use in all workstations of common software that is compatible with the software running in the server. A number of vendors sell packages that include server software, plus the workstation software that is required to work with the servers. The entire package, or sometimes just the server portion of the software, is referred to as a *network operating system.* This title is not strictly accurate. On the workstations, server-related software is subordinate to the native operating system. On the server itself, server software may include an operating system optimized to provide high performance for the specific application. In other cases, the server runs a standard operating system, and the server software is a supplemental set of system and application programs running under the server's operating system. All of this is further confused because the user can buy the server hardware and the server software from one vendor or from two vendors. Table 5-1 compares five of the most widely used server software packages.

**TABLE 5-1**  Features of Five LAN Operating Systems (●= yes; ○ = no).

| | IBM PC LAN Program 1.30 | IBM OS/2 LAN Server 1.00 | 3Com 3+Open 1.0 | 3Com 3+Share 1.3.1 | Novell SFT NetWare 286 version 2.15 |
|---|---|---|---|---|---|
| Price | $245 per user | $1040 for server $830 per OS/2 workstation $245 per DOS workstation* | $995 for 5 users $2995 for unlimited users | $595 for 5 users $2495 for unlimited users | $4695 for up to 100 users |
| Minimum server requirements | | | | | |
| Hardware | 80286 or 80386 | 80286 or 80386 | 80286 or 80386 | 80286 or 80386 | 80286 or 80386 |
| Software | DOS 3.3 or 4.0 | OS/2 EE 1.1 | OS/2 1.0 | DOS 3.1 or higher | |
| Memory | 640K for extended services 350K for basic services | 5 Mb | 4 Mb | 640K | 1 Mb† |
| DOS workstation memory used by the network operating system | 81—190K | 81—190K | NBP: 25K XNS: 100K | NBP: 25K XNS: 100K | 46—60K |
| Peer-to-peer resource sharing | ● | ● | ○ | ● | ○ |
| Disk caching | ● | ● | ● | ● | ● |
| E-mail | ● | ● | [●] | [●] | ○ |
| Disk diagnostics | ○ | ○ | ○ | ○ | ● |
| Supports multiple file servers | ● | ● | ● | ● | ● |
| Server can act as a workstation | ● | ● | ● | ● | ○ |
| Administrator access from remote station | ● | ● | ● | [●] | ● |

**TABLE 5-1**  *(cont.)*

| | IBM PC LAN Program 1.30 | IBM OS/2 LAN Server 1.00 | 3Com 3+Open 1.0 | 3Com 3+Share 1.3.1 | Novell SFT NetWare 286 version 2.15 |
|---|---|---|---|---|---|
| **Traffic monitoring** | | | | | |
| Reports current log-ons | ● | ● | ● | ● | ● |
| Reports shared resources | ● | ● | ● | ○ | ● |
| Error log | ● | ● | ● | ● | ● |
| Audit trail | ○ | ● | ● | ○ | ● |
| User chargeback accounting | ○ | ○ | ○ | ○ | ● |
| **Security** | | | | | |
| Passwords attached to users | ● | ● | ● | ● | ● |
| Passwords attached to resources | ● | ● | ● | ● | ● |
| Time restrictions | ○ | ○ | ● | ○ | ● |
| Station address restrictions | ○ | ○ | ○ | ○ | ● |
| **Network hardware supported** | | | | | |
| Ethernet | ○ | ○ | ● | ● | ● |
| Token Ring | ● | ● | ● | ● | ● |
| ARCnet | ○ | ○ | ● | ○ | ● |
| **Connectivity options** | | | | | |
| AppleTalk | ○ | ○ | ● | ● | ● |
| LU 6.2 | ● | ● | ● | ● | ● |
| SNA | ● | ● | ● | ● | ● |
| DECnet | ○ | ○ | ● | ● | ○ |
| TCP/IP | ○ | ○ | ● | ● | ○‡ |
| X.25 | ○ | ○ | ● | ● | ● |

*Requires IBM PC LAN program.
†1024K bytes (1 megabyte) if attaching a 70-megabyte hard disk drive or less; 2048K bytes (2 megabytes) if attaching a 70-megabyte or larger hard disk drive.
‡TCP/IP gateway available from third-party vendors.
 [ ] = Optional.
Source: *Byte*, July 1989.

## Server Hardware

Disk and file servers are the most popular type of servers on the market, and there are many vendors. To give some idea of the breadth of products, Table 5-2 provides a sample of products with their characteristics and prices, as of late 1988. Although most of the entries are self-explanatory, a few need clarification. "Compatible LAN" refers to the LAN interface boards that are accommodated. Thus, if a server is compatible with StarLAN, it will take a communications board that includes the physical interface for StarLAN, and the medium access control and logical link control logic for StarLAN.

**TABLE 5-2** Local Area Network Servers

| Vendor | Product | Compatible LAN | Maximum Ports (Serial/Parallel) | Operating System | RAM Size (bytes) | Memory Cache Size (bytes) | Minimum RAM for System Software (bytes) | Microprocessor/Clock Rate | Memory Channel Bus Width (bits) | Disk Capacity (bytes) | Disk Seek Time (msec) | Disk Transfer Rate (bit/sec) | Tape Backup Capacity (bytes) | Minimum/Maximum Price |
|---|---|---|---|---|---|---|---|---|---|---|---|---|---|---|
| Alloy Computer Products, Inc. Framingham, Mass. | Cluster Plus | Ethernet, token ring, 10NET, Arcnet, AlloyNet | 2/3 | MS-DOS 3.3 and NetWare | 640K to 16M | 8M to 15M | 200K to 1M | IntelCorp. 80286/NA | 16/16 | 150M to 600M | 16 to 27 | 10M | 120M | $15,000/$28,000 |
| Apple Computer, Inc. Cupertino, Calif. | AppleShare File Server | LocalTalk, EtherTalk | None/none | Macintosh OS | 1M to 4M (Mac Plus & SE); 1M to 16M (Mac II) | 3M to 15M | 1M | Motorola Corp. 68020/NA | 32/32 | 20M to 43M | NA | NA | 40M | $3,600 for Model SE, $6,300 for Mac II, $3,700 for Mac Plus |
| AT&T Basking Ridge, N.J. | Starlan 6386 WorkGroup System | Ethernet, Starlan, token ring | 33/9 | Unix System V/386, Release 3.1, 3.2, MS-DOS 3.2, OS/2, Microsoft Corp.'s Xenix | 1M to 16M | 12M | 4M | Intel 80386/16M or 20MHz | 32/32 or 16 | 8M to 33M (for 20MHz); 40M to 135M (for 16MHz) | 20 or 30 | 5M (40M and 60M disk); 10M (80M, 135M, 300M disks) | 40M, 60M, 125M | $4,800 (16MHz, 40M disk) to $6,400 (16MHz, 135M disk); $6,000 (20MHz, 80M disk); $11,400 (20MHz, 300M disk) |
| | Starlan 3B2, Model 700 Server | Starlan, Ethernet | 90/11 | Unix System V, Release 3.2 | 8M to 64M | None | 8M | Western Electric 32200/22MHz (up to 4 micro processors per server) | 32/32 | 600M to 15.9G | 18 | 12M to 36M | 40M, 60M, 120M | $64,000/$69,000 |
| Banyan Systems, Inc. Westborough, Mass. | Corporate Network Server | Ethernet, token ring, VistaLAN, LANStar | 30/NA | Unix System V, Release 3 | 4M to 24M | 32K | 4M | Intel 80386/20MHz | 32/16 | 80M to 2.5G | 20 | NA | 150M | $32,000/$94,000 |
| | Desktop Server | Ethernet, token ring, VistaLAN, LANStar | 30/NA | Unix System V, Release 2 | 2M to 5M | None | 2M | Motorola 68000/NA | 16/16 | 52M to 146M | 20 | NA | 16M | $13,000 average |

| Vendor | Product | Compatible LAN | Maximum Ports (Serial/Parallel) | Operating System | RAM Size (bytes) | Memory Cache Size (bytes) | Minimum RAM for System Software (bytes) | Microprocessor/Clock Rate | Memory/Channel Bus Width (bits) | Disk Capacity (bytes) | Disk Seek Time (msec) | Disk Transfer Rate (bit/sec) | Tape Backup Capacity (bytes) | Minimum/Maximum Price |
|---|---|---|---|---|---|---|---|---|---|---|---|---|---|---|
| Compaq Computer Corp. Houston | Deskpro 386/25 | Ethernet, token ring, Arcnet, Novell, Inc. NetWare, 3Com Corp. 3+ | 2/2 | MS-DOS 3.3, OS/2 | 1M to 16M | 512K | 2M plus network control software | Intel 80386/25MHz | 32/16 | 110M to 1.2G | 18 to 25 | 3.5M | 13M or 40M | $13,000/NA |
| Convergent Technologies, Inc. San Jose, Calif. | SPC Model 100 | Ethernet, token ring | 28/none | Unix System V, Release 3 | 2M to 12M | None | 2M | Intel 80386/20MHz | 32/32 or 16 | 40M to 405M | 18 to 23 | 26.4M | 60M to 150M | $9,000/$21,000 |
| | Server PC Model 200 | Ethernet, token ring | 43/none | Unix System V, Release 3 | 4M to 64M | 64K | 2M | Intel 80386/16MHz | 32/32 or 16 | 80M to 975M | 18 to 28 | 26.4M | 60M to 150M | $12,000/$75,000 |
| Data General Corp. Westborough, Mass. | MV Family Super Minis | DG/PC Integration, Rational Data Systems PC/VS | 12 to 1000/12 to 1000 | AOS/VS | 4M to 64M | NA | 4M | Proprietary/ NA | NA/NA | 12M to 20G | 12 to 20 | 14M | 163M | $10,000/NA |
| DSC Nester Systems, Inc. San Jose, Calif. | Planstar | Arcnet | None/none | Starplus Plus | 1M | None | 512K | Motorola 68000/12 to 16MHz | 16/16 | 68M to 1.1G | 25 | 1.5M | 150M | $8,000/$10,000 |
| | NEXOS 386 Server | Ethernet, token ring, Arcnet | 5/2 | NEX/OS | 2M to 16M | 8M | 640K | Intel 80386/20MHz | 32/16 | 70M to 1.4G | 26 | 2M | 60M to 150M | $15,000/$25,000 |
| EasyNet Systems, Inc. Mississauga, Ontario | EasyServer | Any NETBIOS | 1/1 | MS-DOS 3.X | 640K to 4M | None | 240K plus network control software | Intel 80286/12MHz | 16/16 | 40M to 200M | 28 | NA | 60M to 130M | $7,300/$12,000 |

*(continued)*

**TABLE 5-2** *(cont.)*

| Vendor | Product | Compatible LAN | Maximum Ports (Serial/Parallel) | Operating System | RAM Size (bytes) | Memory Cache Size (bytes) | Minimum RAM for System Software (bytes) | Microprocessor/Clock Rate | Memory/Channel Bus Width (bits) | Disk Capacity (bytes) | Disk Seek Time (msec) | Disk Transfer Rate (bit/sec) | Tape Backup Capacity (bytes) | Minimum/Maximum Price |
|---|---|---|---|---|---|---|---|---|---|---|---|---|---|---|
| Faultnot Technologies, Inc. East Kingston, N.H. | 286/386Server | Ethernet, token ring, Arcnet Starlan, VistaLAN | 9/6 | NetWare or Banyan VINES | 1M to 16M | 3M | 1M | Intel 80286/10M or 12MHz; Intel 80386, 32 for 80386 120M or 25MHz | 16 for source | 72M to 1.4G | 28 | 500K | 60M or 120M standard; up to 400M optional | $12,300 (no disk)/$50,000 (with 288M disk) |
| Hewlett-Packard Co. Cupertino, Calif. | HP Vectra RS/16PC | Ethernet, token ring, Starlan | 1/1 | HP Vectra DOS 3.3, OS/2, Xenix 386 | 1M to 16M | 1M | 2M | Intel 80386/16MHz | 32/16 | 40M to 100M | 17 | 7.5M | 40M | $6,600/$8,500 (with 310M bytes of disk) |
| | HP Vectra RS/20PC | Ethernet, token ring, Starlan | 1/1 | HP Vectra DOS 3.3, OS/2, Xenix 386 | 1M to 16M | 1M | 2M | Intel 80386/20MHz | 32/NA | 40M to 620M | 17 | 7.5M | 40M | $7,200/$11,600 (with 310M bytes of disk) |
| Hyundai Electronics America Santa Clara, Calif. | Super 286 File Server | Ethernet, token ring | 1/1 | MS-DOS 3.2 | 1M to 4M | None | 1.5M | Intel 80286 | 16/16 | 40 to 120M | 28 | NA | None | $2,000/$30,000 (with 40M byte disk) |
| IBM Rye Brook, N.Y. | Personal System/2 Model 60 | Token Ring or PC LAN | 3/1 | OS/2 and PC DOS 3.3 | 1M to 15M | 128K to 14M | 1M to 3M | Intel 80286/10MHz | 16/16 | 44M to 159M | 30 or 40 | NA | Tape and 200M optical disk | NA |
| | Personal System/2 Model 80 | Token-Ring and PC LAN | 3/1 | OS/2 and PC DOS 3.3 | 1M to 16M | 128K to 15M | 1M to 3M | Intel 80386 (16 or 20 MHz) | 32/32 or 16 | 44M to 314M | 23 to 40 | 19M | Tape and 200M optical disk | NA |
| NCR Corp. Dayton, Ohio | PC 916 | Any | 1/1 | Any | 2M to 8M | None | Depends on operating system | Intel 80386/4.77M to 16MHz | 32/8 or 16 | 30M to 70M | 30 to 40 | NA | NA | $5,000/$7,500 |
| Novell, Inc. Provo, Utah | 386 AE/155x2 | Ethernet, token ring | 2/1 | NetWare | 4M to 16M | 12M | 2M | Intel 80386/16MHz | 32/32 or 16 | 155M to 2G | 16 | NA | 120M | $9,000/$14,000 |

| Vendor | Product | Compatible LAN | Maximum Ports (Serial/Parallel) | Operating System | RAM Size (bytes) | Memory Cache Size (bytes) | Minimum RAM for System Software (bytes) | Microprocessor/Clock Rate | Memory/Channel Bus Width (bits) | Disk Capacity (bytes) | Disk Seek Time (msec) | Disk Transfer Rate (bit/sec) | Tape Backup Capacity (bytes) | Minimum/Maximum Price |
|---|---|---|---|---|---|---|---|---|---|---|---|---|---|---|
| | 386 AE/320x2 | Ethernet, token ring | 2/1 | NetWare | 4M to 16M | 12M | 2M | Intel 80386/16MHz | 32/32 or 16 | 320M to 2G | 16 | NA | 120M | NA |
| Racore Computer Products, Inc. Los Gatos, Calif. | LANpac 386 | Ethernet, token ring | 2/1 | Unix, Xenix, MS-DOS, OS/2 | 2M to 16M | None | Depends on operating system | Intel 80386/16M or 200MHz | 32/8 or 16 | 80M to 360M | NA | 4.29M | 60M to 120M | $5,000/NA |
| Sytek, Inc. Mountain View, Calif. | Model 4430 Network Server | Ethernet, Sytek 6000 | 1/2 | NetWare | Up to 2.5M | NA | 1M | Intel 80386/16MHz | 32/8, 16.32 | 135M | 16.5M | NA | 125M | $11,500/$14,000 |
| The Network Connection, Inc. Alpharetta, Ga. | Triumph | Ethernet, token ring, Arcnet, Starlan, VistaLAN | 2/3 | MS-DOS 3.3; OS/2; Microsoft LAN Manager, Novell NetWare, Unix Version V, Release 3 | 1M to 16M | Up to 16.5M | 2M to 4M (depending on operating system and network control software) | Intel 80286/10MHz or 12MHz; Intel 80386/16M, 20M, or 25MHz | 16 (80286) and 32 (80386)/16 (both processors) | 20M to 2.64G | 0.6 | 1M | 10M to 2.2G | $6,800 (for 130M disk)/$19,600 (for 2.6G disk) |
| 3Com Corp. Santa Clara, Calif. | 3S/200 | Ethernet, token ring | 5/2 | 3Com 3+ | 2M to 3M | 2M | 1M | Intel 8186/8MHz | 16/8 | 106M to 900M | 28 | 10M | 150M | $8,500/$10,500 |
| | 3S/400 | token ring, AppleTalk | 12/2 | 3Com 3+ | 2M to 14M | 13M | 1M | Intel 80386/16MHz | 32/16 | 150 to 900M | 16 | 10M | 150M | $12,500/$14,500 |
| Univation, Inc. Milpitas, Calif. | Univation 386 | Ethernet, Arcnet, Sytek (broadband), Omninet, any NETBIOS | 1/1 | LifeNet | 2M to 16M | 900K to 15M | 1M | Intel 80386/NA | 32/16 | 80M to 170M | 20 | 2.8M | 60M | $7,000/14,000 |

(continued)

151

## TABLE 5-2 (cont.)

| Vendor | Product | Compatible LAN | Maximum Ports (Serial/Parallel) | Operating System | RAM Size (bytes) | Memory Cache Size (bytes) | Minimum RAM for System Software (bytes) | Microprocessor/Clock Rate | Memory/Channel Bus Width (bits) | Disk Capacity (bytes) | Disk Seek Time (msec) | Disk Transfer Rate (bit/sec) | Tape Backup Capacity (bytes) | Minimum/Maximum Price |
|---|---|---|---|---|---|---|---|---|---|---|---|---|---|---|
| | LifeServer 386 | Same as Univation 386 | 1/2 | LifeNet | 2M to 16M | 900K to 15M | 1M | Intel 80386/16M or 20MHz | 32/16 | 170M, 300M or 600M | 20 | 2.8M | 60M | $17,000/$27,000 |
| Wang Laboratories, Inc. Lowell, Mass. | LS-100 | Ethernet, token ring, VistaLAN, LANStar | 4/3 | Unix Version V, Release 3 | 4M to 24M | NA | 4M | Intel 80386/20MHz | 32/16 | 150M | NA | NA | | $21,000/$30,000 |
| | LS-50 | Ethernet, token ring, VistaLAN, LANStar | 2/2 | Unix System V, Release 3 | 4M to 16M | None | 4.5M | Intel 80386/20MHz | 32/16 | 68M to 136M | NA | NA | 60M to 150M | $11,000/$17,000 |
| Xerox Corp. Stamford, Conn. | Xerox 8000 Series | Ethernet | 4/1 | Pilot proprietary | 512K to 3.6M | None | 512K | Proprietary/7.3MHz | 32/NA | 10M to 2.1G | 25 to 70 | 4M | 48M to 130M | $10,000/$24,000 (includes 310M disk) |
| Zenith Data Systems Mt. Prospect, IL | Z-LAN 500 File Server | Token ring, Arcnet, Ethernet | 1/none | Novell NetWare 286 Advanced 2.1 | 1M to 16M | None | 640K | Intel 80386/16MHz | 32/16 | 40M to 160M | 18 | NA | NA | $2,700/$8,000 |

Arcnet = Datapoint Corp. Arcnet

LANStar = Northern Telecom, Inc. LANStar

NA = Information not available

NETBIOS = Network Basic I/O System

Starlan = AT&T Starlan

Omninet = Corvus Systems, Inc. Omninet

10NET = 10NET Communications 10NET

VistaLAN = Allen-Bradley Co. VistaLAN

This chart includes a representative selection of vendors in the local net server market. Most vendors offer other local net servers, and many vendors not included offer a full range of competitive products.

Source: *Network World*, September 21, 1988

The "Maximum Ports" column indicates the number of ports available for connecting devices such as printers and modems. These ports allow the server to act as a printer server or a modem server or both, as well as a disk and file server. The "Minimum RAM for System Software" column refers to the amount of main memory storage needed to hold the server's operating system.

## Terminal Support

In recent years, the advent of personal computers has tended to eclipse the role of display terminals. Increasingly, personal computers are displacing all varieties of display terminals. This trend is due to two fundamental considerations:

- Personal computer costs, especially for low-end configurations, have dropped to the point where they are nearly competitive with display terminals of reasonable quality and features.
- Manufacturers have discovered that the flexibility of a personal computer inherent in its programmability makes it ideal for "personalizing" it in a specific application to improve productivity and accuracy, lower operator fatigue, and so on.

Nevertheless, the display terminal will be an important piece of equipment in many offices for some time to come. Indeed, as Figure 5-4 shows, in organizations relying on mainframes, the number of display terminals in use is actually growing. Figure 5-5 suggests that the principal application for such terminals is routine clerical tasks, which do not require the versatility of a personal computer.

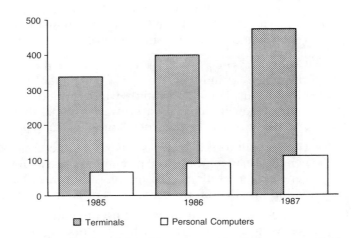

**Figure 5-4** Number of terminals and personal computers installed at sites with IBM and compatible mainframes. *(Source: Focus Research Systems, February 1988.)*

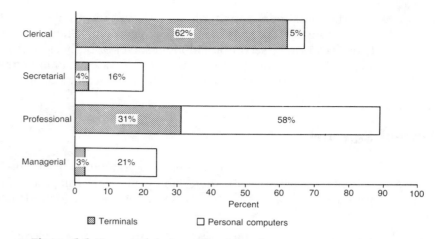

**Figure 5-5** Users and their workstations. *(Source: Input, Mountain View, CA, June 1988.)*

## Terminal Types

Terminals can be classified as either scroll mode or page and forms mode. The *scroll-mode terminal* is the least complex terminal type. It is based on a simple form of teleprinter, the teletype (TTY), which uses a roll of paper that unwinds as printing occurs. After the print head is moved to the next line, it cannot be moved back. A scroll-mode display terminal uses a screen in place of paper, but the concept is the same. Characters are displayed in lines sequentially from the top of the screen to the bottom. When the screen is filled, adding a new line causes the top line to scroll off the screen, and all lines move up one position. This simulates the effect of unwinding the roll of paper.

Four common characteristics of scroll-mode terminals follow:

- User input is on a line basis. Lines can be either a fixed length (number of characters) or unlimited length. In the latter case, a line that exceeds the physical display length simply wraps around to the next line. A system-defined newline character is always a signal that user input is complete and the host may begin processing the data.

- Host output to the display is also on a line basis, although the host may generate many lines before prompting the user for more input. If the host generates more lines than the physical screen can display, the top lines will be scrolled off the screen and possibly lost to the user.

- A type-ahead feature allows the user to enter data while host output is being written to the screen. When the display of computer output is complete, the user input is displayed below it.

- Transmission is usually asynchronous. That is, characters are transmitted one at a time, and very little logic is needed at either end to coordinate the transmission.

There are two significant disadvantages to the scroll-mode terminal. The first is that user input can consist of only one line at a time. In a number of applications, such as word processing, the user wants to deal with the entire screen at one time and be able to enter and alter information on the screen prior to transmission of the entire screen. The second disadvantage is the potential loss of data that is scrolled off the top of the screen. With a TTY, users could read host output as fast as it was typed, and the paper held a permanent copy. With display screens, users can rarely read data as quickly as it appears on the screen, and any lines scrolled off the top of the screen may be lost (depending on the application).

*Page-mode terminals* were designed to alleviate these problems. The basic characteristics of a page-mode terminal follow:

- User input can be multiple lines. A newline does not designate an end to user input, just an end to the line. Another key sequence is used to indicate that the user input is finished and the data can be processed by the host. The system must keep track of how many lines of data are part of the current input.

- Host output is in pages, where a page is defined as the number of characters per line and the number of lines per screen that the physical screen can display. The host will pause between pages until the user indicates that he or she is ready for the next page.

A special type of page-mode terminal is the *forms-mode terminal.* Forms-mode terminals are used for a special class of applications. These applications are designed so that the user inputs only the necessary data—he or she is not required to input commands to process the data or to designate the meaning of the data. This is analogous to filling out a form—you supply only the answers; the form supplies the questions, and the location of the answer defines its meaning. The basic characteristics of a forms-mode terminal follow:

- Host output is on a page basis, as with the page-mode terminal, except the page is divided into distinct fields, each with defined attributes.

- User input is on a field basis. The application restricts the type of data entered in a field and controls how it is displayed. Order of input is not significant, and local editing of user input is permitted. Transmission consists of only the user-supplied portion of a page.

The protocol for terminal-host interaction becomes very complex for forms mode. In the host-to-terminal direction, it must define the form structure and the field attributes. This includes the location on the screen where each field belongs and how it is displayed. In the terminal-to-host direction, it must label each item of user data to indicate which field it represents, and it must designate whether the user input is on a new form or is just changed fields from a previous form.

For page- and forms-mode terminals, transmission is usually synchronous. A data link control protocol is used and data is transmitted in blocks that include control information. Often, such terminals communicate using a polling discipline. That is, the terminal waits until it is specifically polled by the host computer before sending data.

The logic for controlling asynchronous, scroll-mode terminals is considerably less complex than that for page- and forms-mode terminals. Traditionally, LAN vendors have provided much better support for the former.

## Asynchronous Scroll-Mode Terminal Support

### Terminal Server

The simplest way to handle asynchronous scroll-mode terminals is to provide what appears to be a transparent connection between the terminal and an asynchronous port on a host computer. This is sometimes referred to as the terminal server approach, and is illustrated in Figure 5-6a. Communication between the terminal server and terminals is managed by an asynchronous transmission module in the server. As characters come in from a terminal, they are placed in an input buffer by the asynchronous transmission module. When a carriage return is received, or when a timeout occurs, the contents of the buffer are passed to LLC for transmission. The data is transmitted across the LAN to another terminal server attached to a host. Data arriving from the LAN is delivered in blocks from LLC to another asynchronous transmission module, which takes characters from the block and transmits them one at a time to the host. A similar process occurs in the reverse direction. Thus, it appears to both the host computer and the terminal that there is a direct physical connection between them.

This scheme is supplemented by logic that allows the terminal to communicate directly with its local terminal server. When a terminal is first turned on, it is in command mode. Any data from the terminal is interpreted as a command to the terminal server. One such command is a Connect command, by which the terminal user requests a connection to a particular host. After the connection is made, the terminal is in data mode, and any entered data is transmitted to the host.

### PAD Approach

The approach just outlined is simple and effective. Its main drawback is evident in Figure 5-6a. Because the connection is transparent, there must be one asynchronous port on the host for each terminal connection. This is referred to as the "milking machine" approach, and is clearly wasteful of host hardware. It would be preferable if the link to the host was a multiplexed link that could carry traffic from a number of terminals at the same time (Figure 5-6b). This

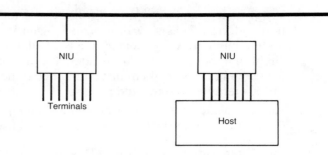

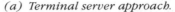

*(a) Terminal server approach.*

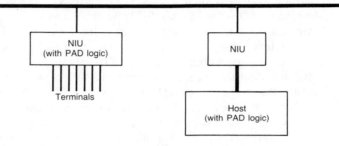

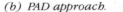

*(b) PAD approach.*

**Figure 5-6** LAN terminal support.

latter approach is referred to as the packet assembler/disassembler (PAD) approach.

The PAD solves the two fundamental problems associated with the attachment of terminals to a network:

- Many terminals cannot implement the protocol layers for attaching to a network in the same manner as a host. The PAD facility provides the intelligence for communicating with a host.
- There are differences among terminal types. The PAD facility provides a set of parameters to account for those differences.

However, the PAD facility is limited: It deals with only asynchronous, scroll-mode terminals. To handle a broader range of terminal types across networks, a much more powerful facility, known as a *virtual terminal service,* is needed. We explore this topic later in this section.

The operation of the PAD is in many ways similar to that of the terminal server. As its name suggests, the PAD collects characters transmitted from a terminal and assembles them into a packet for transmission. Incoming packets are disassembled and the characters from the packet are delivered to the terminal one at a time. There are two key differences from the terminal server:

- A network-level protocol is used to enable the host to receive traffic from many terminals through a single physical port. In essence, the traffic from any given terminal is associated with a dedicated logical connection to the host, referred to as a *virtual circuit.* Each virtual circuit is assigned a unique number. All packets from a particular terminal include the virtual circuit number in the packet header. The host contains logic to discriminate among the virtual circuits and hence to be able to keep track of the various terminals connected to it.

- Various characteristics associated with each terminal can be set, either by the host computer system or by the terminal user.

This latter point provides the PAD with a certain degree of flexibility. The most common set of characteristics used in PAD products is defined in an international standard known as X.3, which lists 22 parameters that determine the behavior of the PAD (Table 5-3). Because a PAD may serve more than one terminal, a set of these parameters is maintained for each terminal. Most of these parameters are self-explanatory, but items 3 and 4 deserve further comment. As the PAD receives characters from a terminal, it places them in a buffer whose length equals the maximum data field size of an X.25 packet. When the buffer is full, the packet is sent. However, we need to be able to send shorter blocks of data. For example, when a user enters a command in the form of a line of characters followed by a carriage return, the user expects that line to be transmitted to the computer. Parameter 3 is set to indicate which control characters should trigger the transmission of a packet. In a similar fashion, the PAD can be set by parameter 4 to transmit whatever is in the buffer if the user pauses for a given period of time.

**TABLE 5-3**    PAD Parameters (X.3)

| Number | Description | Selectable Values |
|--------|-------------|-------------------|
| 1 | Whether terminal operator can escape from data transfer to PAD command state | 0: not allowed<br>1: escape character<br>32–126: graphic characters |
| 2 | Whether PAD echoes back characters received from terminal | 0: no echo<br>2: echo |
| 3 | Terminal characters that will trigger the sending of a partially full packet by the PAD | 0: only send full packets<br>1: alphanumeric<br>2, 4, 8, 16, 32, 64: other control characters |
| 4 | Timeout value that will trigger the sending of a partially full packet by the PAD | 0: no timeout<br>1–255: multiple of 50 ms |
| 5 | Whether PAD can exercise flow control over terminal output, using X-ON, X-OFF | 0: not allowed<br>1: allowed |
| 6 | Whether PAD can send service signals (control information) to terminal | 0: not allowed<br>1: allowed |
| 7 | Action(s) taken by PAD on receipt of break signal from terminal | 0: nothing<br>1: send interrupt<br>2: reset<br>4: send break signal |

**TABLE 5-3**   *(cont.)*

| Number | Description | Selectable Values |
|--------|-------------|-------------------|
| | | 8: escape<br>16: discard output |
| 8 | Whether PAD will discard DTE data intended for terminal | 0: normal delivery<br>1: discard |
| 9 | Number of padding characters inserted after carriage return (to terminal) | 0: determined by data rate<br>1–255: number of characters |
| 10 | Whether PAD inserts control characters to prevent terminal line overflow | 0: no<br>1–255: yes, line length |
| 11 | Terminal speed (bps) | 0–18: 50 to 64,000 |
| 12 | Whether terminal can exercise flow control over PAD, using X-ON, X-OFF | 0: not allowed<br>1: allowed |
| 13 | Whether PAD inserts line feed after carriage return sent or echoed to terminal | 0: no line feed<br>1, 2, 4: various conditions |
| 14 | Number of padding characters inserted after line feed (to terminal) | 0: no padding<br>1–255: number of characters |
| 15 | Whether PAD supports editing during data transfer (defined in parameters 16—18) | 0: no<br>1: yes |
| 16 | Character delete | 0–127: selected character |
| 17 | Line delete | 0–127: selected character |
| 18 | Line display | 0–127: selected character |
| 19 | Terminal type for editing PAD service signals (such as character delete) | 0: no editing signals<br>1: printing terminal<br>2: display terminal |
| 20 | Characters that are not echoed to terminal when echo is enabled | 0: no echo mask<br>Each bit represents certain characters |
| 21 | Parity treatment of characters to/from terminal | 0: no parity treatment<br>1: parity checking<br>2: parity generation |
| 22 | Number of lines to be displayed at one time | 0: page wait disabled<br>1–255: number of lines |

## TELNET

A capability similar to the PAD is available in the TCP/IP protocol suite, namely TELNET. Recall that TELNET provides remote terminal access across a network to a host. Figure 5-7 shows the architecture involved. The terminals attach to the LAN through a network interface unit that implements the relevant portions of the TCP/IP protocol suite. A terminal-handling program handles the primitive functions of moving data between the terminal and the NIU. This handler connects to a portion of TELNET known as User TELNET. The user at the terminal can engage in a dialogue with User TELNET to request connection to a particular remote host. When a connection is requested, User TELNET sets up a logical TCP connection to a Server TELNET module in the remote host. Server TELNET is responsible for linking a terminal connection to a particular service or application, such as the operating system or a transaction processing monitor. The use of TCP ensures that traffic is reliably exchanged between the terminal and the host application.

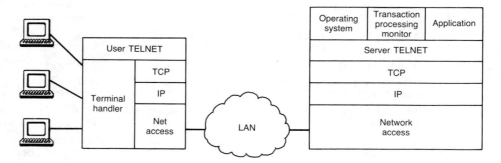

**Figure 5-7** TELNET architecture.

As with the PAD approach, TELNET is designed primarily for scroll-mode terminals. It provides a greater number of terminal characteristics that can be modified. In addition, it provides a mechanism by which a group of users can define new characteristics to be set for particular terminals.

## Virtual Terminal Service

The use of a PAD or TELNET is effective for asynchronous, scroll-mode terminals. However, for support of a wide variety of terminals, a more powerful approach is needed. The most attractive approach is an international standard issued by ISO, known as the virtual terminal service.

### Virtual Terminal Approach

A virtual terminal service is an application that provides a mechanism for exchanging data between a terminal and a computer across a communications facility. It also provides mechanisms for the terminal and the host to agree on the data stream format they will use for that data exchange and performs translations between the characteristics of the terminal and the agreed-upon format.

Figure 5-8 illustrates the process involved. Upon user input, the characteristics of a real terminal are transformed into the agreed-upon format, or "virtual terminal." This formatted data is transmitted over a network to a host system. In the host computer, the virtual terminal structure is translated into the terminal format normally used by the host. The reverse process is performed for host-to-terminal traffic. Thus, a virtual terminal service must understand the virtual terminal format and be able to use a data transfer mechanism, such as that provided in the OSI architecture.

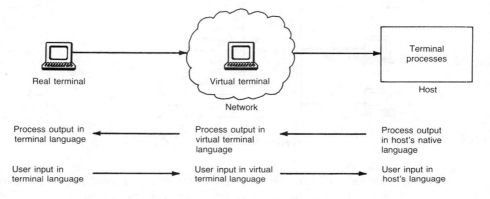

**Figure 5-8** Virtual terminal model.

A useful feature of a virtual terminal service is the capability to negotiate about the characteristics of the virtual terminal or the details of the data transfer. This allows users and processes to define a remote terminal access service that provides service as close as possible to what the terminal user expects.

Figure 5-9 relates the virtual terminal service to the OSI architecture. Terminals are connected locally to a device that may be a terminal cluster controller, some other sort of communications processor, or a general-purpose computer. Some terminal-handler software module is needed to communicate with the terminals; this is usually part of the operating system. The purpose of this module is to link the terminal user to some application in the system. In this case, the user is linked to the virtual terminal service. This service is at the application layer of the OSI architecture and makes use of the lower six layers of OSI to establish a connection with a virtual terminal service module on a remote computer.

On the remote computer, the virtual terminal service module provides an interface to various applications. To the application, terminal traffic coming in through the virtual terminal service module appears to be coming from a local terminal through the usual terminal-handler software. Thus, for both the user and the application, it appears as though the user is locally connected to the remote computer.

## ISO Virtual Terminal Service

The ISO virtual terminal service is an application-layer service defined within the framework of the open systems interconnection (OSI) model. The stan-

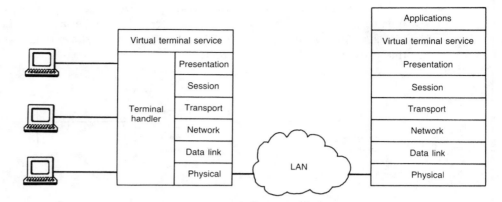

**Figure 5-9** Architecture for virtual terminal service.

dard defines a model for a virtual terminal, which is an abstract representation of a real terminal. The standard defines operations that can be performed, such as reading text from the virtual keyboard, writing text on the virtual screen, and moving a cursor to a particular position on the virtual screen. The standard also defines a virtual terminal protocol for the exchange of data and control messages between a terminal and an application by the virtual terminal service. The protocol standard specifies the display data stream structure and the control messages by which the two sides can agree on the details of the terminal capabilities to be supported.

Rather than defining a single virtual terminal for all possible applications, the standard provides its users with tools to define a virtual terminal suited to the application at hand and the physical limitations of the terminal. For example, if the physical terminal is monochrome, the two sides agree not to use color information. Table 5-4 lists some key aspects of the ISO standard. We examine each of these in turn.

The ISO standard provides different *classes of service*. Each class meets the needs of a specific range of applications and terminal functions. So far, Basic, Forms, and Graphics classes have been identified. Of these, only the Basic class is fully defined and supported by vendors. We can expect to see the other classes available in the next few years.

The Basic class is a character-oriented service. In its simplest form, it meets the terminal access requirements of applications such as line editing and operating system command language interaction, which can be satisfied with simple scroll-mode terminals. The basic class also supports page-mode terminals and provides for the exchange of data in blocks instead of character-at-a-time. An extension to the Basic class provides a primitive set of forms-related services. It allows the definition and addressing of individual fields and the transmission of selected fields. With this capability, the service can transfer just the variable fields on a form. However, there is no facility for defining or using field attributes.

**TABLE 5-4**  Aspects of the ISO Virtual Terminal Service

**Classes of Service**
Basic
Forms
Graphics

**Modes of Operation**
Two-way alternate
Two-way simultaneous

**Delivery Control**
No delivery control
Simple delivery control
Quarantine delivery control

**Echo Control**
Local echo
Remote echo

The Forms class handles all operations associated with forms-mode terminals, such as the IBM 3270 terminals. This would allow any forms-mode terminal from any vendor to interact with forms-mode applications on any host from any vendor. Finally, the Graphics class deals with graphics and image-processing terminals.

The virtual terminal standard supports two *modes of operation:* two-way alternate (half duplex) and two-way simultaneous (full duplex). When a terminal sets up a connection to a host, the mode of operation is agreed upon between the two virtual service modules.

The two-way alternate mode enforces the discipline that only one side at a time can transmit. This prevents data from the computer appearing on the terminal display screen while the user is entering text from the keyboard. The two-way alternate mode is typical of synchronous forms-mode terminals such as the 3270. Most normal enquiry and response applications are naturally two-way alternate, for example.

The two-way simultaneous mode permits both sides to transmit at the same time. An example of the utility of this is the control terminal for a complex real-time system such as a process control plant. For such an application, the terminal must be capable of being updated rapidly with status changes even if the operator is typing in a command.

*Delivery control* allows one side to control the delivery of data to the other side to coordinate multiple actions. Normally, any data entered at a terminal is automatically delivered to the application on the other side as soon as possible, and any data transmitted by the application is delivered to the terminal as soon as possible. In some cases, however, one side may require explicit control over when certain data is delivered to its peer.

For example, suppose a user is logged on to a time-sharing system through the virtual terminal service. The time-sharing system may issue a single prompt character (e.g., >) when it is ready for the next command. The terminal side of the virtual terminal service, however, may choose to deliver data to the terminal for display only after several characters have been received, rather than one character at a time. Because this single prompt character must be displayed, and because the terminal side cannot reasonably be expected to know what the prompt character is, some mechanism is needed to force delivery. Another example is the use of special function keys, which are found on many terminals. These keys can be set up to perform multiple actions, resulting in the transmission of multiple messages to the host. Sometimes it is desirable that all of the functions of the key be presented to the peer user simultaneously.

Three types of delivery control can be specified with any transmission:

- *No delivery control:* This is the default type. Data is made available to the peer at the convenience of the virtual terminal service.

- *Simple delivery control:* The service user (terminal or application) can issue a request that all undelivered data be delivered. Optionally, the invoking side may also request acknowledgment of the delivery to the other side.

- *Quarantine delivery control:* The remote virtual terminal service module holds all incoming data until it is explicitly released for delivery by the other side. For example, an application could send a screen-full of data in several small blocks but instruct the other side to defer delivery so that the entire screen update is displayed at once. Another example is the function key action mentioned previously.

*Echo control* manages the updating to a display of characters typed on a keyboard. In real terminals, characters typed on the keyboard may be displayed on the screen locally by the terminal as they are typed or may be echoed back to the display by the computer. The former option is less flexible but is often chosen when the communication link is half duplex and echoing back would therefore not be practical. The latter option is used when the communication line is full duplex and when greater control over the screen is required. For example, a time-sharing system may want to suppress the display of the terminal user's password and identification code but display all other characters.

In addition to the aspects of the virtual terminal service listed in Table 5-4, a major feature of the service is the use of *terminal parameters*. These are similar to those used in X.3 in that they provide a way to define various characteristics of the terminal, but the parameters in the ISO standard are much more complex and powerful than those of X.3. They allow the user to define various characteristics of displayable characters, such as font, size, intensity, and color. Control objects can be defined to control formatting on the display and to trigger various events such as ringing an alarm. Characteristics of other devices such as printers can also be specified.

# Distributed Applications

The LAN server has become quite popular in recent years, particularly on personal computer LANs, where the capability to share expensive resources among inexpensive machines is especially desirable. The difficulty with this approach, however, is that no standards are defined for these servers. Thus, the user must decide which server scheme to use and limit purchases to hardware and software compatible with that scheme.

A far more attractive approach, in the long run, is to use standardized applications that support cooperative processing. Such applications can be used between user stations or between a user station and a server. We have seen one example of this, namely the TCP/IP protocol suite, which supports file transfer, electronic mail, and remote terminal access. However, as we discussed in Chapter 3, the standards based on the OSI model are positioned to dominate the market in the future. Thus, a user contemplating the types of distributed applications that will meet projected requirements would do well to plan for a OSI-based solution. In this section, we present two of the most important OSI-based distributed applications: electronic mail and file transfer. There are many others, but a plan that incorporates these two applications will meet many of the requirements of an organization.

## Electronic Mail

### Principles

Electronic mail, also known as a computer-based message system (CBMS), is a facility that allows users at terminals to compose and exchange messages. The messages need never exist on paper unless the user (sender or recipient) wants a paper copy of the message. Like voice mail, electronic mail solves many problems of communications between people by eliminating the necessity for both parties of an exchange to be available at the same time. In addition, electronic mail addresses the problem of the office paper explosion. Offices generate a tremendous amount of paperwork, most of it in the form of internal memos and reports: Over 80 percent of all business documents are textual or numeric or both (no graphics) and originate and remain within the same organization.

With an electronic mail facility, each user is registered and has a unique identifier, usually the person's last name and possibly the location. One mailbox is associated with each user. The electronic mail facility is an application program available to any user logged onto the system. A user may invoke the facility, prepare a message, and send it to any other user. The act of sending simply involves putting the message in the recipient's mailbox. The mailbox is maintained by the electronic mail facility and is like a file directory. Any incoming mail is simply stored as a file under that user's mailbox directory. The user reads messages by invoking the mail facility and reading rather than sending. In most systems, when a user logs on, he or she is informed if there is any new mail in that user's mailbox. Table 5-5 lists some of the common features provided by an electronic mail facility.

The simplest form of electronic mail is the single-system facility (Figure 5-10). This facility allows all the users of a shared computer system to exchange messages. Many public mail systems are single-computer systems, with

**TABLE 5-5**   Typical Electronic Mail Facilities

### Message Preparation

| | |
|---|---|
| Word processing | Facilities for the creation and editing of messages. Usually these do not need to be as powerful as a full word processor, because electronic mail documents tend to be simple. However, most electronic mail packages allow off-line access to word processors: the user creates a message using the computer's word processor, stores the message as a file, then uses the file as input to the message preparation function of the word processor. |
| Annotation | Messages often require some sort of short reply. A simple technique is to allow the recipient to attach annotation to an incoming message and send it back to the originator or to a third party. |

### Message Sending

| | |
|---|---|
| User directory | Used by the system. May also be accessible to users so that they can look up addresses. |
| Timed delivery | Allows the sender to specify that a message be delivered before, at, or after a specified date, time or both. A message is considered delivered when it is placed in the recipient's mailbox. |
| Multiple addressing | Copies of a message are sent to multiple addressees. The recipients are designated by listing each in the header of the message or by using a distribution list. The latter is a file containing a list of users. Distribution lists can be created by the user and by central administrative functions. |
| Message priority | A message may be labeled at a given priority level. Higher-priority messages will be delivered more rapidly, if possible. Also, the recipient will be notified or receive some indication of the arrival of high-priority messages. |
| Status information | A user may request notification of delivery or of actual retrieval by the recipient. A user may also query the current status of a message (e.g., queued for transmission, or transmitted but receipt confirmation not yet received). |
| Interface to other facilities | These would include other electronic systems such as telex and physical distribution facilities such as couriers and the public mail service (e.g., U.S. postal service). |

### Message Receiving

| | |
|---|---|
| Mailbox scanning | Allows the user to scan the current contents of mailbox. Each message may be indicated by subject, author, date, priority, and so on. |

**TABLE 5-5** *(cont.)*

**Message Receiving**

| | |
|---|---|
| Message selection | The user may select individual messages from the mailbox for display, printing, storing in a separate file, or deletion. |
| Message notification | Many systems notify an on-line user of the arrival of a new message and indicate to a user during log on that messages are in his or her mailbox. |
| Message reply | A user may reply immediately to a selected message, avoiding the necessity of keying in the recipient's name and address. |
| Message rerouting | A user who has moved, either temporarily or permanently, may reroute incoming messages. An enhancement is to allow the user to specify different forwarding addresses for different categories of messages. |

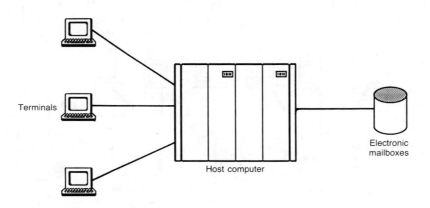

**Figure 5-10** Single-system electronic mail.

a single host system maintaining all the mailboxes of all the users. In the private context, a single time-shared computer system often supports single-computer mail.

With a single-system electronic mail facility, messages can be exchanged only among users of that particular system. Clearly, this is too limited. In a distributed environment, we would like to be able to exchange messages with users attached to other systems. Thus, we would like to treat electronic mail as a distributed application. Figure 5-11 illustrates this arrangement. Now there are multiple systems, each with its own set of mailboxes. In addition, a protocol for transmitting messages from one system to another allows a user on one system to send mail to a user on another system; the protocol illustrated in this example is X.400, which is discussed in the next section. Another popular electronic mail protocol is SMTP, which is part of the TCP/IP protocol suite. The figure also shows that some systems, such as terminals and personal computers, do not have local mailboxes, but make use of mailboxes on a mail server. Thus, a user from a terminal or personal computer would need to log on to the mail server to send and receive mail.

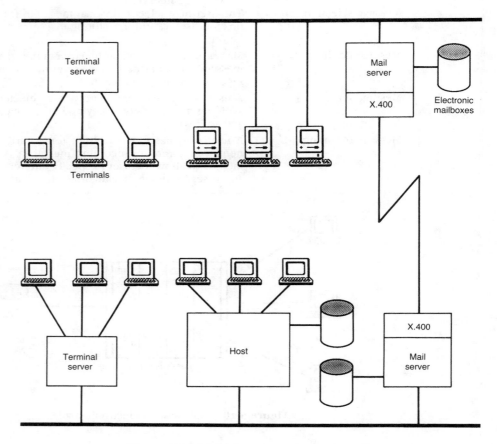

**Figure 5-11** Multiple-system electronic mail.

Figure 5-12 suggests the internal computer software configuration required. Let us refer to a single-system mail facility as a *native mail* facility. For native mail, three major modules are needed. Users will interact with native mail through terminals; hence, terminal-handling software is needed. Mail is stored as files in the file system, so file-handling software is needed. Finally, there must be a native mail package that contains all the logic for providing mail-related service to users.

To extend this system to *distributed mail,* two more modules are needed. Because we will communicate across a network or transmission system, communication I/O logic is needed (for example, OSI or SNA communications software). Mail transfer logic is also needed; this module invokes the communications function, specifies the recipient's network address, and requests whatever communication services are needed (for example, priority). Note in

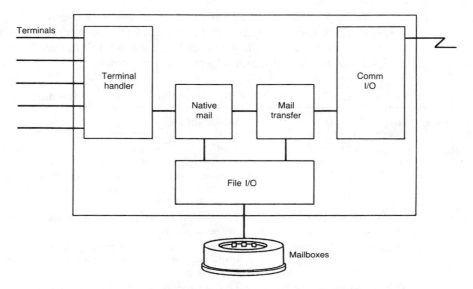

**Figure 5-12** Structure of an electronic mail system.

Figure 5-12 that the user does not directly interact with the mail transfer module. Ideally, the user interface for local and remote mail should be the same. If the user designates a local recipient, the message is stored in a local mailbox. If a remote recipient is designated, the native mail module passes the message to the mail transfer module for transmission across the network. Incoming mail from the network is routed to the appropriate mailbox and henceforth treated the same as other messages in the mailbox.

Many vendors now offer a network version of their basic electronic mail facility, but the user can send mail only to users on systems from the same vendor. Several forms of interconnection are needed. It is most desirable to provide an interconnection between a private electronic mail network and a public electronic mail service. Also desirable is the capability to interconnect private systems based on computers from different vendors. To provide these interconnections, a set of standards is needed, a topic to which we now turn.

## CCITT X.400 Family of Standards

In 1984, CCITT (Consultative Committee International Telegraph and Telephone) issued the X.400 family of standards for message-handling systems (MHS) that encompasses the requirements of what we have referred to as network electronic mail; the standards were revised in 1988. The standards do not deal with the user interface or services available directly to the user (what we have referred to as native mail). They do, however, specify what services are available for sending messages across the network and thus provide the base for building the user interface.

Table 5-6 lists the nine standards that comprise the X.400 family. All the standards fit into the framework of an MHS model, which is described in the first specification, X.400. We describe that model first, then look at some key aspects of the specification of services and protocols.

**TABLE 5-6**   The CCITT X.400 Family of Standards for Message Handling Systems

| Number | Title | Description |
|--------|-------|-------------|
| X.400 | System and Service Overview | Defines the message handling system model consisting of user agents and message transfer agents, discusses naming and addressing, defines interpersonal messaging and message transfer services, and discusses protocols for implementation. |
| X.402 | Overall Architecture | Defines the overall architecture and serves as a technical introduction to it. |
| X.403 | Conformance Testing | Specifies the criteria for acceptance of an implementation as conforming to the X.400 family of recommendations. |
| X.407 | Abstract Service Definition Conventions | Defines techniques for formally specifying the distributed information processing tasks that arise in message handling. |
| X.408 | Encoded Information Type Conversion Rules | Specifies the conversion between different types of encoded information to allow dissimilar devices to exchange messages. The encoded information types handled include Telex, Teletex, ASCII terminals, facsimile, and videotex. |
| X.411 | Message Transfer System: Abstract Service Definition and Procedures | Defines the services provided by the message transfer system and the procedures employed by the MTS. Also defines the services provided by the message transfer agent. |
| X.413 | Message Store: Abstract Service Definition | Defines the services provided by the message store. |
| X.419 | Protocol Specifications | Defines the protocols for accessing the message transfer system and for accessing a message store. Also defines protocols used between message transfer agents to provide for the distributed operation of the MTS. |
| X.420 | Interpersonal Messaging System | Defines the services provided by interpersonal messaging and the procedures for providing those services. |

The message-handling system model is defined in X.400. This model provides a framework for all the other recommendations. The model defines two types of entities: user agent (UA) and message transfer agent (MTA). The user agent operates on behalf of a user. It interacts directly with the user, performing functions for preparing messages and submitting messages for routing to the destination(s). In the process, the source UA interacts with destination UAs, which perform the delivery function. The UAs also assist the user in dealing with other message functions, such as filing, replying, retrieving, and forwarding.

The UA submits messages to an MTA for transmission across the network. The X.400 series specifies the interaction of the UA with the MTA and other UA entities but does not specify the interaction between the UA and its user.

The message transfer agent accepts messages from UAs for delivery to other UAs. Sometimes the MTA delivers the message directly to the destination UA. In other cases, the message must be relayed through a series of MTAs to the destination. For example, if only some MTAs have access to the proper long-distance communication paths, a message addressed to a distant UA might be relayed in several stages. Using relays also eliminates the need to have all UAs and MTAs available on a 24-hour basis. The store-and-forward action makes it feasible to treat electronic mail components like any other office equipment that gets turned off at night.

Figure 5-13 shows the way in which messages are constructed and transmitted. The user prepares the body of a message outside the scope of the X.400 family, using a word processor or editor. The user presents this body to the user agent software, together with a description, which might include recipient, subject, and priority. The user agent appends a *header* containing this qualifying information to the message, forming a complete message. This message is submitted to a message transfer agent. The MTA appends an *envelope* to the message; the envelope contains the source and destination addresses plus other control information needed for relaying the message through the network.

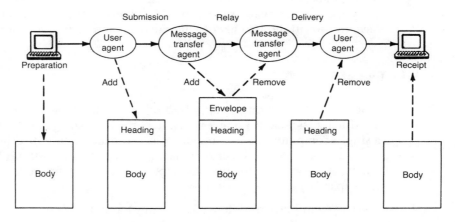

**Figure 5-13** X.400 message flow.

The X.400 series of standards defines the mechanisms for the exchange of messages and the services available to users of the system. In this case, the users are either terminal users who invoke electronic mail facilities or application programs that exchange messages. Corresponding to the two types of entities in the X.400 model (UA and MTA), the services are organized into two groups: message transfer services provided by MTAs and interpersonal messaging services provided by UAs.

Both sets of services are divided into three categories: basic, essential optional, and additional optional. *Basic services* are inherent in the message-handling system and must be implemented. The remaining services are known as optional user facilities, which may be invoked at the option of the user, in some cases on a per-message basis and in others for an agreed-upon contractual period. *Essential optional user facilities* must be offered by the service provider, but it is up to the user to select or not select the option. Finally, *additional optional user facilities* may or may not be offered by the provider; if offered, the user can decide whether or not to use each option.

Table 5-7 lists the *message transfer services.* The MTAs attempt to deliver messages to one or more recipients and can be asked to notify the originator's UA of the success or failure of each attempt. For example, the originator may request that delivery take place no earlier than a specified time. Or the recipient may request that a message be temporarily held in the system prior to delivery. Another example of a message transfer service is when the originator designates a message as urgent.

*Interpersonal messaging services* are provided by the UA and are listed in Table 5-8. In this case, optional services receive two designations, one for origination and one for reception. Note that many of the services that are additional (need not be offered) for origination are essential for reception. For example, UAs are not required to allow a user to mark a message as private but must be able to appropriately handle a received message marked private. Among the most fundamental interpersonal messaging services are specification of primary and secondary recipients and the subject of the message. Other services have to do with how to handle the message and instructions for notification.

## File Transfer

One of the first facilities supported on computer networks was file transfer. The file transfer facility is an extension of the file management system found in a single-computer system. In many cases, the facility is concerned solely with moving a complete file across a data link or network, with no knowledge of what is done with the file upon receipt. Many file transfer facilities also include the capability for the initiator to

- Get (and perhaps delete after getting) a remote file
- Overwrite an existing remote file (error if no file exists)
- Write to a new remote file (error if file already exists)
- Write to a remote file, overwriting any existing one or creating a new one
- Append, with similar options to write facilities, as just described

Some earlier facilities, and many facilities now used for micro-to-micro and micro-to-mainframe links, offer little more than this set of facilities. More recently, sophisticated file transfer facilities, both vendor specific and standard, have been developed. These typically include support for the following requirements:

**TABLE 5-7**  Message Transfer Layer Services (X.400)

### Basic Services

| | |
|---|---|
| Access management | Enables UA to submit and have messages delivered to it |
| Content type indication | Specified by originating UA |
| Converted indication | Specifies any conversions performed on message being delivered |
| Submission/delivery time stamp | Submission and delivery time are supplied with each message |
| Message identification | Unique identifier for each message |
| Nondelivery notification | Message cannot be delivered |
| Registered encoded information types | Allows UA to specify types that can be delivered to it |
| Original encoded information types | Specified by submitting UA and supplied to receiving UA |

### Essential Optional Services

| | |
|---|---|
| Alternate recipient allowed | Deliver to alternate if designated recipient cannot be found |
| Deferred delivery | Deliver no sooner than specified date and time |
| Deferred delivery cancellation | Abort delivery of deferred message |
| Delivery notification | Notify originator of successful delivery |
| Disclosure of other recipients | Disclose list of recipients to recipient |
| Grade of delivery selection | Request urgent, normal, or nonurgent |
| Multidestination delivery | Specify more than one recipient |
| Conversion prohibition | Prevents MTS from conversion |
| Probe | Determines if a message could be deliverable |

### Additional Optional Services

| | |
|---|---|
| Prevention of nondelivery notification | Suppress potential nondelivery notice |
| Return of contents | Return message contents if nondelivery |
| Explicit conversion | Specifies particular conversion |
| Implicit conversion | Performs necessary conversion on all messages without explicit instruction |
| Alternate recipient assignment | Requests designation of requesting UA as alternate recipient |
| Hold for delivery | Requests that messages intended for this UA be held in MTS until later time |

UA = user agent
MTS = message transfer agent

- The need to support *file access* (reading or writing random parts of a suitably structured file).
- The need to support a wide range of *file types and structures,* not just plain text or binary, with access to parts of a complex structure.
- The need to support reading and writing (where applicable) of *attributes* of a file (e.g., date last written and access control). This, together with creating and deleting files, is called *file management.*

- The need to encourage or require implementors to use disk or tape storage for checkpointing to protect against host crashes. (Checkpointing is the process of taking periodic snapshots of a database so that if a crash occurs, the database can be recovered at the last checkpoint.)

**TABLE 5-8**    Interpersonal Messaging Services (X.400)

| | |
|---|---|
| **Basic Services** | |
| IP-message identification | Assign reference identifier to each message content sent or received |
| Typed body | Allows nature and attributes of message body to be conveyed along with body |
| **Essential Optional Services (for Both Origination and Reception)** | |
| Originator indication | Identifies the user that sent message |
| Primary and copy recipients indication | Allows UA to specify primary and secondary recipients |
| Replying IP-message indication | Specifies an earlier message to which this is a reply |
| Subject indication | Description of message |
| **Additional (for Origination) and Essential (for Reception) Optional Services** | |
| Blind copy recipient indication | List of recipients whose identities are not to be disclosed to primary or copy recipients |
| Auto-forwarded indication | Marks a message as containing an automatically forwarded message |
| Authorizing user's indication | Indicates one or more persons who authorized the message |
| Expiry date indication | Conveys a date and time after which the originator considers the message invalid |
| Cross-referencing indication | Specifies one or more other messages related to this one |
| Importance indication | Specifies low, normal, or high |
| Obsoleting indication | Specifies previous messages that are obsolete and superseded by this one |
| Sensitivity indication | Specifies personal, private, or company-confidential |
| Reply request indication | Asks for response; may also specify date, time, and other recipients |
| Forwarded IP-message indication | Marks a message as containing a forwarded message |
| Body part encryption indication | Body part of message is encrypted |
| Multipart body | Enables sending message with multiple parts, each with its own attributes |
| **Additional Optional Services (for both Origination and Reception)** | |
| Nonreceipt notification | Requests that originator be informed if message is not received by its intended recipient |
| Receipt notification | Requests that originator be notified of receipt of message by intended recipient |

## Principles

Figure 5-14 shows the elements of a file transfer. The object is to move a file or a portion of a file from wherever it is (the source file) to somewhere else (the destination file). The files are stored in the file system, normally on disk, in general-purpose host computers. The host computer has hardware for connection to a network and communications software that includes the file transfer logic.

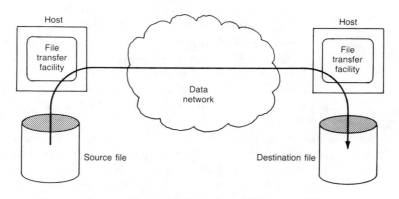

**Figure 5-14** File transfer.

Typically, the file transfer facility is used interactively by an on-line user. It may also be invoked by some other application program. For example, a program at a sales office may automatically connect to a headquarters computer every evening to transfer a sales record file. In any case, the user (human or another application) connects to the local facility to transfer all or part of a file. There are three possibilities. The user at A may want a file at B to be transferred to A; this would give the user local access to the contents of the file. The user may have prepared a file locally (at A) and want it sent to B. Finally, the user may request that a file be exchanged between B and a third system, C. This is referred to as a third-party transfer and involves the file transfer modules at A, B, and C.

A general-purpose file transfer facility must operate in a mixed-vendor, mixed-file environment. We would like to be able to exchange files between different vendor equipment (e.g., IBM and DEC) and to exchange files between systems that use different formats (e.g., ASCII characters and EBCDIC characters). Before suggesting an effective way to handle this situation, let us consider what will be transferred. There are three possibilities:

- *Data in the file:* If just the contents of the file are sent, we are not really dealing with a file transfer. This is more in the nature of an electronic mail facility.

- *Data plus file structure:* This, at minimum, is what is usually meant by a file transfer.

- *Data, file structure, and file attributes:* Examples of attributes are an access control list, an update history, and the author of the file.

In general, the file transfer facility will operate somewhere on the spectrum between the second and third items. The task we face is in the conversion between different systems. The following considerations apply:

- *Data:* We have already given one example of differences here—ASCII versus EBCDIC character codes. If a text file is transferred from a system that uses one code to a system that uses the other code, either the sending or receiving system must do the conversion.
- *File structure:* Different file management and database packages use different file structures, such as hierarchical versus relational databases. Even if both systems are using the same file structure, different packages use different internal formats and structures to store the file structure that is seen by the user. Again, either the sending or receiving system must do the conversion.
- *File attributes:* There are two issues here. First, one file management system may support an attribute that is not supported by the other (e.g., data last altered). In this case, the attribute must be ignored. Second, even if both systems provide this attribute, its format or location in the file structure may differ. In this case, either the sending or receiving system must do the conversion.

The conversion requirement poses a serious problem. Consider, for example, a network of five different computers in which the file characteristics of each are unique in terms of content, structure, or attributes. On each system, we want to implement a file transfer facility that can exchange files with the remaining four systems (Figure 5-15a). Further suppose that all conversions are done by the sending system. It follows that each system must be equipped with four conversion packages, one for each system with which it can exchange files. Thus, in this network, a total of twenty conversion packages must be implemented.

A better approach is to use the concept of a virtual filestore. A *virtual filestore* is a general-purpose file structure with a set of attributes, formats, and allowable actions. The virtual filestore defines the files that can be exchanged between systems. Therefore, on each system all that is needed is a conversion between the local (real) files and virtual files (Figure 5-15b). In our example, the number of implementations needed is now only five, one in each system.

Figure 5-16 shows the nature of the conversion. Defined actions (e.g., read, write, create, or destroy) on the virtual file are interpreted as actions on the real file and implemented as such. For this approach to work, a definition of the virtual filestore must be standardized and used by all vendors. If this definition is kept very simple, it will be relatively easy for implementors to convert incoming virtual files and virtual file commands into files and commands that can be handled by the local file system. Unfortunately, many characteristics and features of a real file would then have no equivalent in the

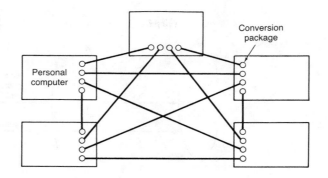

*(a)  Separate conversion packages.*

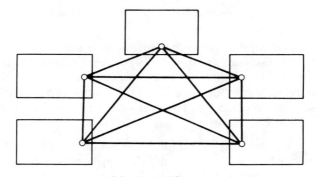

*(b)  Virtual filestore.*

**Figure 5-15**  Conversion software for file transfer.

virtual file and would therefore not be supported for file transfer. On the other hand, if the virtual filestore definition contained a wide range of file types and functions, it would be relatively easy to convert files from real to virtual, but the standard itself would be difficult to implement because of its complexity. The standard described next leans more toward the latter philosophy.

## ISO FTAM Standards

In 1988, ISO issued a standard that defines a flexible and powerful file transfer facility. It is known as file transfer, access, and management (FTAM). The standard specifies a virtual filestore that defines the types of files that can be exchanged, the service provided to the user, and the mechanisms for implementing those services.

In FTAM, each file is associated with a number of attributes. Two classes of attributes are defined: file attributes and activity attributes. File attributes represent properties of the file itself; these are the types of attributes often found on file management systems on time-sharing systems. Three groups of file attributes are defined in FTAM. The kernel group is the minimum that must be

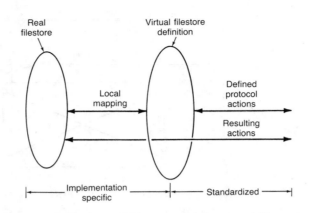

**Figure 5-16** The real filestore and the virtual filestore.

supported; they provide the basic information needed for the act of file transfer. The storage group defines concepts related to the physical storage of files; they are concerned with physical properties of the file, such as size, as well as information about users of the file. The security group provides for file-related security information. The attributes are listed in Table 5-9. Some of them merit further comment:

- *Contents type:* The internal structure of the file (unstructured, sequential, or hierarchical) and the data type (text or binary).
- *Permitted actions:* Actions (defined subsequently) that are permitted on this file.
- *Access control:* List of permitted users and the actions each is permitted to perform.
- *Encryption name:* Name of the algorithm used to encrypt the file contents.
- *Legal qualifications:* Text conveying information about the legal status of the file and its usage.

Activity attributes form the other class of attributes. These are relevant only to the file activity in progress. The file activity attributes for each file action have a different set of values. As with file attributes, activity attributes are divided into kernel, storage, and security groups. Among these are

- *Current access context:* The view of the file's access structure for the purposes of communication (hierarchical, sequential, or unstructured).
- *Current concurrency control:* The restrictions on simultaneous access to the file for particular actions during the current activity. For example, if someone is reading a file, others may be allowed to read the file. If someone is writing (updating) a file, the file may be locked so that no one else can access it until the update is complete.

Table 5-10 lists the allowable actions on files and file elements. Some ac-

**TABLE 5-9**   FTAM Attributes

| File Attribute | Activity Attribute |
|---|---|
| **Kernel Group** | |
| File name | Active contents type |
| Contents type | Current access request |
| | Current location |
| | Current processing mode |
| | Current application entity title |
| **Storage Group** | |
| Storage account | Current account |
| Date and time of creation | Current access context |
| Date and time of last modification | Current concurrency control |
| Date and time of last read access | |
| Date and time of last attribute modification | |
| Identity of creator | |
| Identity of last modifier | |
| Identity of last reader | |
| Identity of last attribute modifier | |
| File availability | |
| Permitted actions | |
| File size | |
| Future file size | |
| **Security Group** | |
| Access control | Active legal qualifications |
| Encryption name | Current initiator identity |
| Legal qualifications | Current access passwords |

tions are defined on a complete file; these fall within the scope of file management. The other actions are related to the access of subsets of the file, referred to as file access data units.

The FTAM standard defines a set of services available to users for accessing and manipulating virtual files. These services are used in a series of stages:

- *Association stage:* Allows the user and the filestore provider to establish each other's identity. During this stage, the user's authority to access a particular file management system is determined. It is equivalent to logging on to a remote host.

- *File selection stage:* Identifies the file that is needed and the user's authority to access the file. The file may be selected from existing files, or it may be created. During this stage, the user may read and, if authorized, alter the attributes of the file.

**TABLE 5-10**   Allowable Actions on FTAM Files

### Actions on Complete Files

| | |
|---|---|
| Create file | Creates new file; establishes its attributes. |
| Select file | Creates relationship between initiator and file. |
| Change attribute | Changes a current file attribute. |
| Read attribute | Gets value of requested attribute. |
| Open file | Establishes suitable regime for the performance of the actions for file access on the selected file. File may be opened for read or read/write. |
| Close file | Terminates the open regime. |
| Delete file | Deletes the selected file. |
| Deselect file | Terminates file selection. |

### Actions for File Access

| | |
|---|---|
| Locate | Locates specified FADU. |
| Read | Locates and reads an FADU. |
| Insert | Inserts FADU relative to current location. |
| Replace | Replaces currently located FADU. |
| Extend | Adds data to the end of the DU associated with the root node of the currently located FADU. |
| Erase | Specified FADU is erased. |

DU = Data Unit
FADU = File Access Data Unit

- *File open stage:* Temporarily assigns a file to a user. Concurrency controls (whether other users may read the file or write to the file) may be established during this stage.
- *Data transfer stage:* Allows the user to access the file or a portion of the file. During reading or writing, the user may define checkpoints to be used for recovery.

As a final point, FTAM can be used with file servers, in the same manner as we saw with electronic mail. Figure 5-17 shows a typical configuration.

# Choosing LAN Software

The choice of software for a LAN installation is not an easy one. A wide variety of proprietary and standardized products work on a variety of personal computers, minicomputers, mainframes, and servers. In addition, the manager is faced with a chicken-and-egg problem: Choose the computers and LAN that best meet the organization's requirements and then select the best software for the configuration, or choose the software that best matches the organization's

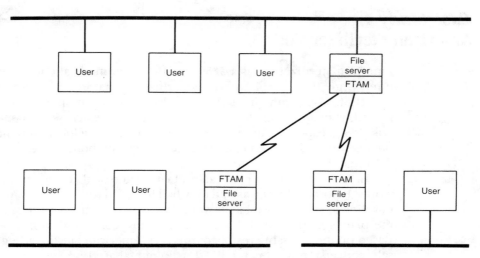

**Figure 5-17** File servers and multiple lans.

application needs and then select the best hardware and LAN that support that software?

If there were a widely implemented, functionally-rich set of standards for distributed processing software, the choice would be much easier. The manager could focus on choosing a LAN configuration and a set of computers, with the expectation that whatever is chosen will support the standard software. This point may be reached or at least more closely approached in the next few years, but for now we are a long way from this paradise. This section provides a few helpful hints.

If an organization needs personal computer support, a good approach is to dictate a uniform strategy for personal computer networking. This strategy should limit the type of personal computer LANs to one type or several compatible types (e.g., several members of the 802.3 family), and involve uniform software across all the LANs. For example, if servers will be used, the same server software should be used on all LANs in the organization. This simplifies user training (remember Figure 1-14!) and maintenance and reduces the number of vendors one has to deal with. In today's market, standards are not far enough advanced to be able to dispense with proprietary server software, so servers will probably be an element of any personal computer LAN strategy.

Whether the organizations networking needs are met solely by personal computer LANs, or whether other types of LANs and computers are involved, the organization should have a plan that moves eventually to international standards. In the long run, this is the solution with the lowest cost and least hassle. As we discussed in Chapter 3, the move to international standards may not make sense in the short run. In that case, a TCP/IP solution or even an SNA solution is at least better than any other proprietary, nonstandard approach.

## Case Study 4
## American Sterilizer Co.[1]

American Sterilizer Co. is a $250-million-a-year medical equipment manufacturer. Until 1985, all of American Sterilizer's data processing was handled by two IBM 4341 mainframes. Both on-line and batch applications were supported, with approximately 750 terminals in place across the company's various sites. Response time for interactive use varied widely, depending on the processing load. The company was unhappy with both the response time and the reliability of the facility.

In 1986, the company began evaluating personal computers and local networks. Before the year was out, they had installed a pilot system in Apex, North Carolina to see how well a network could support their business needs. All of the plant's COBOL-based applications were converted to run on IBM PCs. Based on the favorable results of this test, American Sterilizer began a wholesale conversion from centralized mainframe-based processing to distributed processing based on local area networks and personal computers.

By early 1988, the company had terminated the lease on one of its two mainframes and installed 550 personal computers to replace 550 terminals. Local networks were installed in the company's three headquarters in Eire, Pennsylvania, in a manufacturing plant in Montgomery, Alabama, and in a number of regional sales offices. All of the personal computers are IBM PC compatible, and the local networks are baseband coaxial cable. An X.25 packet-switching network interconnects the various sites. Applications converted to run on the personal computers include personnel and payroll systems, accounts payable, and large portions of service order entry. Although the applications had to be modified to work with a different database management system, most of the COBOL logic was unchanged.

This initial phase of the implementation has already resulted in dramatic improvements. In 1987, the company saved $600,000 compared with what it spent in 1985 on rentals and maintenance of mainframe hardware and software. During the second phase of the project, the company plans to replace the remaining mainframe and terminals with an additional 350 personal computers. This will require converting the rest of the software, including such batch applications as materials requirements planning and the manufacturing support system. Savings of over $1 million a year are expected.

In addition to cost savings, the use of personal computers and LANs provides performance and reliability benefits. The company's experience is that response time on interactive applications is shorter and more consistent on the personal computers compared to the mainframe. Whereas mainframe performance suffers due to changing loads, users on the LAN have consistently good performance because their applications are running on their individual personal computers. In the LAN environment, the only shared usage occurs when

[1] This case study is based on material in M. Petrosky, "User Sends Mainframes Packing," *Network World*, April 11, 1988.

various users access data files maintained on server personal computers. Because these access functions are of short duration compared to applications that run in the personal computers, there is little impact on response time.

Reliability has also improved. An occasional software crash or power interruption on the mainframe brought all processing to a halt, whereas such a fault on a personal computer affects only one user or a few users. The mainframe systems were not equipped with an uninterruptible power supply because it was too costly. Now all shared file server microcomputers are equipped with such a feature.

The experience of American Sterilizer is representative of the experience of many medium-sized companies: Compared to the combination of terminals and mainframes, the combination of personal computers and LANs provides cost, performance, and reliability benefits.

# Summary

To be useful, a LAN must be more than simply a means of moving bits from one point in a building to another. Networking software is needed to use cooperative, distributed applications and share expensive resources. This software should be vendor-independent and LAN-independent to provide the user with the maximum flexibility as needs and configurations evolve.

An important element in virtually all LAN software strategies is the use of servers. A server is a separate system that controls one or more network resources, providing access to users on the LAN. The most important type of server is the disk and file server. This type of server provides a shared storage space for files. In its simplest form, as a disk server, it merely provides dedicated space on a shared disk for each user to store files. More sophisticated file servers have some or many of the features of a sophisticated file management system on a time-sharing computer. A printer server controls one or more printers on behalf of network users. Print requests are queued and printed in order. A modem server provides one modem or a pool of modems that can be accessed by a LAN user to establish a data connection over a telephone line.

LAN software is needed also to support terminals that connect to the LAN by an NIU. The simplest approaches are for asynchronous terminals. These can be supported by a simple terminal server, which requires one host port for each active terminal. A more efficient technique uses a protocol that supports multiple logical terminal-to-host connections on a single physical link to the host computer. The most common protocol for this approach is based on the use of a packet assembler/disassembler (PAD) device. Another commonly used protocol is TELNET, which is part of the TCP/IP protocol suite. For more complex synchronous terminals, far more software is required. The virtual terminal service, which is an international standard, satisfies this requirement.

As standardized software becomes more widely available, a more attractive approach to providing distributed applications than the server approach is to use international standards. In the area of electronic mail, the X.400 series of standards allow the linkage of a number of single-system mail facilities across a network, enabling a user to send a message to any other user on any system on the network. Another important distributed application is file transfer, for which the file transfer, access, and management (FTAM) standard has been created.

# Chapter 6

# The Internetworking Requirement: Bridges, Routers, and Gateways

LOCAL AREA NETWORKS (LANs) and wide area networks (WANs) grew out of the computer user's need to have access to resources beyond those available in a single system. In a similar fashion, the resources of a single network are often inadequate to meet users' needs. Thus, in many business environments, a number of networks are used. For a variety of reasons, discussed subsequently, it is impractical in most cases to merge multiple networks into a single network. Rather, what is needed is the capability to interconnect various networks so that any two devices on any of the constituent networks can communicate.

An interconnected set of networks, from a user's point of view, may appear simply as a larger network. If each of the constituent networks retains its identity and special mechanisms are needed for communicating across multiple networks, the entire configuration is often referred to as an *internet,* and each of the constituent networks as a *subnetwork.* These terms are briefly defined in Table 6-1.

Table 6-1 also defines three sorts of devices used to interconnect subnetworks in an internet. These devices provide a communications path and the necessary logic so that data can be exchanged between subnetworks. The differences between them have to do with the types of protocols used for the internetworking logic. In this chapter, we examine each of these devices in turn.

Figure 6-1 shows the projected growth in the use of the two most important types of internetworking devices, bridges and routers. Bridges are further broken down into those that connect LANs in the same site (local bridges) and those that make use of telecommunications facilities to interconnect LANs at different sites (remote bridges). These projections reflect the rapid growth in the use of internetworking. Another indication of the importance placed on internetworking is shown in Figure 6-2. Particularly in larger organizations, most LAN users feel that the capability to link LANs to WANs is important or critical.

**TABLE 6-1**   Internetworking Terms

| | |
|---|---|
| Communication network | A facility that provides a data transfer service among stations attached to the network. |
| Internet | A collection of communication networks interconnected by bridges, routers, and/or gateways. |
| Subnetwork | Refers to a constituent network of an internet. This avoids ambiguity because the entire internet, from a user's point of view, is a single network. |
| Bridge | A device used to connect two LANs that use identical LAN protocols. The bridge acts as an address filter, picking up packets from one LAN that are intended for a destination on another LAN and passing those packets on. The bridge does not modify the contents of the packets and does not add anything to the packet. The bridge operates at layer 2 of the OSI model. |
| Router | A device used to connect two networks that may or may not be similar. The router employs an internet protocol present in each router and each host of the network. The bridge operates at layer 3 of the OSI model. |
| Gateway | A device used to connect two sets of computers that use two different communications architectures. The gateway maps from an application on one computer to an application that is similar in function but differs in detail on another computer. The bridge operates at layer 3 of the OSI model. |

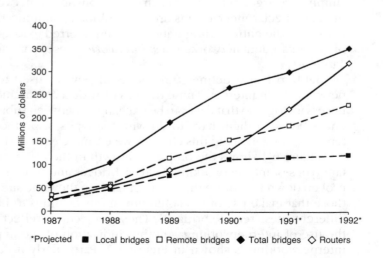

**Figure 6-1**  Sales of bridges and routers. (*Source:* Data Communications, *July 1989.)*

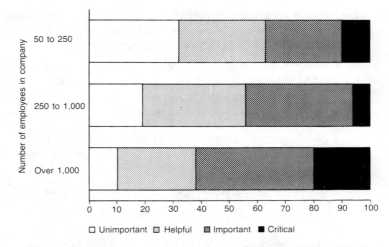

**Figure 6-2** LAN users rate importance of linking LANS to WANs.
*(Source: The Market Information Center, Marlborough MA, February 1988.)*

# Bridges

## Principles of Operation

The simplest internetworking device is the bridge. This device is used between local area networks (LANs) with identical protocols for the physical and link layers (e.g., all conforming to IEEE 802.3 or all conforming to FDDI). Because the devices all use the same protocols, the amount of processing required at the bridge is minimal.

Because the bridge is used with LANs that have the same characteristics, the reader may ask, why not simply have one large LAN? Depending on circumstance, there are several reasons for the use of multiple LANs connected by bridges:

- *Reliability:* The danger in connecting all data processing devices in an organization to one network is that a fault on the network may disable communication for all devices. By using bridges, the network can be partitioned into self-contained units.

- *Performance:* In general, performance on a LAN declines with an increase in the number of devices or the length of the wire. A number of smaller LANs will often give improved performance if devices can be clustered so that intranetwork traffic significantly exceeds internetwork traffic.

- *Security:* The establishment of multiple LANs may improve security of communications. It is desirable to keep different types of traffic (e.g., accounting, personnel, or strategic planning) that have different security needs on physically separate media. At the same time, the different types of users with different levels of security need to communicate through controlled and monitored mechanisms.

- *Geography:* Clearly, two separate LANs are needed to support devices clustered in two geographically distant locations. Even in the case of two buildings separated by a highway, it may be far easier to use a microwave bridge link than to attempt to string coaxial cable between the two buildings.

To understand the action of a bridge, first let us recall how communication takes place among devices attached to a single LAN. Figure 2-3 shows an example using a bus-topology LAN; the principle is similar for tree and ring topologies. Data on the bus is transmitted in packets. So, if station C wants to transmit a message to station A, for example, C breaks its message into small pieces that are sent, one at a time, in packets. Each packet header includes, among other control information, the address of A. Based on some medium access control technique (e.g., CSMA/CD or token bus), C transmits each packet onto the bus. The packet travels the length of the bus in both directions, reaching all other stations. When A recognizes its address on a packet, it copies the packet and processes it.

Now suppose we want to link LANs X and Y, which use the same protocols. This is accomplished in Figure 6-3 using a bridge attached to both local networks. The functions of the bridge are few and simple:

- Read all packets transmitted on X and accept those addressed to any station on Y.
- Using the medium access control protocol for Y, retransmit each packet on Y.
- Do the same for Y-to-X traffic.

Several design aspects of a bridge are worth highlighting:

- The bridge makes no modification to the content or format of the packets it receives, nor does it encapsulate them with an additional header. Each packet to be transferred is simply copied from one LAN and repeated with exactly the same bit pattern on the other LAN. We can do this because the two LANs use the same LAN protocols.
- The bridge must contain addressing and routing intelligence. At a minimum, the bridge must know which addresses are on each network in order to know which packets to pass. Further, more than two LANs may be interconnected by a number of bridges. In that case, a packet may have to be routed through several bridges in its journey from source to destination.
- A bridge may connect more than two networks.

In summary, the bridge provides an extension to the LAN that requires no modification to the communications software in the stations attached to the LANs. To all stations on the two (or more) LANs, it appears that there is a single LAN on which each station has a unique address. The station uses that unique

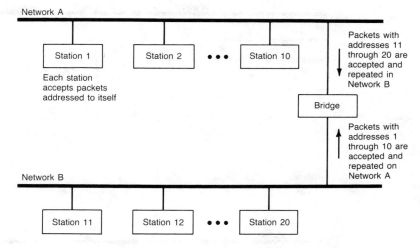

**Figure 6-3** Bridge operation.

address and need not explicitly discriminate between stations on the same LAN and stations on other LANs; the bridge takes care of that.

In the layout in Figure 6-3, we assume that the two LANs are close enough to each other that a bridge can be directly connected to both LANs. This is often the case with two LANs in the same building. In other cases, even though two LANs are at the same site, they are not sufficiently close to allow one bridge to directly link to both. And, invariably, when two LANs are geographically remote, a single bridge is insufficient. For these situations, two bridges are needed, as illustrated in Figure 6-4. The figure is labeled "Remote bridges," which implies that the two LANs are at different geographic sites; the principle is the same when two LANs at the same site use two bridges. As before, a bridge attached to a LAN scans packets on the LAN for those addressed to another LAN. In this case, the bridge captures each such packet and transmits it across some sort of communications facility (leased line, dial-up line, or wide area network) to a partner bridge. The partner bridge accepts packets from the communications facility and forwards them to its LAN. The same process occurs in the reverse direction.

A final point: Note in Figure 6-5a that the bridge encompasses only layers 1 and 2 of the OSI model. In effect, the bridge operates as a layer-2 relay. Layers 3 and above must be identical in the two end systems for successful end-to-end communications.

## Routing with Bridges

In each of the configurations of Figures 6-3 and 6-4, the bridge makes the decision to relay a frame on the basis of the destination MAC address. In a more complex configuration, the bridge must also make a routing decision.

Consider the configuration of Figure 6-6. Suppose that station 1 transmits a

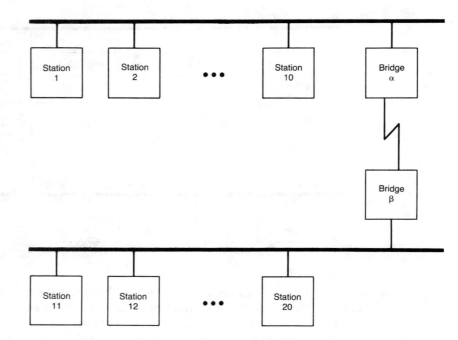

**Figure 6-4** Remote bridges.

frame on LAN A intended for station 5. The frame will be read by both bridge 101 and bridge 102. For each bridge, the addressed station is not on a LAN to which the bridge is attached. Therefore, each bridge must make a decision of whether or not to retransmit the frame on its other LAN, to move the frame closer to its intended destination. In this case, bridge 101 should repeat the frame on LAN B, whereas bridge 102 should refrain from retransmitting the frame. After the frame has been transmitted on LAN B, it will be picked up by both bridges 103 and 104. Again, each must decide whether or not to forward the frame. In this case, bridge 104 should retransmit the frame on LAN E, where it will be received by the destination, station 5.

Thus we see that, in general, the bridge must be equipped with a routing capability. When a bridge receives a frame, it must decide whether or not to forward it. If the bridge is attached to more than two networks, it must decide whether to forward the frame and, if so, on which LAN the frame should be transmitted.

The routing decision may not always be a simple one. In Figure 6-7, bridge 107 is added to the previous configuration, directly linking LAN A and LAN E. Such an addition may be made for higher overall internet availability. In this case, if station 1 transmits a frame on LAN A intended for station 5 on LAN E, either bridge 101 or bridge 107 could forward the frame. It would appear preferable for bridge 107 to forward the frame because it will involve only one "hop," whereas if the frame travels through bridge 101, it must suffer two hops. Another consideration is that there may be changes in the configuration. For

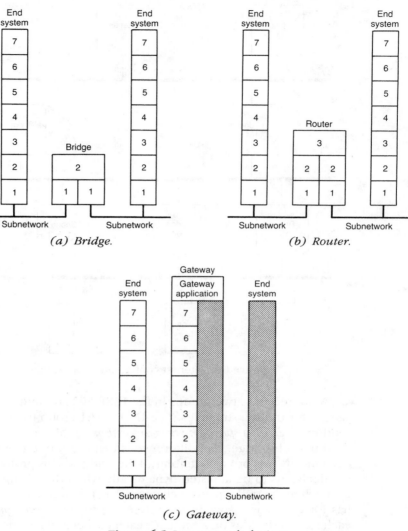

*(a) Bridge.*                    *(b) Router.*

*(c) Gateway.*

**Figure 6-5** Internetwork devices.

example, bridge 107 may fail, in which case subsequent frames from station 1 to station 5 should go through bridge 101. So we can say that the routing capability must take into account the topology of the internet configuration and may need to be dynamically altered.

A variety of routing strategies have been proposed and implemented in recent years. The simplest and most common strategy is *fixed routing*. In this strategy, each bridge contains a table that dictates the routing decision for all incoming packets. The table is set during configuration and must be changed manually when the configuration changes. This strategy is suitable for small internets and relatively stable internets. Most bridge vendors offer this capability.

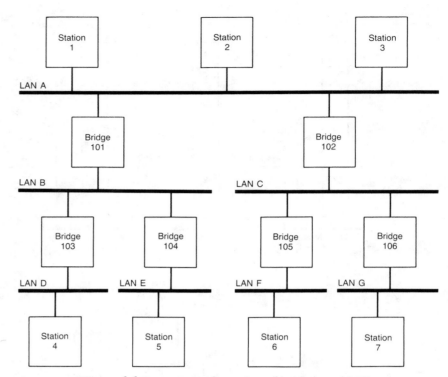

**Figure 6-6** Internet configuration of bridges and LANs.

More recently, two groups in the IEEE 802 committee developed specifications for routing strategies. The IEEE 802.1 group has issued a standard for routing based on a *spanning tree algorithm*. In this case, a routing table is also used in each bridge. The difference is that the routing table can be changed dynamically by a protocol among all the bridges. This protocol allows the routing decisions to be adjusted dynamically when the configuration changes or even when the traffic pattern changes. The token ring committee, IEEE 802.5, has issued its own specification, referred to as *source routing*. In this case, each station decides on a route for each packet and attaches the routing information to the packets. The bridges simply read the routing information to determine what action, if any, to take.

The relative merits of the two IEEE algorithms are a matter of some dispute. In most situations, either algorithm will work satisfactorily. If the user has an internet that is too large or dynamic to be handled by static routing, either standard is preferable to a proprietary one.

## Bridge Products

The market for bridges is expanding rapidly and the number of products on the market is also growing. All of the products provide the basic bridge function of

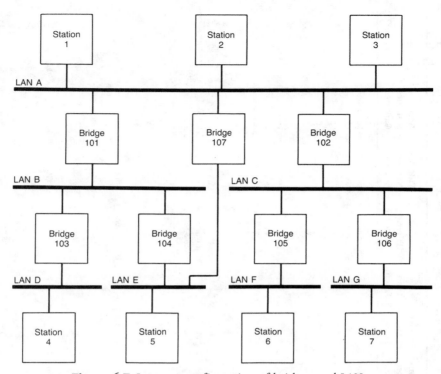

**Figure 6-7** Internet configuration of bridges and LANs, with alternate routes.

moving packets between similar LANs. Most now offer a variety of other features. Some products support multiple bridges between two LANs and permit load balancing. Some support priority packet processing by permitting high-priority traffic, such as interactive applications, to take precedence over low-priority traffic, such as file transfers. Table 6-2 gives details on most current vendors.

# Routers

## Principles of Operation

The bridge is only applicable to a configuration involving a single type of LAN. Of course, in many cases, an organization needs access to devices on a variety of networks. For example, as Figure 1-10 illustrates, an organization may have a tiered LAN architecture, with different types of LANs used for different purposes. In addition, access may be needed to devices on a wide area network. Examples of the latter are a database for query and transaction applications and a customer's computer for transferring ordering information.

**TABLE 6-2** Bridge Products

| Vendor | Product | Bridge Type | Local Net Interconnect | Spanning Tree Protocol | Learning Bridge | Local Net Transmission Media | Transmission Speed (bit/sec) | Number of Link Ports | Load Balancing | Filtering Based On | Wide-Area Network Interface | Network Statistics Gathered | Price |
|---|---|---|---|---|---|---|---|---|---|---|---|---|---|
| Advanced Computer Communications Santa Barbara, Calif. (805) 963-9431 | ACS 4030 Remote Ethernet Bridge | Remote | Ethernet to Ethernet | Optional | Yes | Thin/thick Ethernet | Up to 128K | 4 | Yes | Destination address | RS-232C, RS422/449 | Packets filtered, forwarded, refused, rejected | $5,475 |
| | ACS 4110T1 Remote Ethernet Bridge | Remote | Ethernet to Ethernet | Yes | Yes | Thin/thick Ethernet | 1.544M, 2.048M | 2 | Yes | Destination address | RS-232-C, RS 422/ 449, CCITT V.35, T-1 | Packets filtered, forwarded, refused, rejected | $7,500 |
| Applitek Corp. Wakefield, Mass. (617) 246-4500 | N110/E Ethernet Bridge | Remote | Ethernet to Ethernet via UniLan | No | Yes | Thin/thick Ethernet, fiber optic; baseband or broadband operation | Info. not available | 1 Ethernet, 1 UniLan | No | Source and destination address | UniLan | Transmit/receive packets, collisions, run packets, jabbers, late packets | $12,100 to $13,750 |
| | Bridge-master | Local | Broadband Ethernet to Ethernet | No | Yes | Thin/thick Ethernet, fiber optic; broadband operation | 10M | 1 Ethernet to 1 Ethernet | No | Destination address | None | Transmit/receive packets, collisions, run packets, jabbers, late packets | $9,950 |
| Artel Communications Corp. Hudson, Mass. (508) 562-2100 | Manbridge | Local and remote | Ethernet to Ethernet via DS3 transmission facilities | No | Yes | Thin/thick Ethernet; TA34 coaxial for DS3 | 10M local; 45M remote | 1 | No | Source and destination address | DS3 | Tokens generated, bit errors per hour, jabber, packet distribution list, utilization reports | $25,000 |
| | Fiberway 802.3 Bridge | Local and remote | Ethernet to Ethernet via Artel's Fiberway | No | Yes | Thin/thick Ethernet, fiber optic | 10M, 50M | 1 | No | Source and destination address | DS3 | Tokens generated, bit errors per hour, jabber, packet distribution list | $23,450 |

| Vendor | Product | Bridge Type | Local Net Interconnect | Spanning Tree Protocol | Learning Bridge | Local Net Transmission Media | Transmission Speed (bit/sec) | Number of Link Ports | Load Balancing | Filtering Based On | Wide-Area Network Interface | Network Statistics Gathered | Price |
|---|---|---|---|---|---|---|---|---|---|---|---|---|---|
| AT&T Morristown, N.J. (201) 631-6000 | Starlan Network 1:10 Bridge | Local | Starlan to Ethernet | Yes | Yes | Thin/thick Ethernet, twisted pair | 1M for Starlan; 10M for Ethernet | 2 | No | Destination address | NA | Spanning Tree, network alarms, packets forwarded, packet and network errors | $4,500 |
| | Starlan Network 10:10 Bridge | Local | Ethernet to Ethernet | Yes | Yes | Thin/thick Ethernet, twisted pair, fiber optic | 10M | 2 | No | Destination address | Info. not available | Spanning Tree, network alarms, packets forwarded, packet and network errors | $7,000 |
| BICC Data Networks Inc. Westborough, Mass. (508) 898-2422 | 1410 Managed Bridge | Local | Ethernet to Ethernet | Yes | Yes | Thin/thick Ethernet, fiber optic, twisted pair | 10M | 2 | NA | Source and destination address, packet type, protocol | NA | Packets filtered and forwarded, packets and bytes transmitted, multicast, collisions, deferred transmissions, transmission errors | $7,000; $5,995 for network management software |
| | 1400 Primary Bridge | Local | Ethernet to Ethernet | No | Yes | Thin/thick Ethernet, twisted pair, fiber optic | 10M | 2 | NA | Destination address | NA | Info. not available | $3,395 |
| Cabletron Systems, Inc. Rochester, N.H. (603) 332-9400 | NB35 T1 Bridge | Remote | Ethernet to Ethernet via T 1 | Yes | Yes | Thin/thick Ethernet, twisted pair, fiber optic | 10M, 1.544M | 2 | No | Destination address | T 1 | Receive packet count, packet errors, T-1 receive errors, T-1 transmit and time-out errors | $14,900 for 2 T-1 bridges; $1,400 for each CSU |

*(continued)*

TABLE 6-2 *(cont.)*

| Vendor | Product | Bridge Type | Local Net Inter-connect | Spanning Tree Protocol | Learning Bridge | Local Net Transmis-sion Media | Transmis-sion Speed (bit/sec) | Number of Link Ports | Load Balancing | Filtering Based On | Wide-Area Network Interface | Network Statistics Gathered | Price |
|---|---|---|---|---|---|---|---|---|---|---|---|---|---|
| | NB25E | Local | Ethernet to Ethernet | Yes | Yes | Thin/thick Ethernet, fiber optic, twisted pair | 10M | 2 | No | Destination address | NA | Collisions, transmit/receive errors, inbound/outbound network traffic, aborted transmissions | $5,495 |
| CBIS, Inc. Norcross, Ga. (404) 446-1332 | Network-OS Bridge | Local and Remote | Ethernet, Arcnet, token bus, token ring, to same | No | Yes | Thin/thick Ethernet, twisted pair | 2.5M to 10M local; remote depends on modem used | 1 | No | Destination address | None | Packets sent and received, packet errors, collisions, aborts, buffer counts | $160 for bridge; $360 for cluster bridge |
| Chipcom Corp. Waltham, Mass. (617) 890-6844 | Ether-modem III Bridge | Local | Baseband to broadband Ethernet | Yes | Yes | Thin/thick Ethernet, fiber optic | 10M | 2 | No | Destination address | NA | Info. not available | $8,950 for single-cable 12-MHz or 18-MHz unit |
| | Marathon Bridge | Local | Baseband to broadband Ethernet | No | Yes | Thin/thick Ethernet, broadband coaxial | 10M | 2 | No | Destination address | NA | Info. not available | $9,950; $7,900 for remodulator |
| Cisco Systems, Inc. Menlo Park, Calif. (415) 326-1941 | Hybridge | Local and remote | Ethernet to Ethernet | Yes | Yes | Thick coaxial | 10M local; up to 4M remote | 1; up to 16 T-1s optional | Yes | Source and destination address, packet size and type, protocol | RS-232-C, RS-449, CCITT V.35, T-1 | Bits and packets transmitted, total packets transmitted, errors, broadcast messages | $7,225 |
| CrossComm Corp. Marlborough, Mass. (508) 481-4060 | ILAN | Local and remote | Ethernet to Ethernet via T-1 transmission facilities | Yes | Yes | Thin/thick Ethernet, fiber optic, twisted pair | 10M local; up to 1.544M remote | 4 | Yes | Source and destination address, protocol | RS-449, CCITT V.35, T-1 | Packets transmitted and received, packets filtered, packet errors, multicast | $4,900 to $9,800 |

| Vendor | Product | Bridge Type | Local Net Interconnect | Spanning Tree Protocol | Learning Bridge | Local Net Transmission Media | Transmission Speed (bit/sec) | Number of Link Ports | Load Balancing | Filtering Based On | Wide-Area Network Interface | Network Statistics Gathered | Price |
|---|---|---|---|---|---|---|---|---|---|---|---|---|---|
| Cryptal Communications Corp. Cranston, R.I. (401) 941-7600 | 3000 Series | Remote | Ethernet to Ethernet | Yes | Yes | Thin/thick Ethernet | 10M local; 56K remote | 4 | Yes | Source and destination address | RS-232-C, RS-449, CCITT V.35, fiber optic, microwave | Packets transmitted and received, net errors, link loss | $8,500 to $12,500 |
| Digital Equipment Corp. Maynard, Mass. (617) 897-5111 | LAN Bridge 100 | Local and remote | Baseband and broadband, Ethernet to Ethernet, Ethernet to token ring | Yes | Yes | Baseband and broadband coaxial | 10M | 2 | No | Destination address | None | Network utilization and throughput, top 10 protocols used, top 10 transmitting stations, multicast addresses | $6,500; $7,500 with fiber-optic interface; $15,000 with microwave interface; $5,355 for traffic monitor software |
| FiberCom, Inc. Roanoke, Va. (703) 342-6700 | WB 80 | Remote | Ethernet to Ethernet | Yes | Yes | Thin/thick Ethernet | 10M local; 2.048M remote | 1 local; 2 remote | Yes | Source and destination address | CCITT V.35 and X.21, RS-449, T-1 | Transmit rates, thresholds | $10,400; $1,500 for second wide-area net port |
| | WB-65 | Local | Ethernet to Ethernet | Yes | Yes | Thin/thick Ethernet | 10M | 2 | Yes | Source and destination address | NA | Filter rates, thresholds | $2,650 |
| Gateway Communications, Inc. Irvine, Calif. (714) 553-1555 | G/remote Bridge | Remote | Any supporting Novell, Inc. NetWare | Yes | Yes | Thin/thick Ethernet, twisted pair | Up to 19.2K | 2 | No | Destination address | RS-232 C | None | $1,595 for single link; $2,990 for two links |
| | G/remote Bridge 64 | Remote | Any supporting or using NetWare | No | Yes | Thin/thick Ethernet, twisted pair | Up to 64K | 1 | NA | Destination address | RS-232-C, CCITT V.35 | None | $2,495 for single link; $4,495 for two links |
| Halley Systems, Inc. San Jose, Calif. (408) 432-2600 | Connect-LAN 202 | Local | Token ring to token ring | No | Yes | IBM Type I, II, and III cabling | 4M | NA | Yes | Source and destination address | NA | Packets filtered and forwarded | $12,995 |

*(continued)*

**TABLE 6-2** *(cont.)*

| Vendor | Product | Bridge Type | Local Net Interconnect | Spanning Tree Protocol | Learning Bridge | Local Net Transmission Media | Transmission Speed (bit/sec) | Number of Link Ports | Load Balancing | Filtering Based On | Wide-Area Network Interface | Network Statistics Gathered | Price |
|---|---|---|---|---|---|---|---|---|---|---|---|---|---|
| Hewlett-Packard Co. Roseville, Calif. (916) 786-8000 | HP 28647B | Local | Starlan to Ethernet | Yes | Yes | Thin/thick Ethernet, twisted pair | 1M, 10M | 2 | No | Destination address | NA | Packets per second filtered/forwarded, packets queued, transmission errors | $4,635 |
| | HP 28649A | Local | Token ring to Ethernet | Yes, plus source routing | Yes | Thin/thick Ethernet, twisted pair, IBM Type I, II, III cabling | 4M, 10M | 2 | No | Destination address | NA | Packets transmitted/received and forwarded, frame errors, net alarms | $8,250 |
| Hughes LAN Systems Mountain View, Calif. (415) 966-7400 | 8050 Broadband/Ethernet Bridge | Local | Ethernet to 2M bit/sec broadband | No | Yes | Thin/thick Ethernet, broadband coaxial | NA | 2 | No | Source and destination address, packet type and size, protocol, multicast | NA | Ethernet and broadband packets transmitted and received, transmission retries | $8,125 |
| | 8011 WAN Bridge | Remote | Ethernet to ethernet | No | Yes | Thin/thick Ethernet | 2.048M | 2 | Yes | Source and destination address, packet size and type, protocol | RS-232-C, RS-449, CCITT V.35 | Packets transmitted and received, retries | $7,500 |
| IBM White Plains, N.Y. (914) 696-1900 | IBM PC Network Bridge | Local | Broadband, token ring to same | Yes (single root only) | No | IBM cabling, twisted pair | 2M for PC Network; 4M or 16M for token ring | Info. not available | Yes | Source routing | Info. not available | Broadcast packets and bytes forwarded and received, adapter congestion, nonbroadcast packets and bytes forwarded | $5,000 |

| Vendor | Product | Bridge Type | Local Net Inter-connect | Spanning Tree Protocol | Learning Bridge | Local Net Transmis-sion Media | Transmis-sion Speed (bit/sec) | Number of Link Ports | Load Balancing | Filtering Based On | Wide-Area Network Interface | Network Statistics Gathered | Price |
|---|---|---|---|---|---|---|---|---|---|---|---|---|---|
| | IBM Token-Ring Bridge Program Version 2.1 | Local or remote | Token ring to token ring | Yes (single root only) | No | IBM cabling, twisted pair | 4M or 16M local; remote to T-1 | 1 | Yes | Source routing | CCITT V.35, RS-232-C, X.21 | Broadcast packets and bytes forwarded and received, adapter congestion, nonbroadcast packets and bytes forwarded | $1,595 |
| Infotron Systems Corp. Cherry Hill, N.J. (609) 424-9400 | LAN Span | Remote | Ethernet to Ethernet | No | Yes | Thin/thick Ethernet, twisted pair | 10M local; 9.6K to 2.048M remote | 1 | NA | Source and destination address | RS-449, CCITT V.35, T-1 | Packets/bytes transmitted and forwarded, packets discarded, network traffic, T-1 errors | $11,965 |
| Lanex Corp. Beltsville, Md. (301) 595-4700 | Lanexpress Local Ethernet Bridge (LOC 8023) | Local | Ethernet to Ethernet; baseband and broadband | Yes | Yes | Thin/thick Ethernet | 10M | 2 | Yes | Destination address, protocol, packet size and type | NA | Packets transmitted and received, packets forwarded, network errors, collisions, traffic loading, topology | $4,995; $6,995 for broadband Ethernet |
| | Lanexpress Remote Ethernet Bridge | Remote | Ethernet to Ethernet | Yes | Yes | Thick coaxial, fiber optic | 10M local; 7.5M remote | 2 | Yes | Destination address, protocol, packet size and type | RS-232-C, RS-449, CCITT V.35 | Packets transmitted and received, packets forwarded, network errors, collisions, traffic loading, topology | $5,995 |

*(continued)*

**TABLE 6-2** *(cont.)*

| Vendor | Product | Bridge Type | Local Net Interconnect | Spanning Tree Protocol | Learning Bridge | Local Net Transmission Media | Transmission Speed (bit/sec) | Number of Link Ports | Load Balancing | Filtering Based On | Wide-Area Network Interface | Network Statistics Gathered | Price |
|---|---|---|---|---|---|---|---|---|---|---|---|---|---|
| Microcom Corp. Norwood, Mass. (617) 762-9310 | LAN Bridge | Remote | Ethernet to Ethernet; Token ring to token ring | No | Yes | Thin/thick Ethernet, twisted pair | 10M and 4M local; 9.6K to 2.048M remote | 4 | No | Source and destination address, packet size | RS-232-C, CCITT V.35, T-1 | Packets sent and received, multicast packets sent and received, packets discarded, packets sent and received, time-outs | $6,198 to $14,699 |
| Netronix Inc. Petaluma, Calif. (707) 762-2703 | Netronix Bridge | Local | Broadband Ethernet to Ethernet; broadband Ethernet to Starlan | No | Yes | Thin/thick Ethernet, twisted pair, fiber optic | 2M, 10M | 2 | No | Destination address | NA | Packet size, collisions, packet counts and addresses | $4,950 |
| | Token-Master | Local | Token ring to token ring; token ring to baseband Ethernet | NA | No | Twisted pair, thick coaxial | 4M | 2 | Yes | Destination address | NA | Packet count, packet size, packet address | $5,490 |
| Performance Technologies, Inc., San Antonio, Texas (512) 349-2000 | Power-bridge | Local | Ethernet, token ring, Arcnet, to same | No | Yes | Thin/thick Ethernet, twisted pair | Up to 10M | 1 | No | Source and destination address | NA | Packets sent and received, collisions, aborts, retransmissions, buffer statistics | $495 |
| Racal InterLan Boxborough, Mass. (508) 263-3536 | IB30 | Local | Ethernet to Ethernet | Yes | Yes | Thin/thick Ethernet | 10M | 2 | No | Source and destination address | NA | Packets transmitted and received, packets filtered and net errors | $2,295 to $3,295 |
| Rad Data Communications, Inc., Rochelle Park, N.J. (201) 568-1466 | RTB | Remote | Token ring to token ring | No | Yes | IBM Type I, II, III cabling | 4M local; up to 1.544M remote | 4 | Yes | Source and destination address, protocol, user-selectable filters | CCITT V.35, RS422, T-1 | Transmit/receive packets, packets forwarded, buffer overflow | $3,995 for 1 link; $8,450 for 4 links; $1,400 for CSU |

| Vendor | Product | Bridge Type | Local Net Interconnect | Spanning Tree Protocol | Learning Bridge | Local Net Transmission Media | Transmission Speed (bit/sec) | Number of Link Ports | Load Balancing | Filtering Based On | Wide-Area Network Interface | Network Statistics Gathered | Price |
|---|---|---|---|---|---|---|---|---|---|---|---|---|---|
| | REB/LEB | Local and remote | Ethernet to Ethernet | No | Yes | Thick coaxial | 10M local; up to 1.544M remote | 2 local; 4 remote | Yes | Source and destination address, protocol, user-selectable filters | RS-232-C, CCITT V.35, T-1 | Good and bad packets, collisions, alignment errors, overflow, packets forwarded, packets blocked | $3,995 for 1 link; $12,445 for 2 local and 4 remote links; $1,400 for CSU |
| Raycom Systems, Inc. Boulder, Colo. (303) 530-1620 | Bridge+ Fiber | Remote | Ethernet to Ethernet (Starlan, thin Ethernet) | Yes | Yes | Single or multimode fiber optic | 10M | 1 | No | Source and destination address | Single or multimode fiber-optic interface | Packets transmitted and received, packets filtered and net statistics | $7,875 to $8,160 |
| | Bridge + 1.5 T-1 | Remote | Ethernet to Ethernet (Starlan, thin Ethernet) | Yes | Yes | Thin/thick Ethernet | Up to 1.544M | 1 | No | Source and destination address | RS-449/422, RS-232-C, CCITT V.35 | Packets transmitted and received, packets filtered and net statistics | $6,975 to $7,260 |
| Retix Santa Monica, Calif. (213) 399-2200 | Model 2265M Bridge | Local | Ethernet to Ethernet | Yes | Yes | Thin/thick Ethernet | 10M | 2 | NA | Source and destination address, packet type | NA | Total collisions, excessive collisions, packets received, multicast packets received, short packets received | $3,250 |
| | Retix 4880 High Performance Remote Bridge | Remote | Ethernet to Ethernet | Yes | Yes | Thin/thick Ethernet | 10M local; 1.544M remote | 2 | Yes | Source and destination address, packet type | RS-449, CCITT V.35, X.21, T-1 | Packets filtered and forwarded, serial channel traffic volume | $10,400 |
| Shiva Corp. Cambridge, Mass. (617) 864-8500 | TeleBridge | Remote | Apple Computer Inc. LocalTalk to RS-232-C | No | Yes | Twisted pair | 230.4K local; 1.2K to 57.6K remote | 2 | No | Destination address | RS-232 C | Packets transmitted and received, packets forwarded, net errors | $499 |

*(continued)*

## TABLE 6-2 *(cont.)*

| Vendor | Product | Bridge Type | Local Net Interconnect | Spanning Tree Protocol | Learning Bridge | Local Net Transmission Media | Transmission Speed (bit/sec) | Number of Link Ports | Load Balancing | Filtering Based On | Wide-Area Network Interface | Network Statistics Gathered | Price |
|---|---|---|---|---|---|---|---|---|---|---|---|---|---|
| | NetBridge | Local | Apple LocalTalk to LocalTalk | No | Yes | Twisted pair | 230.4K | 2 | No | Destination address | NA | Packets transmitted and received, packets forwarded, net errors | $499 |
| Simple Net Systems, Inc. Brea, Calif. (714) 996-5088 | Laser-Bridge | Local | Fiber Distributed Data Interface to Ethernet | Yes | Yes | Fiber optic | 100M | 2 | Yes | Source and destination address, packet type, protocol | NA | Packets transmitted and received, address bits, retransmitted packets, packets not delivered | $9,500; $295 for dual-ring connection; $1,095 for Novell, Inc. Internetwork Packet Exchange (IPX) option |
| 3Com Corp. Santa Clara, Calif. (408) 562-6400 | IB/3 | Remote | Baseband or broadband Ethernet to same | Yes | Yes | Thick coaxial | 9.8K to 2.048M | 8 | Yes | Source and destination address, packet size and type, protocol, user-selectable filters | RS-232-C, RS 422/ 449, CCITT V.35 | Packets transmitted and received, lost packets, oversized packets, bytes transmitted, framing errors, collisions, deferred packets, carrier loss, buffer overflow, network utilization percentage | $10,500 for 2 ports |

| Vendor | Product | Bridge Type | Local Net Interconnect | Spanning Tree Protocol | Learning Bridge | Local Net Transmission Media | Transmission Speed (bit/sec) | Number of Link Ports | Load Balancing | Filtering Based On | Wide-Area Network Interface | Network Statistics Gathered | Price |
|---|---|---|---|---|---|---|---|---|---|---|---|---|---|
| | IB/2000 | Local | Ethernet to Ethernet | Yes | Yes | Thick coaxial | 10M | 2 | NA | Source and destination address, packet size and type, protocol, user-selectable filters | NA | Packets transmitted and received, lost packets, oversized packets, bytes transmitted, framing errors, collisions, deferred packets, carrier loss, buffer overflow, network utilization percentage | $5,250 |
| TRW, Inc. Information Networks Division Torrance, Calif. (213) 254-6871 | NB2000 | Local and remote | Ethernet to broadband Ethernet | Yes | Yes | Thick/thin Ethernet, twisted pair, fiber optic | 9.6K to 2.048M | 3 | Yes | Source and destination address, protocol | RS-232-C, RS-449/422, T-1 | Transmission errors, packets dropped, multicast packets, network activity | $5,395 |
| T3 Technologies, Inc., Research Triangle Park, N.C. (919) 467-4000 | Metro-Bridge | Remote | Multiple Ethernet to Ethernet | No | Yes | Transceiver cable connection | 22M or 44M | 1DS3 | NA | Source and destination address | DS3 | Network utilization, packet size, histogram, bit error rate | $24,980; $2,500 for MetroView network management software |
| Ungermann-Bass, Inc. Santa Clara, Calif. (408) 496-0111 | Net/One Token Ring to Ethernet Data Link Bridge | Local | Token ring to Ethernet | Yes | Yes | Thin/thick Ethernet, fiber optic, twisted pair | 10M | 1 | Info. not available | Source and destination address, packet type, protocol | NA | Packets transmitted and received | $9,450 |
| | Net/One Ethernet to Ethernet Data Link Bridge | Local and remote | Ethernet to Ethernet | Yes | Yes | Thin/thick Ethernet, fiber optic, twisted pair | 10M | NA | Yes | Source and destination address, packet size and type, protocol | RS-232-C, RS-449, CCITT V.35 | Info. not available | $9,450 |

*(continued)*

**TABLE 6-2** *(cont.)*

| Vendor | Product | Bridge Type | Local Net Interconnect | Spanning Tree Protocol | Learning Bridge | Local Net Transmission Media | Transmission Speed (bit/sec) | Number of Link Ports | Load Balancing | Filtering Based On | Wide-Area Network Interface | Network Statistics Gathered | Price |
|---|---|---|---|---|---|---|---|---|---|---|---|---|---|
| Vitalink Communications Corp. Fremont, Calif. (415) 794-1100 | TransRING 500 | Remote | Token ring to token ring | Yes | Yes | Twisted pair | 2.048M | 8 | Yes | Source and destination address, packet size and type, protocol, priority, multicast, user-selectable filters | CCITT V.35, RS-449, T-1, Switched 56 | Packets transmitted/received, bytes transmitted/received, packets discarded, traffic composition, errors | $23,250 |
| | TransLAN III | Remote | Ethernet to Ethernet | Yes | Yes | Thin/thick Ethernet, twisted pair, fiber optic | 10M local; 2.048M remote | 8 | Yes | Source and destination address, packet size and type, multicast, priority, user-selectable filters | RS-232-C, RS-449, CCITT V.35, T-1, Switched 56 | Packets transmitted/received, bytes transmitted/received, packets discarded, link errors, local net errors | $12,500 for 1 port; $2,500 for 4 ports; $1,250 for bridge software |
| Wellfleet Communications, Inc. Bedford, Mass. (617) 275-2400 | Link Node | Local and remote | Ethernet to Ethernet | Yes | Yes | Thin/thick Ethernet, twisted pair | 2.4K to 2.048M | 16 | Yes | Source and destination address, protocol, type field, multicast bit field | RS-232-C, RS-449/422, T-1 | Packets transmitted/received, packets filtered/forwarded, circuit status, T-1 errors, retransmissions | $9,000 for 1 port, $2,000 per additional Ethernet port, $2,000 per additional synchronous port |
| | Connector Node | Local and remote | Ethernet to Ethernet | Yes | Yes | Thin/thick Ethernet, twisted pair | 2,400 to 2.048M | 52 | Yes | Source and destination address, protocol, type field, multicast bit field | RS-232-C, RS-449/422, T-1 | Packets transmitted/received, packets filtered/forwarded, circuit status, T-1 errors, retransmissions | $9,000 for 1 port; $2,000 per additional Ethernet port; $2,000 per additional synchronous port |

CSU = Channel service unit

NA = Not applicable

This chart includes a representative selection of vendors in the local-area network bridge market. Most vendors offer other local net bridges, and many vendors not included offer a full range of competitive products.

Source: *Network World*, July 10, 1989.

A router[1] is a general-purpose device that connects dissimilar networks and operates at layer 3 of the OSI model. The router must cope with a variety of differences among networks, including:

- *Addressing schemes:* The networks may use different schemes for assigning addresses to devices. For example, an IEEE 802 LAN uses either 16-bit or 48-bit binary addresses for each attached device; an X.25 public packet-switching network uses 12-digit decimal addresses (encoded as four bits per digit for a 48-bit address). Some form of global network addressing, as well as a directory service, must be provided.

- *Maximum packet sizes:* Packets from one network may have to be broken into smaller pieces to be transmitted on another network, a process known as *segmentation.* For example, Ethernet imposes a maximum packet size of 1500 bytes; a maximum packet size of 1000 bytes is common on X.25 networks. A packet transmitted on an Ethernet system and picked up by a router for retransmission on an X.25 network may have to segment the incoming packet into two smaller ones.

- *Interfaces:* The hardware and software interfaces to various networks differ. A router must be independent of these differences.

- *Reliability:* Various network services may provide anything from a reliable end-to-end virtual circuit to an unreliable service. The operation of the routers should not depend on an assumption of network reliability.

The operation of the router, as Figure 6-5b indicates, depends on a protocol at OSI layer 3 (network layer), sometimes known as an *internet protocol.* Figure 6-8 depicts a typical example, in which two departmental LANs are interconnected by a higher-speed backbone. The figure shows the operation of the internet protocol for data exchange between host A on one departmental LAN (subnetwork 1) and host B on another departmental LAN (subnetwork 3) through the backbone LAN (subnetwork 2). The figure shows the format of the data packet at each stage. Each host must have the same internet protocol at layer 3. In addition, as with the bridge, each host must have compatible protocols at layers 4 through 7 to communicate successfully. The intermediate routers need compatible protocols only up through layer 3.

From the higher layers of software in A, the network layer at A receives blocks of data to be sent to B. The network layer attaches a header that specifies the global internet address of B. That address is in two parts: network identifier and station identifier. Let us refer to this block as the internet protocol (IP) data unit. Next, the network layer recognizes that the destination (B) is on another subnetwork. So the first step is to send the data to a router, in this case router A. To do this, the network layer appends to the IP data unit another header to construct a packet for subnetwork A. In this case, this is done at the

---

[1] A router is also referred to as an intermediate system, interworking unit, network relay, or sometimes even gateway. In this book, the use of the term *gateway* is confined to its more common meaning of an application-level device.

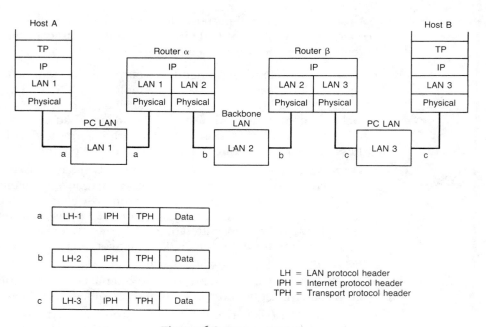

**Figure 6-8** Router operation.

LLC and MAC levels, so we can refer to the added information as the LAN protocol header. This header contains the address of router **A**.

Next, the packet travels through subnetwork 1 to router **A**. The router removes the LAN protocol header and analyzes the IP header to determine the ultimate destination of the data, in this case B. The router must now make a routing decision. There are two possibilities:

1. The destination station Y is connected directly to one of the subnetworks to which the router is attached.

2. To reach the destination, one or more additional routers must be traversed.

In this example, the data must be routed through router **B** before reaching the destination. So router **A** constructs a new packet by appending a LAN protocol header to the IP data unit containing the address of router **B**. When this packet arrives at router **B**, the LAN protocol header is stripped off. The router determines that this IP data unit is destined for B, which is connected directly to a network to which the router is attached. The router therefore creates a packet with a destination address of B and sends it out onto LAN 3. The data finally arrive at B, where the LAN protocol and internet headers can be stripped off.

At each router, the data unit, before it can be forwarded, may need to be segmented to accommodate a smaller maximum packet size limitation on the outgoing network. The data unit is split into two or more segments, each of which becomes an independent IP data unit. Each new data unit is wrapped in a lower-layer packet and queued for transmission. The router may also limit the length of its queue for each network to which it is attached to avoid having a slow network penalize a faster one. After the queue limit is reached, additional data units are simply dropped.

The process just described continues through as many routers as it takes for the data unit to reach its destination. As with a router, the destination host recovers the IP data unit from its network wrapping. If segmentation has occurred, the IP module in the destination host buffers the incoming data until the entire original data field can be reassembled. This block of data is then passed to a higher layer in the host.

This service offered by the internet protocol is unreliable because the protocol does not guarantee that all data will be delivered or that the data that is delivered will arrive in the proper order. It is the responsibility of the next higher layer, the transport layer, to recover from any errors. This approach provides a great deal of flexibility. In the internet protocol approach, each unit of data is passed from router to router in an attempt to get from source to destination. Because delivery is not guaranteed, there is no particular reliability requirement on any of the subnetworks. Thus, the protocol will work with any combination of subnetwork types. Because the sequence of delivery is not guaranteed, successive data units can follow different paths through the internet. This allows the protocol to react to congestion and failure in the internet by changing routes.

## Standards for the Internet Protocol

The International Standards Organization (ISO) has issued a standard for an internet protocol, the Protocol for Providing the Connectionless-Mode Network Service (IS 8473). This is often referred to as ISO-IP.

As part of its suite of standards, generally referred to as the TCP/IP protocol suite, the U.S. Department of Defense (DOD) has issued a standard for an internet protocol, DOD-IP. Actually, DOD-IP predates and is the inspiration for ISO-IP. Although the formats and details of DOD-IP and ISO-IP differ, they provide essentially the same functionality.

Because DOD-IP and the other military standards have been around longer, they are more widely used than the ISO standards. In particular, there are a number of vendors who provide TCP/IP-based products and routers employing DOD-IP. International standards are gradually gaining wider acceptance, however, and clearly represent the wave of the future. We can expect a rapid increase in ISO-IP based LANs and routers over the next year or two.

## The Routing Function

The routing function is typically accomplished by maintaining a routing table in each host and router. For each possible destination network, this table gives the next router to which the IP data unit should be sent.

The routing table may be static or dynamic. In a simple configuration, such as a collection of PC LANs and a single backbone LAN, a static table is adequate. For a more complex configuration, involving a number of LANs at different locations and perhaps one or more wide area networks, the static table has several drawbacks. It does not allow alternate routing for load leveling and it does not provide for rapid reconfiguration in the event of a router failure.

A dynamic table is more flexible in responding to both error and congestion events. For this technique, a protocol must allow the routers to exchange information about congestion and the topology of the configuration. This area is still experimental; the required router-to-router protocols are still evolving.

## Router Products

As with bridges, a variety of routers are on the market. Most support either the military standard IP or the OSI-based internet protocol. Table 6-3 gives details of most of the current vendors.

## Summary

There is a place for both bridges and routers in planning the development of an internet. Bridges are simple, easy to configure, and have no impact on host software. In an environment where all the communicating devices are on similar LANs, this is the appropriate solution. In a mixed environment, the more complex routers are needed. Even then, however, bridges may be used to interconnect some of the LANs.

# Gateways

Bridges and routers can be used to solve internetwork problems when all devices implement compatible protocols from the OSI model or the TCP/IP protocol suite. This is the ideal situation toward which a business organization should strive. In many cases, however, a business has installed a proprietary network architecture such as SNA. Because of the investment in the proprietary system, it is expensive and disruptive to attempt to replace all communications software with OSI-based software. On the other hand, the user wants to use OSI to gain access to products from a variety of vendors.

The gateway is a way to permit the coexistence of OSI-based and proprietary products and gives the manager the tool needed to plan and implement a smooth migration to an exclusive OSI strategy. As Figure 6-5c illustrates, a gateway is a device that connects different network architectures by performing a conversion at the application level. The gateway itself must utilize all seven layers of the OSI model plus all the layers of the proprietary architecture.

The gateway is used as a staging area for a two-step transfer of data. Let us consider a file transfer as an example. Figure 6-9 shows a network to which are attached two sets of devices: those that implement the OSI protocols and those that implement a proprietary architecture, in this case, SNA. In the OSI world, the file transfer standard (described in Chapter 5) is file transfer, access, and management (FTAM). Two OSI hosts can exchange files using FTAM. Similarly, two hosts with the same proprietary architecture can exchange files using the proprietary file transfer application.

If a mixed transfer is attempted from an OSI host to a proprietary-software host, the sending host automatically (without user intervention) sends the file to a gateway using FTAM. The gateway accepts the file, then transfers it to the intended destination using the proprietary file transfer protocol. A transfer in the reverse direction proceeds similarly. In like manner, other applications, such as electronic mail and document architecture, can also be supported with a gateway. Thus, the gateway must contain both the OSI version and the proprietary version of any application requiring gateway services.

There are several key limitations with the use of a gateway:

1. The gateway is a potential bottleneck. In an environment with large numbers of both types of hosts, there may be considerable traffic through the gateway. To overcome performance limitations, a user might need more than one gateway. This complicates the host software, which must now decide which gateway to use for each transfer.

2. The service provided for an application is the "least common denominator." For example, FTAM supports the use of priorities. If the proprietary file transfer protocol does not support priorities, the priority discipline is imposed only between the OSI host and the gateway. From the gateway to the other host, no priority scheme is used.

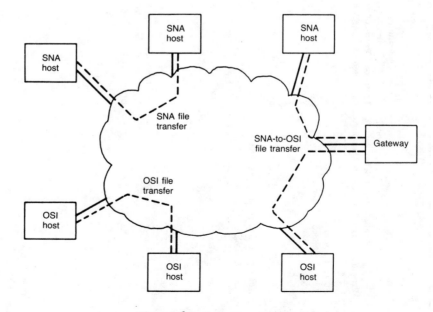

**Figure 6-9** Gateway operation.

**TABLE 6-3** Router Products

| Vendor | Product | Product Type | Local Nets Connected | Local Net OS Supported | Protocols Supported | Spanning Tree Protocol Support | Self-Learning/Load Balancing | Source/Nonsource Routing | Number of Link Ports | Transmission Speed (bit/sec) | Maximum Local Net/Wide Area Net Interfaces per Unit | Wide-Area Network Interfaces | Net Management Supported | Price |
|---|---|---|---|---|---|---|---|---|---|---|---|---|---|---|
| Advanced Computer Communications Santa Barbara, Calif. (805) 963-9431 | ASC 4140 | Routing bridge | 802.3 to same | NA | NA | Yes | Yes/Yes | NA | 2 | 2,400 to 1,544M | 1/2 | RS-232C, RS-422/449, CCITT V.35 | SNMP and 802.1 | $7,500 |
| | ASC 4130 | IP router | 802.3 to same | NA | TCP/IP, DDN, EGP, RIP | No | Yes/Yes | NA | 2 | 2,400 to 1,544M | 1/2 | RS-232C, RS-442/449, CCITT V.35 | SNMP and 802.1 | $7,500 |
| AT&T Morristown, N.J. (201) 631-6000 | AT&T StarGroup Software X.25 Router | Router | AT&T StarGroup on any local net | NA | OSI | No | No/No | Nonsource | None | 56K | 10 0/20 X.25 | X.25 | None | $1,275 for software; $1,595 for hardware |
| Cicso Systems, Inc. Menlo Park, Calif. (415) 326-1941 | AGS | Router | 802.3 to 802.5 | NA | TCP/IP, OSI, XNS, DDN, X.25, DECnet, Apple Computer, Inc.'s AppleTalk, IPX | Yes | Yes/Yes | Source | 14T-1s | Up to 4M | 8/14 | RS-232C, RS-449, CCITT V.35 | SNMP | $15,000 |
| Communication Machinery Corp. Santa Barbara, Calif. (805) 963-9471 | DRN-3200 DDN Gateway | Router | 802.3 to X.25 | NA | TCP/IP, DDN, X.25 | NA | NA | NA | 1 | 1,200 to 64K | 1/1 | RS-232C, RS-449, CCITT V.35 | None | $11,990 |
| Cryptal Communications Corp. Cranston, R.I. (401) 941-7600 | Series 3000 Bridge-Router | Routing bridge | 802.3 to same | Novell, Inc. NetWare; Unix | NA | Yes | Yes/Yes | NA | 2 | Up to 10M | 2/2 | RS-232C, RS-449/530, CCITT V.35, fiber optic, microwave | SNMP | $8,500 |

| Vendor | Product | Product Type | Local Nets Connected | Local Net OS Supported | Protocols Supported | Spanning Tree Protocol Support | Self-Learning/Load Balancing | Source/Nonsource Routing | Number of Link Ports | Transmission Speed (bit/sec) | Maximum Local Net/Wide Area Net Interfaces per Unit | Wide-Area Network Interfaces | Net Management Supported | Price |
|---|---|---|---|---|---|---|---|---|---|---|---|---|---|---|
| Digital Pathways, Inc., Mountain View, Calif. (415) 964-0707 | Secure Bridge Ethernet | Routing bridge | 802.3 to same | Info. not available | NA | No | Yes/Yes | Info. not available | 4 | 9.6K to 2.048M | 2/4 | RS-232C, RS-422, CCITT V.35, fiber optic | Proprietary | $6,590 for 1 link; $7,950 for 4 links |
| Gateway Communications, Inc. Irvine, Calif. (714) 553-1555 | G/Remote Bridge 64 | Routing bridge | IPX to X.25 | NetWare | NA | No | Yes/No | Nonsource | 1 | 64K | 3/1 | RS-232C, CCITT V.35 | None | $2,495 |
| | G/Remote bridge | Routing bridge | All | NetWare | NA | No | Yes/No | Nonsource | 2 | 19.2K | 255/64 | RS-232C | None | $2,995 for 2-link Starter Kit; $1,595 per link thereafter |
| Halley Systems, Inc. San Jose, Calif. (408) 432-2600 | Connect-LAN 100 Ethernet Router | Routing bridge | 802.3 to same | NetWare, 3Com Corp. 3+, Banyan Systems, Inc. VINES | NA | No | Yes/Yes | NA | 4 | Up to 2,048M | 2/4 | RS-232C, RS-422, CCITT, V.35 X.21, T-1/DS1, fiber optic | 802.1 | $8,995 to $15,250 |
| | Connect-LAN 202 Local | Routing bridge | 802.5 to same | IBM PC LAN, NetWare, VINES, 3+, Unger-mann-Bass Net/One | NA | No | Yes/Yes | Both | NA | NA | 2/NA | NA | 802.1 | $12,995 |

(continued)

**TABLE 6-3** *(cont.)*

| Vendor | Product | Product Type | Local Nets Connected | Local Net OS Supported | Protocols Supported | Spanning Tree Protocol Support | Self-Learning/ Load Balancing | Source/ Non-source Routing | Number of Link Ports | Transmission Speed (bit/sec) | Maximum Local Net/ Wide Area Net Interfaces per Unit | Wide-Area Network Interfaces | Net Management Supported | Price |
|---|---|---|---|---|---|---|---|---|---|---|---|---|---|---|
| IBM White Plains, N.Y. (914) 696-1900 | Token-Ring Network Bridge Program Version 2.1 | Routing bridge | 802.5 to same | PC LAN, OS/2 LAN Server, anything supporting source routing | NA | Yes | No/Yes | Source | 1 | 4M to 16M local; 9.6K to 1.544M remote | 2/1 | RS-232C, CCITT V.35, X.21 | IBM LAN Manager Version 2 and Entry | $1,595 |
| Network Equipment Technologies, Inc. Redwood City, Calif. (415) 366-4400 | LanExchange 50 | Router | 802.3 to 802.5 | NA | TCP/IP, DECnet, XNS, X.25, AppleTalk | Yes | Yes/Yes | Source | 24 | 1,200 to 4M | 24/24 | RS-232C, RS-449, CCITT V.35 | SNMP | $21,000 for one link |
| Network Resource Corp. San Jose, Calif. (408) 263-8100 | AT 2000 | Router | 802.3 to AppleShare | NA | AppleTalk | Yes | Yes/No | NA | 1 | 2M to 10M | 1/NA | NA | None | $995 |
| Proteon, Inc. Westborough, Mass. (508) 898-2800 | p4100 Series Router | Router | Ethernet Versions 1 and 2 to 802.3; 802.5 to Proteon ProNet-4 and ProNet-50 | NA | TCP/IP, XNS, IPX | No | Yes/Yes | Source | 4 | Up to 64K | 4/4 | RS-232C, RS-449, CCITT V.35 | SNMP | $3,795 minimum |
| | p4200 Series Router | Router | Ethernet Versions 1 and 2 to 802.3; 802.5 to Proteon ProNet-4 and ProNet-50 | NA | TCP/IP, XNS, IPX | No | Yes/Yes | Source | 14 | Up to 64K; or 56K to 2.048M | 7/14 | RS-232C, RS-449, CCITT V.35 | SNMP | $7,900 minimum |

| Vendor | Product | Product Type | Local Nets Connected Supported | Local Net OS Supported | Protocols Supported | Spanning Tree Protocol Support | Self-Learning/Load Balancing | Source/Nonsource Routing | Number of Link Ports | Transmission Speed (bit/sec) | Maximum Local Net/Wide Area Net Interfaces per Unit | Wide-Area Network Interfaces | Net Management Supported | Price |
|---|---|---|---|---|---|---|---|---|---|---|---|---|---|---|
| RAD Network Devices, Inc. Rochelle Park, N.J. (201) 587-8822 | RTB | Routing bridge | 802.5 to same | NETBIOS compatible | NA | No | Yes/Yes | Both | 4 | 4.8K to 2.048M | 1/4 | RS-422, CCITT V.35 | 802.1 | $5,995 to $8,950 |
| | REB | Routing bridge | 802.3 to same | NETBIOS-compatible | NA | No | Yes/Yes | NA | 4 | 4.8K to 2.048M | 2/4 | RS-422, X.25, CCITT V.35, fiber optic | 802.1 | $5,495 to $12,945 |
| 3Com Corp. Santa Clara, Calif. (408) 562-6400 | IB/2000 | Local routing bridge | 802.3 to same | All | NA | Yes | Yes/NA | NA | 2 | 10M | 2/Info. not available | Info. not available | 3Com NCS | $5,250 |
| TRW., Inc. Information Network Division Torrance, Calif. (213) 254-6871 | NB2000 | Routing bridge | 802.3 to same | NA | NA | Yes | Yes/Yes | NA | 3 | 9.6k to 2048M | 4/3 | RS-232C, RS-449, T-1, DSI | Proprietary | $5,395; $2,395 for Network Management Software |
| Ungermann-Bass, Inc. Santa Clara, Calif. (408) 496-0111 | Net/One Ethernet to Ethernet | Routing bridge | 802.3 to same | Net/One PC, NetWare, IBM LAN Manager | NA | Yes | Yes/Yes | NA | 2 | 10M local | 2/2 | Rs232C, RS-449, CCITT V.35 | Proprietary | $9,450 |
| | Net/One Token Ring to Ethernet | Routing bridge | 802.3 to 802.5 | Net/One PC, NetWare, IBM LAN Manager | NA | No | Yes/No | Source | 2 | 10M on 802.3; 4M on 802.5 | 2/None | NA | Proprietary | $9,450 |

*(continued)*

**TABLE 6-3** *(cont.)*

| Vendor | Product | Product Type | Local Nets Connected | Local Net OS Supported | Protocols Supported | Spanning Tree Protocol Support | Self-Learning/ Load Balancing | Source/ Nonsource Routing | Number of Link Ports | Transmission Speed (bit/sec) | Maximum Local Net/ Wide Area Net Interfaces per Unit | Wide-Area Network Interfaces | Net Management Supported | Price |
|---|---|---|---|---|---|---|---|---|---|---|---|---|---|---|
| Vitalink Communications Corp. Fremont, Calif. (415) 794-1100 | TransPATH | Router/bridge | 802.3 or 802.5 | Any compliant with Ethernet Version 2.0, 802.3, 802.5 | NA | TCP/IP routed; all others bridged | Yes/Yes | Both (optional) | Up to 8 | 9.6K to 2.048M | 1/Up to 8 | RS-449, CCITT V.35, V.36, DS1 | SNMP and WAN Manager | $12,500 to $20,000 |
| Wellfleet Communications, Inc. Bedford, Mass. (617) 275-2400 | Link Node/ Concentrator Node | Router | Ethernet Versions 1 and 2; 802.3 to same | NA | TCP/IP, XNS, IPX, OSI, AppleTalk | Yes | Yes/Yes | NA | 26 on Concentrator Node; 8 on Link Node | 1.2K to 6M | 26 on Concentrator Node; 8 on Link Node/52 on Concentrator Node; 16 on Link Node | RS-232C, RS-449, CCITT V.35, T-1 DS1 | SNMP and 802.1 | $10,000 for Link Node; $18,000 for Concentrator Node |
| Zenith Electronics Corp. Glenview, Ill. (312) 391-7000 | Z LAN 500/4000 BRG | Routing bridge | Z-LAN | Z LAN | NA | No | No/Yes | NA | NA | 4M | Info. not available/ Info. not available | RS-232C, T-1, DS1, CCITT V.35 | Proprietary | $8,000 |

APPC = Advanced Program to Program Communications
DDN = Defense Data Network
EGP = Extended Gateway Protocol
IPX = Novell's Internetwork Packet Exchange
NA = Not applicable
RIP = Routing Information Protocol
SNMP = Simple Network Management Protocol
XNS = Xerox Corp.'s Xerox Network Systems
Source: *Network World*, August 7, 1989.

The market for gateways is projected to grow rapidly. This is because OSI-based products are becoming increasingly prevalent and cost-competitive, while there is (and will remain for some time) a large installed base of systems based on proprietary communications architectures, especially SNA. Although the gateway is not ideal, it is a way for the manager and user to cope with a mixed environment.

# Case Study 5
# The Houston Chronicle[2]

## Background

The Houston Chronicle is a very large newspaper produced in five daily editions (circulation: 420,000) and one Sunday edition (circulation 530,000). The entire newspaper is produced electronically. This includes administrative and editorial tasks, advertising, and prepress page makeup. Graphics content is heavy and virtually all activities are, or will soon be, integrated through various LANs and computers. Although electronic publishing presents some challenges specific to its industry, the Houston Chronicle's enterprise-wide integrated network can certainly stand as a model for any large-scale business network.

Two main challenges faced the publisher:

- The variety of tasks and data rate requirements inevitably meant a complex configuration of LANs and other communications facilities. These needed to be integrated to allow ease of communication.
- The networking configuration had to handle very large blocks of data in a relatively interactive manner to support several hundred workstations, servers, and terminals.

The range of applications that the network must support is impressive. Because of the high graphic content of the paper, several users cooperating in the production of a page need to be able to share image files, each tens of megabytes large. It would not take the movement of many of these files to bring all but the fastest networks to their knees.

Another key area requiring support is advertising sales, the lifeblood of the paper. This activity must be carried out simultaneously with production of the paper. Ad sales requires access to large client and ad databases, word processing, graphic design functions, and administrative functions. Often these activities must occur in real time while the salesperson is on the phone with one of the newspaper's advertisers.

---

[2] This case study is based on material in P. Stephenson's, "The Houston Chronicle: A LAN Keeps a Metropolitan Daily Printing All the News that Fits," *LAN Magazine,* August 1989.

## The Networking Environment

Four basic work groups are tied together over the networks. In addition to the need for a high degree of interactive cooperation among the members of each group, there is the need for a significant amount of data sharing and message passing between groups. The four groups are pagination, display advertising, classified advertising, and editorial. As an example of the requirements of these groups, let us look at a representative networking scenario that involves all of them: display advertising.

1. An ad taker, working at a Sun Microsystems 3/60 UNIX workstation, receives the advertiser's phone call.

2. Information on the advertiser, ad rates, billing, and other administrative and accounting data reside on an IBM 3081 mainframe. The ad taker accesses the advertising information on the mainframe from the UNIX workstation and "rates" the ad, determining the fee for this type of ad for this advertiser.

3. The accounting and billing information on the mainframe is updated to reflect the ad purchased by the customer.

4. The graphic image of each ad is maintained on a file server, a Sun 4/280 system. If new art or changes to existing art are required, the ad is retrieved by an artist for design or modification. The new ad is placed back on the file server.

5. Based on information in the mainframe, a layout specialist is alerted that this ad will be placed in the next edition. The specialist retrieves the ad from the file server. There is no traditional pasteup or manual page makeup; the entire procedure is done electronically. It is fast and efficient. It also eases last-minute changes and additions.

A similar process occurs for classified ads.

## The Networking Configuration

The networking configuration includes token ring and 802.3 networks and a broadband backbone. The system supports several hundred workstations and there is 100% redundancy of CPUs, drives, and bridges. Data transfer rates vary from 3 Mbps to 1 Gbps (gigabit per second = one billion bits per second). Figure 6-10 shows a part of this large and complex internet.

To get an appreciation of the networking configuration, let us use an individual Sun 3/60 workstation as a starting point. This is a powerful 3-MIPS UNIX computer with 8M of main memory. Each workstation contains an 802.3 interface that allows the workstation to be connected to the internet through the building's twisted pair wiring layout. Star topology 802.3 twisted pair systems support the workstations and provide connection to the rest of the configuration and to each other using "bridges." Although these products are

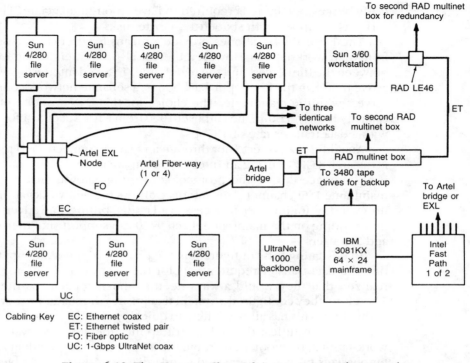

**Figure 6-10** The *Houston Chronicle's* enterprise-wide network.

referred to as bridges by the vendor, in many cases they connect dissimilar LANs. However, they do this at a MAC level and do not involve the complex routing capability and the use of a separate network-layer header found in the typical router. Thus, they are closer to what are referred to in this book as bridges than they are to pure routers.

The bridges connect the workstation to one of the four Artel FiberWay LANs. FiberWay is a high-speed (100 Mbps) fiber optic ring. The token-passing protocol it uses is proprietary, but is in many ways similar to FDDI. Had a suitable FDDI product been available at the time of installation, the publisher would probably have chosen the standard product over this proprietary scheme.

Sun 4/280 file servers connect directly to a FiberWay backbone through an interface device known as the Artel EXL Node. This interface unit allows the device to interface as though it were interfacing to Ethernet. Each Node connects up to eight file servers. Each file server, in turn, connects to a total of four EXL Nodes on four different fiber optic LANs. This redundancy of connection provides great reliability and tremendous capability to respond to local peaks in traffic.

The file servers contain information for advertising, editorial, and pagination. There is significant storage space required for large graphics files, especially because each file is required to have an on-line backup. Thus, each file server is equipped with sixteen 1.2-Gbyte disks.

The FiberWay backbones provide a means for users to access file servers from their workstations. However, there is also a tremendous amount of traffic between the file servers and the mainframe. To avoid interfering with the interactive traffic on the fiber optic backbones, a separate network connects the file servers with the mainframe. The choice for this LAN was one of the highest capacity LANs yet built: the UltraNet 1000 from UltraNet of San Jose, California, with a data transfer rate of 1 Gbps.

An additional, direct (not through any LAN) connection to the mainframe is through TCP/IP using an Intel 9770 Fastpath connectivity control unit. This is an interface device and protocol-converting gateway that connects to the mainframe I/O channel. This interface allows the Sun workstation user to call up a window for immediate access to ad rating, billing, and advertiser information residing on the mainframe. Each 9770 can support six Ethernet interfaces and 255 users.

In designing this configuration, the planners did not attempt to tightly define the data transfer requirements for their set of applications. Rather, they realized that they would always need as much capacity as they could get. Therefore, they configured a system that pushes the state-of-the art technology to the limit. This has allowed them to quickly get to the point where they could exploit to the fullest the rich set of application software available on their workstations. In another environment, a more cautious, gradual approach that emphasizes proven systems and standardized products might be more appropriate. But, for the *Houston Chronicle,* their aggressive approach to local area networking has been a resounding success.

## Summary

An isolated LAN has become a rarity. Most organizations need multiple LANs, which must be interconnected to provide an integrated data communications facility. In addition, most organizations need links from devices on LANs to the outside world, including links to remote LANs and to resources available on wide area networks. Hence, there is a need for internetworking: the capability to link LANs and other networks in such a way that data can be exchanged between any two stations on any of the networks. Three types of devices are used for internetworking: bridges, routers, and gateways.

A bridge is used between local area networks with identical protocols for the physical and link layers (e.g., all conforming to IEEE 802.3 or all conforming to FDDI). Because the devices use the same protocols, the amount of processing required at the bridge is minimal.

For configurations that involve more than a single type of LAN or wide area networks or both, a more complex device known as a router is required. The router is a general-purpose device that operates at layer 3 of the OSI model. It allows data to be routed from a station on any one network to a station on any other network, regardless of the types of networks involved.

Finally, a gateway is a specialized device that interconnects two sets of devices that use two different communications architectures. For example, an SNA/OSI gateway would allow cooperation between applications on OSI machines and applications on SNA machines.

There is a potential role for all three types of devices in a networking environment. The choice depends on the details of the networks, applications, and communication software involved.

# Chapter 7

# LAN Security

T HE REQUIREMENTS OF *INFORMATION SECURITY* in an organization have undergone two major changes in the last several decades. Prior to the widespread use of data processing equipment, the security of valuable information was provided primarily by physical and administrative means. An example of the former is the use of rugged filing cabinets with a combination lock for storing sensitive documents. An example of the latter is personnel screening procedures used during the hiring process.

With the introduction of the computer, the need for automated tools for protecting files and other information stored on the computer became evident. This is especially the case for a shared system, such as a time-sharing system. The need is even more acute for systems that can be accessed over a public telephone or data network. The generic name for the collection of tools designed to protect data and thwart hackers is *computer security*.

The second major change that affects security is the introduction of distributed systems and the use of networks and communications facilities for carrying data between terminal user and computer and between computer and computer. *Network security* measures are needed to protect data during its transmission.

Computer and network security can be defined as the protection of network resources against unauthorized disclosure, modification, utilization, restriction, or destruction. Security has long been an object of concern and study for both data processing systems and communications facilities. With computer networks, these concerns are combined. And for local area networks, the problems may be most acute.

Consider a large LAN installation with terminal and personal computer access to data files and applications distributed among a variety of host computers and servers. The LAN may also provide access to and from long-distance telephone networks through a modem server, and access to other data networks through bridges and routers. The complexity of the task of providing security in such an environment is clear. The subject is broad, and encompasses physical and administrative controls as well as automated ones. In this chapter, we confine ourselves to the consideration of automated security controls.

We begin by examining the types of threats faced by computer-communications complexes. Then the bulk of the chapter deals with tools and techniques that enhance security. The first and most important of these is encryption. The various approaches to encryption and the problems and benefits of each are discussed. Next, the use of encryption in a LAN environment is examined.

The chapter then moves to the subject of access control. This is primarily a computer security rather than a network security issue, but must be faced by those with either a network or a security management responsibility. The chapter closes with a discussion of the most recent security threat, the computer virus.

# Security Threats

A publication of the National Bureau of Standards identified some of the threats that stimulated the upsurge of interest in security[1]:

- Organized and intentional attempts to obtain economic or market information from competitive organizations in the private sector.
- Organized and intentional attempts to obtain economic information from government agencies.
- Inadvertent acquisition of economic or market information.
- Inadvertent acquisition of information about individuals.
- Intentional fraud through illegal access to computer data banks with emphasis, in decreasing order of importance, on acquisition of funding data, economic data, law enforcement data, and data about individuals.
- Government intrusion on the rights of individuals.
- Invasion of individual rights by the intelligence community.

These are examples of specific threats that an organization or an individual (or an organization on behalf of its employees) may feel the need to counter. The nature of the threat that concerns an organization will vary greatly depending on the circumstances. Fortunately, we can approach the problem from a different angle by looking at the generic types of threats that might be encountered.

Table 7-1 lists the types of threats that might be faced in the context of network security. The threats can be divided into the categories of passive threats and active threats, as shown in the table and in Figure 7-1.

---

[1] D. Branstad, editor, *Computer Security and the Data Encryption Standard,* National Bureau of Standards, Special Publication No. 500-27, February 1978.

**TABLE 7-1**   Potential Network Security Threats

**Passive Threats**

The monitoring of data or recording of data or both
while the data is being transmitted over a
communications facility.

| | |
|---|---|
| Release of message contents | Attacker can read the user data in messages. |
| Traffic analysis | The attacker can read packet headers to determine the location and identity of communicating hosts. The attacker can also observe the length and frequency of messages. |

**Active Threats**

The unauthorized use of a device attached to a
communications facility to alter transmitting data or
control signals or to generate spurious data or
control signals.

| | |
|---|---|
| Message-stream modification | The attacker can selectively modify, delete, delay, reorder, and duplicate real messages. The attacker can also insert counterfeit messages. |
| Denial of message service | The attacker can destroy or delay most or all messages. |
| Masquerade | The attacker can pose as a real host or switch and communicate with another host or switch to acquire data or services. |

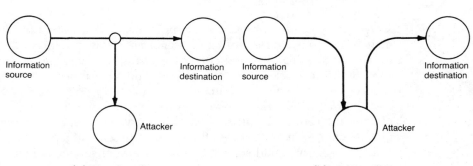

*(a) Passive threat.*                          *(b) Active threat.*

**Figure 7-1**  Passive and active communications security threats.

## Passive Threats

Passive threats involve eavesdropping on or monitoring the transmissions of an organization. The goal of the attacker is to obtain information that is being transmitted. Two types of threats are involved here: release of message contents and traffic analysis.

The threat of *release of message contents* is clearly understood by most managers. A telephone conversation, an electronic mail message, or a transferred file may contain sensitive or confidential information. We want to prevent the attacker from learning the contents of these transmissions.

The second passive threat, *traffic analysis,* is more subtle and often less applicable. Suppose that we had a way of masking the contents of messages or other information traffic so that an attacker, even if he or she captured the message, would be unable to extract the information from the message. The common technique for doing this is encryption, discussed at length subsequently. If we had such protection in place, it might still be possible for an attacker to observe the pattern of these messages. The attacker can determine the location and identity of communicating hosts and can also observe the frequency and length of messages being exchanged. This information might be useful in guessing the nature of the communication taking place.

Passive threats are very difficult to detect because they do not involve alteration of the data. However, it is feasible to prevent these attacks from being successful. The emphasis in dealing with passive threats is on prevention and not detection.

## Active Threats

The second major category of threat is active threats. These involve some modification of the data stream or the creation of a false stream. We can divide these threats into three categories: message-stream modification, denial of message service, and masquerade.

*Message-stream modification* simply means that some portion of a legitimate message is altered or that messages are delayed, replayed, or reordered to produce an unauthorized effect. For example, a message meaning "Allow John Smith to read confidential file accounts" is modified to mean "Allow Fred Brown to read confidential file accounts."

The *denial of service* prevents or inhibits the normal use or management of communications facilities. This attack may have a specific target; for example, an attacker may suppress all messages directed to a particular destination (e.g., the security audit service). Another form of service denial is the disruption of an entire network, either by disabling the network or by overloading it with messages so as to degrade performance.

A *masquerade* takes place when an attacker pretends to be someone else. A masquerade attack usually includes one of the other two forms of active attack. Such an attack can take place, for example, by capturing and replaying an authentication sequence.

Active threats have the opposite characteristics of passive threats. Passive attacks are difficult to detect, but measures are available to prevent their success. On the other hand, it is quite difficult to absolutely prevent active attacks because this would require physical protection of all communications facilities and paths at all times. Instead, the goal is to detect active attacks and recover from any disruption or delays caused by the attack. Because the detection has a deterrent effect, this may also contribute to prevention.

# Principles of Encryption

By far the most important automated tool for network and communications security is encryption. Encryption is a process that conceals meaning by changing intelligible messages into unintelligible messages, using a code or a cipher. A code system uses a predefined table or dictionary to substitute a meaningless word or phrase for each message or part of a message. The simplest code would substitute another letter for each letter of the alphabet. A cipher uses a computable algorithm that translates any stream of message bits into an unintelligible cryptogram. Because cipher techniques lend themselves more readily to automation, these techniques are used in contemporary computer and network security facilities. This section discusses only cipher techniques.

We begin by looking at the traditional approach to encryption, now known as conventional encryption. We then look at a new and quite useful technique known as public-key encryption.

## Conventional Encryption

Figure 7-2a illustrates the conventional encryption process. The original intelligible message, referred to as *plaintext,* is converted into apparently random nonsense, referred to as *ciphertext.* The encryption process consists of an algorithm and a key. The key is a relatively short bit string that controls the algorithm. The algorithm will produce a different output depending on the key used. Changing the key radically changes the output of the algorithm.

After the ciphertext is produced, it is transmitted. Upon reception, the ciphertext can be transformed back to the original plaintext by using a decryption algorithm and the same key that was used for encryption.

The security of conventional encryption depends on several factors. First, the encryption algorithm must be powerful enough so that it is impractical to decrypt a message on the basis of the ciphertext alone. Beyond that, the security of conventional encryption depends on the secrecy of the key, not the secrecy of the algorithm. That is, it is assumed that it is impractical to decrypt a message on the basis of the ciphertext *plus* knowledge of the encryption/decryption algorithm. In other words, we don't need to keep the algorithm secret; we need to keep only the key secret.

This feature of conventional encryption makes it feasible for widespread use. The fact that the algorithm need not be kept secret means that manufacturers can, and have, developed low-cost chip implementations of data encryp-

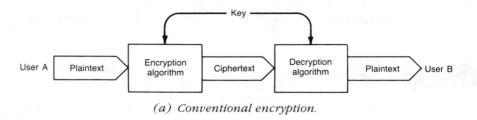

(a) Conventional encryption.

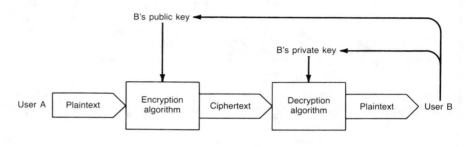

(b) Public-key encryption.

**Figure 7-2** Encryption.

tion algorithms. These chips are widely available and incorporated into a number of products. With the use of conventional encryption, the principal security problem is maintaining the secrecy of the key. This issue is addressed later in this chapter.

## The Data Encryption Standard

The most widely used encryption scheme is based on the data encryption standard (DES), adopted in 1977 by the National Bureau of Standards. For DES, data is encrypted in 64-bit blocks using a 56-bit key. Using the key, the 64-bit input is transformed in a series of steps into a 64-bit output. The same steps, with the same key, reverse the encryption.

DES has enjoyed increasingly widespread use. Unfortunately, DES has also been the subject of much controversy as to how secure it is. The main concern is in the length of the key, which some observers consider to be too short. To appreciate the nature of the controversy, let us quickly review the history of DES.

DES is the result of a request for proposals for a national cipher standard released by NBS (National Bureau of Standards) in 1973. At that time, IBM was in the final stages of a project, called Lucifer, to develop its own encryption capability. IBM proposed the Lucifer scheme, which was by far the best system submitted. It was so good that it considerably upset some people at the National Security Agency (NSA), which until that moment had considered itself comfortably ahead of the rest of the world in the still arcane art of cryptography. DES, as eventually adopted, was essentially the same as Lucifer, with one crucial difference: Lucifer's key size was originally 128 bits, whereas the final standard uses a key of 56 bits. What is the significance of the 72 dropped bits?

There are basically two ways to break a cipher. One way is to exploit properties of whatever mathematical functions form the basis of the encryption algorithm to make a "cryptoanalytic" attack. It is generally assumed that DES is immune to such attacks, although the role of NSA in shaping the final DES standard leaves lingering doubts. The other way is a brute force attack in which you try all possible keys in an exhaustive search. That is, you attempt to decrypt the ciphertext with every possible 56-bit key until something intelligible pops out. With only 56 bits in the DES key, there are $2^{56}$ different keys—a number that is uncomfortably small, and becoming smaller as computers get faster.

According to David Kahn, author of *Codebreakers* (Macmillan, New York, 1967) and a noted expert on cryptography, Lucifer set off a debate in NSA. "The codebreaking side wanted to make sure the cipher was weak enough for the NSA to solve it when used by foreign nations and companies. The codemaking side wanted any cipher it was certifying for use by Americans to be truly good." The resulting bureaucratic compromise was a cipher "weak enough for them to read but strong enough to protect the traffic against the casual observer."

Whatever the merits of the case, DES has flourished in recent years and is widely used, especially in financial applications. Except in areas of extreme sensitivity, the use of DES in commercial applications should not be a cause for concern by responsible managers.

## Commercial Communications Security Endorsement Program

Although DES still has a reasonably useful life ahead of it, it is likely that non-government organizations will begin to look for replacements for what is seen as an increasingly vulnerable algorithm. The most likely replacement is a family of algorithms developed under the NSA Commercial COMSEC (communications security) Endorsement Program (CCEP). CCEP is a joint NSA and industry effort to produce a new generation of encryption devices that are more secure than DES, low in cost, and capable of operating at high data rates. Features of the new CCEP algorithms follow:

- The CCEP algorithms are developed by NSA and are classified. Thus, the algorithms themselves remain secret and are subject to change from time to time.
- Industry participants will produce chip implementations of the algorithms, but the NSA maintains control over the design, fabrication, and dissemination of chips.

Two types of algorithms come under the CCEP heading. Type I algorithms protect classified government information. Equipment using type I CCEP will be available only to government agencies and their designated contractors.

Type II algorithms protect sensitive but unclassified information. Type II gear is intended to replace DES gear. Unlike the type I modules that will handle classified information, the type II equipment is controlled only to the point of sale. Presumably, after a type II module is built into a computer or communications device and sold by a vendor, the customer can do with it as he or she pleases—short of exporting it.

Although the purpose of developing the type II equipment, as with the type I equipment, was to provide a means of protecting government information, the type II modules are available for use in nongovernment, private sector applications. As this equipment becomes more widely available, it is likely to become more widely used, at the expense of DES.

## Public-Key Encryption

One of the major difficulties with conventional encryption schemes is the need to distribute the keys in a secure manner. A clever way around this requirement is an encryption scheme that, surprisingly, does not require key distribution. This scheme is known as public-key encryption and was first proposed in 1976. It is illustrated in Figure 7-2b.

For conventional encryption schemes, the keys used for encryption and decryption are the same. But it is possible to develop an algorithm that uses one key for encryption and a companion but different key for decryption. Furthermore, it is possible to develop algorithms such that knowledge of the encryption algorithm plus the encryption key is not sufficient to determine the decryption key. Thus, the following technique will work.

1. Each end system in a network generates a pair of keys to be used for the encryption and decryption of messages that it will receive.

2. Each system publishes its encryption key by placing it in a public register or file. This is the public key. The companion key is kept private.

3. If A wants to send a message to B, it encrypts the message using B's public key.

4. When B receives the message, it decrypts it using B's private key. No other recipient can decrypt the message because only B knows B's private key.

As you can see, public-key encryption solves the key distribution problem because there are no keys to distribute! All participants have access to public keys, and private keys are generated locally by each participant and therefore need never be distributed. As long as a system controls its private key, its incoming communication is secure. At any time, a system can change its private key and publish the companion public key to replace its old public key.

A main disadvantage of public-key encryption compared to conventional encryption is that algorithms for the former are much more complex. Thus, for a comparable size and cost of hardware, the public-key scheme will provide much lower throughput.

Table 7-2 summarizes some of the important aspects of conventional and public-key encryption.

**TABLE 7-2**   Conventional and Public-Key Encryption

|  | **Conventional Encryption** | **Public-Key Encryption** |
| --- | --- | --- |
| Needed to work | The same algorithm with the same key can be used for encryption and decryption. | One algorithm is used for encryption and decryption with a pair of keys, one for encryption and one for decryption. |
|  | The sender and receiver must share the algorithm and the key. | The sender and receiver must each have one of the matched pair of keys. |
| Needed for security | The key must be kept secret. | One of the two keys must be kept secret. |
|  | It must be impossible or at least impractical to decipher a message if no other information is available. | It must be impossible or at least impractical to decipher a message if no other information is available. |
|  | Knowledge of the algorithm plus samples of ciphertext must be insufficient to determine the key. | Knowledge of the algorithm plus one of the keys plus samples of ciphertext must be insufficient to determine the key. |

# Application of Encryption

For conventional encryption to work, the two parties to an exchange must have the same key, and that key must be protected from access by others. Furthermore, frequent key changes are usually desirable to limit the amount of data compromised if an attacker learns the key. Therefore, the strength of any cryptographic system rests with the key distribution technique, a term that refers to the means of delivering a key to two parties that want to exchange data, without allowing others to see the key. Key distribution can be achieved in a number of ways. For two parties A and B:

1. The key could be selected by A and physically delivered to B.
2. A third party could select the key and physically deliver it to A and B.
3. If A and B have previously and recently used a key, one party could transmit the new key to the other, encrypted using the old key.
4. If A and B each have an encrypted connection to a third party C, C could deliver a key on the encrypted links to A and B.

Options 1 and 2 call for manual delivery of a key, which is awkward. In a distributed system, any given host or terminal may need to engage in exchanges with many other hosts and terminals over time. Thus, each device needs a number of keys, supplied dynamically. The difficulty with Option 3 is that if an attacker ever succeeds in gaining access to one key, all subsequent keys are revealed.

Option 4 is the most attractive and could be handled from a host facility or network control center. Figure 7-3 illustrates a possible implementation. For this scheme, two kinds of keys are identified:

- *Session key:* When two end systems (such as hosts or terminals) want to communicate, they establish a logical connection (e.g., LLC connection or transport connection). For the duration of that logical connection, all user data is encrypted with a one-time session key. At the conclusion of the session, or connection, the session key is destroyed.

- *Permanent key:* A permanent key is used between entities to distribute session keys.

The configuration consists of the following elements:

- *Access control center:* The access control center determines which systems can communicate with each other.

- *Key distribution center:* When the access control center grants permission for two systems to establish a connection, the key distribution center provides a one-time session key for that connection.

- *Network interface unit:* The NIU performs end-to-end encryption and obtains session keys on behalf of its host or terminal.

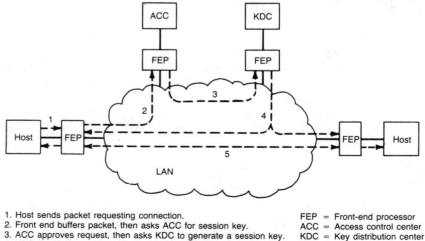

1. Host sends packet requesting connection.
2. Front end buffers packet, then asks ACC for session key.
3. ACC approves request, then asks KDC to generate a session key.
4. KDC distributes session key to both front ends.
5. Buffered packet and subsequent packets transmitted.

FEP = Front-end processor
ACC = Access control center
KDC = Key distribution center

**Figure 7-3** End-to-end encryption across a LAN.

The steps involved in establishing a connection are shown in Figure 7-3. When one host wants to set up a connection to another host, it transmits a connection-request packet (1). The NIU saves that packet and applies to the access control center for permission to establish the connection (2). The communication between the NIU and the access control center is encrypted using a permanent key shared only by the access control center and the NIU. The access control center has one unique key for each NIU and for the key distribution center. If the access control center approves the connection request, it sends a message to the key distribution center, asking for a session key to be generated (3). The key distribution center generates the session key and delivers it to the two appropriate NIUs, using a unique permanent key for each front end (4). The requesting NIU can now release the connection request packet, and a connection is set up between the two end systems (5). All user data exchanged between the two end systems is encrypted by their respective NIUs using the one-time session key.

Figure 7-4 shows the encryption function of the network interface unit (NIU). On the host side, the NIU accepts packets. The user data portion of the packet is encrypted, while the packet header bypasses the encryption process. The resulting packet is delivered to the LAN. In the opposite direction, for packets arriving from the LAN, the user data portion is decrypted and the entire packet is delivered to the host.

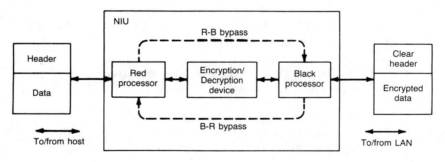

Black data: Data that is encrypted.
Red data: Classified or sensitive data that is not encrypted.

**Figure 7-4** Network interface unit with encryption function.

Several variations on this scheme are possible. The functions of access control and key distribution could be combined into a single system. The separation, however, makes the two functions clear and may provide a slightly enhanced level of security. If we want to let any two devices communicate at will, the access control function is not needed at all; when two devices want to establish a connection, one of them applies to the key distribution center for a session key.

One possible application of public-key encryption is to use it for the permanent key portion of Figure 7-3, with conventional keys used for session keys. Because there are few control messages relative to the amount of user data traffic, the reduced throughput of public-key encryption should not be a handicap. The use of public-key encryption in this fashion means that even the permanent keys do not need to be distributed, further enhancing security.

The automated key distribution approach provides the flexibility and dynamic characteristics needed for a number of terminal users to access a number of hosts and for the hosts to exchange data with each other. A number of LAN vendors offer some version of the scheme shown in Figure 7-3. It is a powerful and reasonably inexpensive means of enhancing network security.

# Access Control

The purpose of access control is to ensure that only authorized users have access to a particular system and its individual resources and that access to and modification of a particular portion of data are limited to authorized individuals and programs. Strictly speaking, access control is a computer security issue, rather than a network security issue. That is, in most cases, access control mechanisms are implemented in a single computer to control the access to that computer. Because much of the access to a computer is through a networking or communications facility, however, it is essential to consider access control as part of LAN security.

## User-Oriented Access Control

Figure 7-5 depicts, generically, measures to control access in a data processing system. These measures are in two categories: those associated with the user and those associated with the data.

A quite common example of user access control on a time-sharing system is the user logon, which requires both a user identifier (ID) and a password. The system allows a user to log on only if that user's ID is known to the system and if the user knows the password associated by the system with that ID. This ID/password system is a notoriously unreliable method of user access control. Users can forget their passwords and accidentally or intentionally reveal their password. Hackers have become very skillful at guessing IDs for special users, such as system control and system management personnel. Finally, the ID/password file is subject to penetration attempts.

A number of measures can be taken to improve the security of the password scheme. Three requirements can be stated:

1. The number of possible password combinations should be large. This reduces the chances for the success of an outsider who either guesses the codes or uses a computer to make repetitive attempts under program control. It is useful to restrict passwords to alphanumeric characters and to use pronounceable combinations of characters, so that users can easily remember them and avoid writing them down. A five-character password

would have over 60 million possible combinations; even with the restriction to containing pronounceable combinations, this is a reasonably secure length, provided points 2 and 3 are met. One note of caution: Users should not be allowed to assign their own passwords. People tend to use personal names, dates, and other information that can be readily guessed.

2. There should be automatic disconnection of the incoming terminal line after a small number of invalid password attempts have been made. The usual limit is three to five attempts. This requires an attacker to hang up and redial after every few tries, increasing the time required to perform a brute-force penetration to years. The programmed attack favored by hackers is thus rendered useless. A related and very valuable feature is automatic deactivation of a user ID if it is used in multiple invalid logon attempts.

3. The operating system should log and report invalid sign-on attempts and other events with security implications. These could include an unauthorized person attempting to run sensitive application programs, such as human resources systems, or using high-powered system utility programs to copy or modify files. This feature reveals whether attempts at computer vandalism are taking place so that further, more positive means can be used to report and apprehend the attackers. Security reports can also be used as evidence in police or FBI investigations and trials.

The problem of user access control is compounded over a communi-

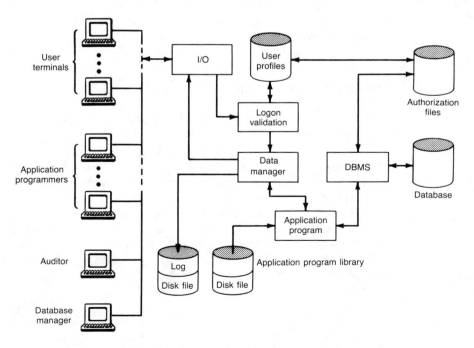

**Figure 7-5** Data processing system security.

cations network. The logon dialogue must take place over the communications medium, and eavesdropping is a potential threat. One approach to this problem is to encrypt the ID/password. All the paraphernalia of encryption, including key management, would be required. If the messages themselves do not require encryption, this is an expensive means of protecting passwords.

User access control in a distributed environment, such as a LAN, can be either centralized or decentralized. In a centralized approach, the network provides a logon service, determining who can use the network and to whom the user can connect. The access control center in Figure 7-3 could perform such a function.

Decentralized user access control treats the network as a transparent communications link, and the usual logon procedure is carried out by the destination host. Of course, the security concerns for transmitting passwords over the network must still be addressed.

In many networks, two levels of access control may be used. Individual hosts may be provided with a logon facility to protect host-specific resources and applications. In addition, the network as a whole may provide protection to restrict network access to authorized users. This two-level facility is desirable for the currently common case, in which the network connects disparate hosts and simply provides a convenient means of terminal-host access. In a more uniform network of hosts, some centralized access policy could be enforced in a network control center.

Techniques that are more elaborate than a simple password/ID have been proposed for user identification. Exotic techniques such as voiceprints, fingerprints, and hand geometry analysis may be foolproof but are at present prohibitively expensive.

## Data-Oriented Access Control

Following successful logon, the user is granted access to one host or a set of hosts and applications. This is generally not sufficient for a system that includes sensitive data in its database. Through the user access control procedure, a user can be identified to the system. Each user can be associated with a profile that specifies permissible operations and file accesses. The operating system can then enforce rules based on the user profile.

The database management system, however, must control access to specific records or even portions of records. For example, anyone in administration may be able to obtain a list of company personnel, but only selected individuals may have access to salary information. The issue is more than just one of level of detail. Whereas the operating system may grant a user permission to access a file or use an application, following which there are no further security checks, the database management system must make a decision on each individual access attempt. That decision depends not only on the user's identity but also on the specific parts of the data being accessed and even on the information already divulged to the user.

A general model of access control exercised by a database management system is the access matrix (Figure 7-6). One axis of the matrix consists of identified subjects that may attempt data access. Typically, this list will consist of individual users or user groups, although access could be controlled for terminals, hosts, or applications instead of users or in addition to users. The other axis lists the objects that may be accessed. At the greatest level of detail, objects are individual data fields. More aggregate groupings, such as records, files, or even the entire database, may also be objects in the matrix. Each entry in the matrix indicates the access rights of that subject for that object.

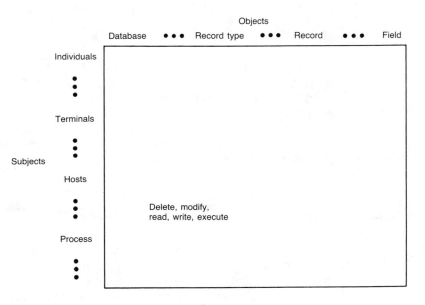

**Figure 7-6** Database access matrix.

In practice, an access matrix is usually sparse and is implemented by decomposition in one of two ways. The matrix may be decomposed by columns, yielding access control lists. Thus, for each object, an access control list will list users and their permitted access opportunities. Decomposition by rows yields capability tickets. A capability ticket specifies authorized objects and operations for a user. Each user has a number of tickets and may be authorized to loan or give them to others. Because tickets may be dispersed around the system, they present a greater security problem than access control lists.

Network considerations for data-oriented access control parallel those for user-oriented access control. If only certain users are permitted to access certain items of data, encryption may be needed to protect those items during transmission to authorized users. Typically, data access control is decentralized; that is, it is controlled by host-based database management systems. If a network database server exists on a network, data access control becomes a network function.

# Viruses and Worms

A new threat has arisen to cause concern to data processing and data communications managers: the virus and its near-relative, the worm. These software creations range from the harmless to the extremely destructive. What is worrisome to the manager responsible for security is the prevalence of these computer contagions. In the first nine months of 1988, an estimated 250,000 computers, from the smallest laptop machines to the most powerful workstation, had been hit with a virus[2].

What was once a rare electronic disease has reached epidemic proportions. Across the U.S., it is disrupting operations, destroying data, and raising disturbing questions about the vulnerability of information systems everywhere.

A virus is a program that can "infect" other programs by modifying them; the modified program includes a copy of the virus program, which can then go on to infect other programs. A worm is a program that makes use of networking software to replicate itself and move from system to system. The worm performs some activity at each system it gains access to, such as consuming processor resources or depositing viruses. At present, the virus presents the more significant threat to data processing facilities, and this chapter provides an introduction.

## The Nature of Viruses

Biological viruses are tiny scraps of genetic code—DNA or RNA—that can take over the machinery of a living cell and trick it into making thousands of flawless replicas of the original virus. Like its biological counterpart, a computer virus carries in its instructional code the recipe for making perfect copies of itself. Lodged in a host computer, the typical virus takes temporary control of the computer's disk operating system. Then, whenever the infected computer comes into contact with an uninfected piece of software, a fresh copy of the virus passes into the new program. Thus, the infection can be spread from computer to computer by unsuspecting users who either swap disks or send programs over a network. In a LAN environment, the capability to access applications and system services on other computers provides a perfect culture for the spread of a virus.

A virus can do anything that other programs do. The only difference is that it attaches itself to another program and executes secretly every time the host program is run. Table 7-3 shows a simple example of how a virus can be implemented so that it spreads. This example indicates only the mechanism by which the virus remains hidden and by which it spreads. If this were all that there were to viruses, they would not cause concern. Unfortunately, after a virus is executing, it can perform any function, such as erasing files and pro-

---

[2] "Invasion of the Data Snatchers," *Time Magazine,* September 26, 1988.

grams. This is the threat of the virus. Table 7-4 lists some of the more common viruses and indicates the damage they can do.

**TABLE 7-3**   Trail of the Virus

A very simple assembly language virus that does nothing more than infect programs might work something like this:

- Find the first program instruction
- Replace it with a jump to the memory location following the last instruction in the program
- Insert a copy of the virus code at that location
- Have the virus simulate the instruction replaced by the jump
- Jump back to the second instruction of the host program
- Finish executing the host program

Every time the host program is run, the virus would infect another program and then execute the host program. Except for a short delay, a user wouldn't notice anything suspicious.

During its lifetime, a typical virus goes through four stages:

1. A dormant phase, in which the virus is idle. Eventually, the virus is activated by some event, such as a date, the presence of another program or file, or the capacity of the disk exceeding some limit. Not all viruses have this stage.

2. A propagation phase, during which the virus places an identical copy of itself into other programs or into certain system areas on the disk. Each infected program now contains a clone of the virus, which will itself enter a propagation phase. This process is illustrated in Figure 7-7, which shows a virus spreading across three user programs.

3. The triggering phase, in which the virus is activated to perform the function for which it was intended. As with the dormant phase, the triggering phase can be caused by a variety of system events, including a count of the number of times that this copy of the virus has made copies of itself.

4. The execution phase, in which the function is performed. The function may be harmless, such as a message on the screen, or damaging, such as the destruction of programs and data files.

Most viruses carry out their work in a manner that is specific to a particular operating system. Thus, they are designed to take advantage of the details, and weaknesses, of particular systems.

## Countering the Threat of Viruses

The ideal solution to the threat of viruses is prevention: don't allow a virus to get into the system in the first place. In general, this goal is impossible to

**TABLE 7-4**   Some Common Viruses

### IBM PC Viruses

Pakistani Brain   One of the most prevalent viruses, so called because it originated in Pakistan. It infects the boot sector on a PC DOS disk and replicates, infecting every floppy disk inserted into the system. The virus takes over the floppy disk controller interface. If it sees a read operation, it pushes the original read operation aside and attempts to read the boot track. If it determines that the boot is uninfected, it modifies the boot to contain the virus. In some versions, the virus starts to mark areas on your disk as bad even through they are good. Eventually, the disk contains nothing but bad sectors.

Jerusalem Virus   This virus infects executable programs, such as .COM or .EXE files. It resides in memory and infects every program that is executed. It destroys file allocation tables, which makes it impossible to access files on disk, and scrambles data on the disk. This virus is spread by floppy disks but attacks hard disks as well.

LeHigh Virus   This virus infects the operating system by getting into the command processor. Whenever a disk access is made, it checks to see if the command processor on that disk is infected. If not, the virus is introduced. If so, a counter controlled by the virus is incremented. When the counter reaches four (or ten, in a more recent version), the virus destroys all the data on the hard disk.

Alemeda Virus   This infects the system's boot sector. It then infects any floppy disk inserted during reboot and destroys the last track on the disk.

### Macintosh Viruses

Scores Virus   This virus replicates for a specified number of days, followed by several days of dormancy. Thereafter, when the user attempts to save information in a file, the virus will not let it, and crashes the system.

nVIR   This virus comes in a variety of forms, of which at least a dozen have been detected. The technique by which it spreads is especially virulent. It invades the System file; once this crucial resource is infected, every application that is subsequently launched is contaminated.

achieve, although prevention can reduce the number of successful viral attacks. The next-best approach is to be able to do the following:

- *Detection:* After the infection has occurred, determine that it has occurred and locate the virus.
- *Purging:* Remove the virus from all infected systems so that the disease cannot spread further.
- *Recovery:* Recover any lost data or programs.

Even this less ambitious goal may be difficult to achieve. Before discussing specific measures, let us look at a useful classification of viruses developed by the Computer Virus Industry Association. As the name suggest, this is a group

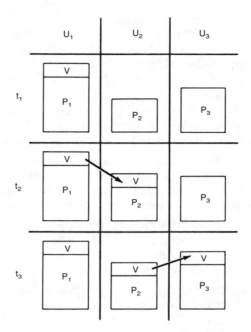

**Figure 7-7** The spread of a virus.

of vendors that design and sell products that prevent or recover from viruses. The association has defined three classes of viruses[3]:

- Those that infect general-purpose programs. These must attach themselves to a program in order to spread. Most of these are detectable and preventable.

- Those that infect operating system files. These must also attach themselves to a program to spread and execute, but they are more difficult to detect because they have already infected the operating system.

- Those that attack the boot sector. These are relatively easy to detect because they cause obvious changes to the boot sector. (The boot sector is the first sector of the disk and is used to boot the operating system into main memory when the computer is turned on. )

Because of the variety of viruses, there is no universal remedy. A number of programs provide some protection, and the security manager would be advised to contact several vendors and assess their products. Some measures that can be taken to ward off viruses follow:

- *Cryptographic checksum.* A checksum is a value produced by a calculation on a block of bits. The value is then stored as part of the block. For example, the binary image of a program could be viewed as a sequence of 16-bit

---

[3] "Antivirus Vendors Form Industry Regulation Group," *Network World,* July 11, 1988.

binary integers. The sum of all of these words, modulo $2^{16}$, is a simple checksum. The advantage of a checksum is that it is a quick way of detecting alterations in a large block of data. If any word or words in the block are changed, the calculated checksum will differ from the stored checksum. To prevent a viral program from modifying both the program and the checksum, an encrypted version of the checksum is stored with the program, with the key maintained separately in a protected manner. Each time the program will be used or transferred to another disk or computer, the checksum is validated to assure that no modifications have occurred.

- *Program monitor.* This is a program that is triggered by any system interrupt and examines each one for suspicious activity. If the program detects anything considered suspicious by the author of the antiviral program, it interrupts the operation and alerts the user.

- *Virus removal.* Some of these programs are specific, looking for the telltale signs in storage of viruses known to the author of the removal program. Others compare snapshots of the system portion of a known clean system with the current system.

- *Backups.* Regular backup of current files is sound practice in any case. Most shared systems (minicomputers and mainframes) provide this service automatically. Unfortunately, many personal computer users are lazy when it comes to this chore. Aside from its value in the event of a disk crash, a backup can be used as a tool in combatting viruses. This technique can be used with virus detection for the purpose of recovery.

The dilemma facing the security manager is this: If sharing of programs and data is prohibited, viruses cannot occur. This, of course, defeats the purpose of a LAN. If sharing is allowed, viruses can occur, and the current repertoire of tools for detecting and preventing viruses is not foolproof.

# Summary

The increasing reliance by business upon data processing systems and the increasing use of networks and communications facilities to build distributed systems have resulted in a strong requirement for computer and network security. Computer security involves mechanisms inside and related to a single computer system. The principal object is to protect the data resources of that system. Network security deals with the protection of data and messages that are communicated. This chapter deals with network security.

The requirements for security are best assessed by examining the various security threats faced by an organization. We can organize these threats into two main categories. Passive threats, sometimes referred to as wiretapping or eavesdropping, are attempts by an attacker to obtain information relating to a communication. In most cases, the most serious such threat is the release of message contents, that is, the disclosure of transmitted files, messages, or documents to an unauthorized party. In some cases, there is also a threat from traffic analysis. That is, the attacker may gain useful information merely from knowledge of the traffic patterns of the communications.

The other category of threats includes a variety of active threats. These involve some modification of the transmitted data or the creation of false transmissions. One type of active threat is message-stream modification: The attacker modifies the contents of a message or the order or timing of messages. Denial of service takes place when an attacker prevents or inhibits the normal use or management of communications facilities. Finally, a masquerade occurs when an attacker pretends to be a legitimate user engaged in an authorized task.

By far the most important automated tool for network and communications security is encryption. Encryption is a process that conceals meaning by changing intelligible messages into unintelligible messages. Most commercially available encryption equipment uses conventional encryption, in which the two parties share a single encryption/decryption key. The principal challenges with conventional encryption are the distribution and protection of the keys. The alternative is a public-key encryption scheme, in which the process involves two keys, one for encryption and a paired key for decryption. One of the keys is kept private by the party that generated the key pair, and the other is made public.

Another important security technique is access control. The purpose of access control is to ensure that access to a particular system and its individual resources and access to and modification of a particular portion of data are limited to authorized individuals and programs. Strictly speaking, access control is a computer security issue, rather than a network security issue. That is, in most cases, access control mechanisms are implemented in a single computer to control access to that computer. Because much of the access to a computer is by means of a networking or communications facility, however, access control mechanisms should operate effectively in a distributed, networking environment.

The most recent threat to be faced by those responsible for system and network security is the computer virus. A virus is a program that can infect other programs by modifying them; the modified program includes a copy of the virus program, which can then go on to infect other programs. After a virus is activated, it can perform functions ranging from the benign to the destructive. Because of the variety of viruses, and their increasingly clever designs, it is difficult to fully counter this threat.

# Chapter 8

# LAN Management

T HE READER SHOULD BY NOW UNDERSTAND the critical and growing importance of networks and distributed processing systems in the business world. The trend is toward larger, more complex networks supporting more applications and more users. As these networks grow, two facts become painfully evident:

- The network and its associated resources and distributed applications become indispensable to the organization.
- More things can go wrong, disabling the network or a portion of the network or degrading performance to an unacceptable level.

A large network cannot be put together and managed by human effort alone. The complexity of such a system dictates the use of automated network management tools. If the network includes equipment from multiple vendors, the urgency of the need for such tools is increased, and the difficulty of supplying such tools is also increased. This is reflected in Figure 8-1, which shows the projected growth for network management products and services (excluding expenditures for public telephone and data networks).

Of course, these comments and Figure 8-1 refer to the total networking facilities of an organization, including local area networks and wide area networks. However, LANs are the core of any organization's networking strategy and must be the focus of any network management program.

In this chapter we attempt to provide a brief overview of a very big and complex subject: network management. Specifically, we focus on the hardware and software tools, and the organized systems of such tools, that aid the human network manager in this difficult task.

We begin by looking at the requirements for network management. This should give some idea of the scope of the task. To manage a network, it is fundamental that one must know something about the current status and behavior of that network. Then we look at the special requirements for LAN management and the tools developed for that purpose.

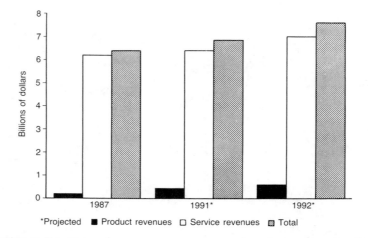

**Figure 8-1** Network management revenues in private networks. *(Source: Business Communications Corp., Norwalk, CT, April 1988.)*

For either LAN management alone or a combined LAN and WAN environment, we need a network management system that includes a comprehensive set of data gathering and control tools and is integrated with network hardware and software. We look at the general architecture of a network management system and examine two approaches: IBM's NetView and the international network management standard.

## Network Management Requirements

Table 8-1 lists key areas of network management as suggested by the International Standards Organization (ISO). These categories provide a useful way of organizing our discussion of requirements.

**TABLE 8-1**   Elements of the ISO Network Management Architecture

| | |
|---|---|
| Fault management | The facilities that detect, isolate, and correct abnormal operation of the OSI environment. |
| Accounting management | The facilities that establish charges for the use of managed objects and identify costs for the use of those managed objects. |
| Configuration and name management | The facilities that exercise control over, identify, collect data from, and provide data to managed objects to assist in the continuous operation of interconnection services. |
| Performance management | The facilities needed to evaluate the behavior of managed objects and the effectiveness of communication activities. |
| Security management | The facilities that address those aspects of OSI security essential to the correct operation of OSI network management and the protection of managed objects. |

# Fault Management

## Overview

To maintain proper operation of a complex network, care must be taken that systems as a whole, and each essential component individually, are in proper working order. When a fault occurs, it is important, as rapidly as possible, to

- Determine exactly where the fault is.
- Isolate the rest of the network from the failure so that the network can continue to function without interference.
- Reconfigure or modify the network in such a way as to minimize the impact of operation without the failed component or components.
- Repair or replace the failed components to restore the network to its initial state.

Central to the definition of fault management is the fundamental concept of a fault. Faults are different than errors. A *fault* is an abnormal condition that requires management attention (or action) to repair. A fault is usually indicated by failure to operate correctly or by excessive errors. For example, if a communications line is physically cut, no signals can get through. Or a crimp in the cable may cause wild distortions so that there is a persistently high bit error rate. Certain errors (e.g., a single bit error on a communications line) may occur occasionally and are not normally considered to be faults. It is usually possible to compensate for errors using the error control mechanisms of the various protocols.

## User Requirements

Users expect fast and reliable problem resolution. Most end users will tolerate occasional outages, but they generally expect immediate notification and the almost immediate correction of the problem. To provide this level of fault resolution requires very rapid and reliable fault detection and diagnostic management functions. The impact and duration of faults can also be minimized by the use of redundant components and alternate communication routes, to give the network a degree of "fault tolerance." The fault management capability itself should be redundant to increase network reliability.

Users expect to be kept informed of network status, including both scheduled and unscheduled disruptive maintenance. Users expect reassurance of correct network operation through mechanisms that use confidence tests or analyze dumps, logs, alerts, or statistics.

After correcting a fault and restoring a system to its full operational state, the fault management service must ensure that the problem is truly resolved and that no new problems are introduced. This requirement is called problem tracking and control. As with other areas of network management, fault management should have minimal effect on network performance.

## Accounting Management

### Overview

In many corporate networks, individual divisions or cost centers (or even individual project accounts) are charged for the use of network services. These are internal accounting procedures rather than actual cash transfers, but they are important to the participating users nevertheless. Even if internal charging is not used, the network manager needs to be able to track the use of network resources by user or user class for a number of reasons, including the following:

- A user or group of users may be abusing access privileges and burdening the network at the expense of other users.
- Users may be making inefficient use of the network, and the network manager can assist in changing procedures to improve performance.
- The network manager is in a better position to plan for network growth if user activity is known in sufficient detail.

### User Requirements

The network manager needs to specify the kinds of accounting information to be recorded at various nodes, the desired interval between sending the recorded information to higher-level management nodes, and the algorithms to be used in calculating charges. Accounting reports should be generated under network manager control.

To limit access to accounting information, the accounting facility must provide the capability to verify users' authorization to access and manipulate that information.

## Configuration and Name Management

### Overview

Modern data communication networks are composed of individual components and logical subsystems (e.g., the device driver in an operating system) that can be configured to perform many different applications. The same device, for example, can be configured to act as either a router or an end system node or both. After it is decided how a device will be used, the configuration manager can choose the appropriate software and set of attributes and values (e.g., a transport layer retransmission timer) for that device.

Configuration management is concerned with initializing a network and gracefully shutting down part or all of the network. It is also concerned with maintaining, adding, and updating the relationships among components and the status of components themselves during network operation.

## User Requirements

Startup and shutdown operations on a network are the responsibilities of configuration management. It is often desirable for these operations on certain components to be performed unattended (e.g., starting or shutting down a network interface unit).

The network manager needs the capability to initially identify the components that comprise the network and to define the desired connectivity of these components. Those who regularly configure a network with the same or a similar set of resource attributes need ways to define and modify default attributes and to load these predefined sets of attributes into the specified network components. The network manager needs the capability to change the connectivity of network components when users' needs change. Reconfiguration of a network is often desired in response to performance evaluation or in support of network upgrade, fault recovery, or security checks.

Users often need or want to be informed of the status of network resources and components. Therefore, when changes in configuration occur, users should be notified of these changes. Configuration reports can be generated either on a routine basis or in response to a request for such a report. Before reconfiguration, users often want to inquire about the upcoming status of resources and their attributes.

Network managers usually want only authorized users (operators) to manage and control network operation (e.g., software distribution and updating).

## Performance Management

### Overview

Modern data communications networks have many and varied components, which must intercommunicate and share data and resources. In some cases, it is critical to the effectiveness of an application that the communication over the network be within certain performance limits.

Performance management of a computer network comprises two broad functional categories—monitoring and controlling. Monitoring is the function that tracks activities on the network. The controlling function enables performance management to make adjustments to improve network performance. Some performance issues of concern to the network manager follow:

- What is the level of capacity utilization?
- Is there excessive traffic?
- Has throughput been reduced to unacceptable levels?
- Are there bottlenecks?
- Is response time increasing?

To deal with these concerns, the network manager must focus on an initial set of resources to be monitored to assess performance levels. This includes associating appropriate metrics and values with relevant network resources as indicators of different levels of performance. For example, what count of re-transmissions on a transport connection is considered to be a performance problem requiring attention? Performance management, therefore, must monitor many resources to provide information in determining network operating level. By collecting this information, analyzing it, and then using the resultant analysis as feedback to the prescribed set of values, the network manager can become more adept at recognizing situations indicative of present or impending performance degradation.

## User Requirements

Before using a network for a particular application, a user may want to know such things as the average and worst case response times and the reliability of network services. Thus, performance must be known in sufficient detail to assess specific user queries.

End users expect network services to be managed in such a way as to consistently afford their applications good response time.

Network managers need performance statistics to help them plan, manage, and maintain large networks. Performance statistics can be used to recognize potential bottlenecks before they cause problems to the end users. Appropriate corrective action can take the form of changing routing tables to balance or redistribute traffic load during peak use or when a bottleneck is identified by a rapidly growing load in one area. Over the long term, capacity planning based on such performance information can indicate the proper decisions to make, for example, with regard to expansion of lines in that area.

## Security Management

### Overview

Security management is concerned with generating, distributing, and storing encryption keys. Passwords and other authorization or access control information must be maintained and distributed. Security management is also concerned with monitoring and controlling access to computer networks and access to all or part of the network management information from the network nodes. Logs are an important security tool; therefore, security management is very involved with the collection, storage, and examination of audit records and security logs, as well as with the enabling and disabling of these logging facilities.

## User Requirements

Security management provides facilities for the protection of network resources and user information. Network security facilities should be available for authorized users only. Users want to know that the proper security policies are in force and effective and that the management of security facilities is itself secure.

# LAN-Specific Network Management

A LAN by itself seems a much more manageable network than one involving wide area components. For one thing, the number of transmission technologies is reduced. Also, everything is at hand; it is much easier to localize faults and to monitor everything because it is all clustered in a small area. Nevertheless, for a local network supporting a substantial amount of equipment, network management is required. In many cases, LAN vendors provide many of the tools needed for network management in a package of hardware and software that can be acquired with the network as an option. In this section, we give an overview of the types of capabilities typically found in such products.

## The Special Importance of LAN Management

Most LANs start out as a homogeneous set of equipment from a single networking vendor. They usually have one main application, such as multiuser accounting, desktop publishing, electronic mail, or host communications. But rapid growth breeds complexity. And, as users come to depend on the LAN, the network's applications expand.

Thus, LANs evolve from being a nice extra to being a critical part of an organization's day-to-day operations. Downtime can cost a corporation dearly as work backs up. Slowdowns, due to increased server and network loads, can lead to wasted time as users wait for transactions to finish or customer accounts to be called up. Unfortunately, most users don't recognize the difficulties of managing LANs until serious problems are encountered. Networks are easy to install and deliver substantial benefits when their size and scope are limited. Network popularity, however, often outpaces users' understanding of network management and methods for spotting and identifying network problems.

The combination of larger size, more internetworking, and multivendor configurations can rapidly change a simple network into a maze that leaves all but the most sophisticated users confused and stymied. Isolating problems and improving performance in complex and feature-laden networks is one of the major challenges in today's LAN environments.

LANs that were once small and easy to use become very easy to misuse when they grow to meet users' ever-expanding needs. For example, one naive user could utilize the wrong boot disk, containing last year's version of network drivers. This could have a catastrophic effect on hundreds of users in a large network installation. Another user innocently using a workstation for a particular database application might discover that by simply exceeding some internal limit, the application unexpectedly starts to use all the resources of the file server.

In another scenario, a network manager installs a file server, which should routinely send out a single packet regarding the health of the file server every 15 minutes. If a mistake is made in setting parameters, the server may send out a flood of packets, which can cause a service brownout due to retransmissions and broadcasts through the network. To the unsophisticated network manager, such a brownout has the same symptoms as a saturated network.

These problems are quite common, and in many instances, the network manager does not know the cause. A sophisticated and easy-to-use network control center can make the job of LAN management much easier.

## LAN Network Control Center

With many local area network products, a network control center (NCC) is provided. Typically, this is a separate dedicated microcomputer attached to the network through a network interface unit (NIU). All of the functions of a LAN network control center involve observation, active control, or a combination of the two. They fall into three categories:

- Configuration functions
- Monitoring functions
- Fault isolation

### Configuration Functions

One of the principal functions of an NCC is to maintain a directory of the names and addresses of resources on the network. This allows users to set up connections by name. A resource may be any device or service—terminals, hosts, peripherals, application programs, or utility programs. For example, a user at a terminal who wants to use the accounts payable package could request it with LOGON ACCOUNTS PAYABLE. Because the directory linking names with addresses can be altered, the manager (with the NCC) can move applications (for load balancing or because a host is down). The directory is maintained at the NCC, but portions or all of it can also be downloaded to NIUs to reduce the network traffic required for directory lookup.

The NCC can also control the operation of the NIUs. The NCC could have the capability to shut down and start up NIUs and to set NIU parameters. For example, an NIU may be restricted so that it communicates only with a certain set of NIUs or destination names. This is a simple way to set up a security scheme. Another example is to assign different priorities to different NIUs or different users.

## Monitoring Functions

In a typical LAN control center, monitoring functions fall into three categories: performance monitoring, network status, and accounting.

Table 8-2 lists the types of measurements reported in a typical LAN facility. These measurements can be used to answer a number of questions. Questions concerning possible errors or inefficiencies include the following:

- Is traffic evenly distributed among network users, or are there source-destination pairs with unusually heavy traffic?
- What is the percentage of each type of packet? Are some packet types of unusually high frequency, indicating an error or an inefficient protocol?
- What is the distribution of data packet sizes?
- What are the channel acquisition and communication delay distributions? Are these times excessive?
- Are collisions a factor in getting packets transmitted, indicating possible faulty hardware or protocols?
- What is the channel utilization and throughput?

These areas are of interest to the network manager. Other questions have to do with response time and throughput by user class and determining how much growth the network can absorb before certain performance thresholds are crossed.

Because of the broadcast nature of LANs, many measurements can be collected passively at the NCC, without adding load to the network. The NCC can be programmed to accept all packets, regardless of destination address. For a heavily loaded network, this may not be possible, and a sampling scheme must be used. In a LAN containing bridges, one collection point per segment is required.

However, not all information can be centrally collected by observing LAN traffic. End-to-end measurements, such as response time, require knowing the time that a packet is generated by a host or terminal and the ability to identify the responding packet. This sort of measurement requires some collection capability at the individual NIUs. From time to time, the NIUs can send the collected data to the NCC. Unfortunately, this technique increases the complexity of the NIU logic and imposes a communication overhead.

Another major area of NCC monitoring is network status. The NCC keeps track of which NIUs are currently activated and the connections that exist. This information is displayed to the network manager on request.

Finally, the NCC can support some accounting and billing functions. This can be done on a device or user basis. The NCC could record the amount of traffic generated by a particular device or user and the resources that a device or user connected to and the length of the connection.

**TABLE 8-2**    Performance Measurement Reports

| Name | Variables | Description |
| --- | --- | --- |
| Host communication matrix | Source x destination | (Number, %) of (packets, data packets, data bytes) |
| Group communication matrix | Source x destination | As above, consolidated into address groups |
| Packet type histogram | Packet type | (Number, %) of (packets, original packets) by type |
| Data packet size histogram | Packet size | (Number, %) of data packets by data byte length |
| Throughput utilization distribution | Source | (Total bytes, data bytes) transmitted |
| Packet interarrival time histogram | Interarrival time | Time between consecutive carrier (network busy) signals |
| Channel acquisition delay histogram | NIU acquisition delay | (Number, %) of packets delayed at NIU by given amount |
| Communication delay histogram | Packet delay | Time from original packet ready at source to receipt |
| Collision count histogram | Number of collisions | Number of packets by number of collisions |
| Transmission count histogram | Number of transmissions | Number of packets by transmission attempts |

## Fault-Isolation Functions

The NCC can continuously monitor the network to detect faults and, to the extent possible, narrow the fault to a single component or small group of components. For example, the NCC can periodically poll each NIU, requesting that it return a status packet. When an NIU fails to respond, the NCC reports the failure and also attempts to disable the NIU so that it does not interfere with the rest of the LAN.

## Responsibility for LAN Management

Who should be responsible for management of the organization's LAN resources? The first decision to make is whether the responsibility should reside in the organization or be contracted. In the latter case, the responsibility could be given to the vendor who supplied the LAN or to an independent consulting firm.

In general, it is wise not to delegate this responsibility to an outsider. The proper functioning of the LAN is so important that the manager must manage the LAN continuously, and be able to respond to faults or performance collapses immediately. Accordingly, as indicated in Figure 8-2, most organizations choose to take on the task themselves.

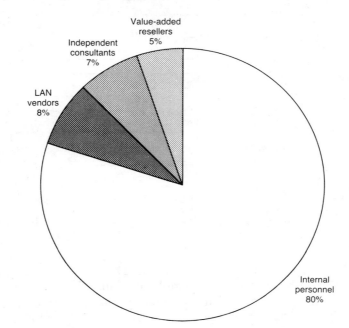

**Figure 8-2** Internal or external LAN management responsibility. *(Source: The Yankee Group, Boston, July 1989. Based on a survey of 170 companies.)*

The next decision to be made is where in the organization the network management task falls. Even if an external management service is used, someone in the organization must be responsible for controlling that service. Figure 8-3 indicates that a variety of strategies are in use. No particular strategy seems superior to the others; the important point is that the network manager should have the authority to purchase needed management hardware and software and control the configuration of the LAN or LANs.

# Network Management Systems

## Architecture of a Network Management System

In the first section in this chapter, we looked at the general functional areas encompassed by network management. In the second section, we examined tools for LAN management. Each of these functional areas and each of these tools can help the network manager operate the network, maintain high availability and low response time, and evaluate network behavior to plan for future

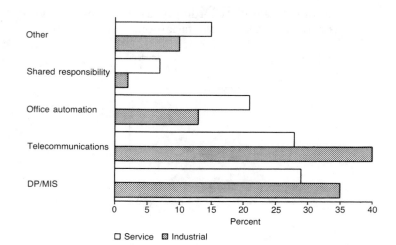

**Figure 8-3** Internal LAN management responsibility. *(Source: The Diebold Group, March 1988.)*

network growth. The difficulty faced by the network manager is the very diversity of these tools. For example, if an installation contains a number of LANs, each of these may be from a different vendor, requiring its own operator interface and training for the LAN management package supplied with the network. In addition, if the organization also controls one or more wide area networks, these too will require management. As networks become more complex and more indispensable to business operations, a more powerful and flexible approach is needed.

From the user's point of view, the best approach would be a set of tools for network management that is integrated as follows:

- A single operator interface with a powerful but user-friendly set of commands for performing most or all network management tasks.

- A minimal amount of separate equipment. That is, most of the hardware and software required for network management is incorporated into the existing user equipment.

We will refer to a system that provides this integration as a *network management system*[1]. A network management system consists of incremental hardware and software additions implemented among existing network components. The software used in accomplishing the network management tasks resides in the host computers and communications processors (e.g., front-end

---

[1] The terminology in this field is far from uniform. In particular, the term *network management system* has been used for a wide range of products, including network technical control systems, network monitoring systems, and even small collections of component-level technical control and performance monitoring equipment. With the increasing availability of the type of product described in this section and with the advent of standards, as discussed later in this chapter, the term is increasingly reserved for the more powerful capability discussed in this section.

processors and network interface units). A network management system views the entire network as a unified architecture, with addresses and labels assigned to each point and the specific attributes of each element and link known to the system. The active elements of the network provide regular feedback of status information to the network control center.

Figure 8-4 shows the architecture of a network management system. Each network node contains a collection of software devoted to the network management task, referred to in the diagram as a network management entity (NME). Each NME performs the following tasks:

- Collects statistics on communications and network-related activities.
- Stores statistics locally.
- Responds to commands from the network control center, including commands to transmit collected statistics to the network control center, change a parameter (e.g., a timer used in a transport protocol), provide status information (e.g., parameter values or active links), and generate artificial traffic to perform a test.

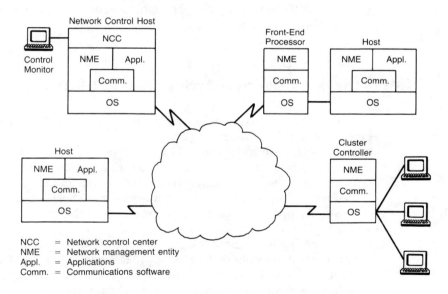

**Figure 8-4** Elements of a network management system.

At least one host in the network is designated as the network control host. In addition to the NME software, the network control host has a collection of software called the network control center (NCC). The NCC includes an operator interface so that an authorized user can manage the network. The NCC responds to user commands by displaying information, issuing commands to NMEs throughout the network, or both. This communication is carried out with an application-level network management protocol that uses the communications architecture in the same fashion as any other distributed application.

Several observations are in order:

1. Because the network management software relies on the host operating system and the communications architecture, most offerings to date are designed for use on a single vendor's equipment. In a network of personal computers, a number of LAN network management packages will tie together personal computers from a number of vendors. Standards in this area are still immature, but in the next few years, we should see the emergence of standardized network management systems designed to manage a multiple-vendor network.

2. As depicted in Figure 8-4, the network control center communicates with and controls what are essentially software monitors in other systems. The architecture can be extended to include technical control hardware and specialized performance monitoring hardware as well.

3. For maintaining high availability of the network management function, two or more network control centers are used. In normal operation, one of the centers is idle or simply collecting statistics, while the other is used for control. If the primary network control center fails, the backup system can be used.

## IBM Network Management Architecture and NetView

As part of its systems network architecture (SNA), IBM has incorporated the elements of a network management architecture. As the types of networks built on SNA have grown in size and complexity and have come to include non-IBM equipment, the software tools for network management have undergone a similar evolution, culminating in the 1986 announcement of NetView, NetView/PC, and open network management. The IBM approach is a bold one. Simply put, IBM wants to provide the single, unifying framework into which all other network management products feed and from which all the equipment in a user's network can be controlled.

It is useful to examine the IBM approach for two reasons. First, the range of capabilities in the IBM scheme provides a good idea of the types of tools desirable in a network management system. Second, the IBM scheme is the most widely used network management system. Because it is linked to SNA, IBM's network management scheme is quickly spreading into customer SNA environments; furthermore, IBM has published specifications that allow other vendors to interface their network management gear to an IBM host-based network management controller. Thus, implementations of the IBM approach have proliferated.

We look first at the various aspects of network management under IBM's scheme and then at the products from which a network management system can be constructed.

## Network Management Categories

As we have seen, network management covers many functions that are necessary to manage a communications network. SNA network management comprises the following major categories:

- Problem management
- Change management
- Configuration management
- Performance and accounting management

Table 8-3 provides a brief definition of each category, and Figure 8-5 shows the key subtasks in each category.

**TABLE 8-3**  Elements of IBM's Network Management Architecture

| | |
|---|---|
| Problem management | The function of dealing with a problem from its detection through its resolution. The steps of problem management are (1) determination, (2) diagnosis, (3) bypass and recovery, (4) resolution, and (5) tracking and control. |
| Change management | The planning, control, and application of changes (additions, deletions, and modifications) to the resources of a network. |
| Configuration management | The facilities and processes necessary to plan, develop, operate, and maintain an inventory of information system resources, attributes, and relationships. |
| Performance and accounting management | The process of quantifying, measuring, reporting, and controlling the usage, responsiveness, availability, and cost of a network. |

*Problem management* is the process of managing network problems from initial detection through final resolution. The initial step is problem *determination:* the automated or manual process that detects a hardware, software, or firmware component problem. *Diagnosis* determines the problem's cause. *Bypass* and *recovery* provide either a partial or a complete bypass until final resolution can be enacted. *Resolution* is the corrective measure taken to eliminate the detected problem or an impending one. *Tracking and control* records the history of the problem.

Each node (host, front-end processor, or cluster controller) in the network is responsible for its own error analysis to determine whether a problem exists and whether local recovery action can be performed. This responsibility extends to controlling line monitors attached to lines emanating from the node. If a problem cannot be resolved locally, the node sends an alert signal to the network control center software to indicate that a component in the network is

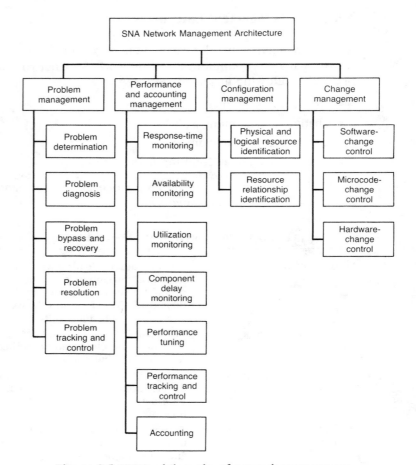

**Figure 8-5** IBM's philosophy of network management.

unavailable and that intervention is required. For example, the network control center may reroute all virtual circuits that pass through the affected area.

*Change management* applies to additions, deletions, and modifications to networked hardware, software, and microcode resources. *Software-change control* documents and controls activities such as installation, removal, modification, and temporary program fixes. *Microcode-change control* keeps tabs on microcode installation, the removal of temporary fixes, engineering changes, and feature changes. *Hardware-change control* notes hardware installation, removal, engineering changes, and other updates.

*Configuration management* is concerned with the generation and maintenance of a configuration database that contains information on all physical and logical network resources and their relationships. *Physical and logical resource identification* records physical network resources, such as host computers, front-end processors, cluster controllers, modems, multiplexers, and protocol converters. Each resource is coded by categories such as line types, serial numbers, inventory numbers, telephone numbers, real and virtual memory allocations, and program numbers. The term *logical resource* refers to SNA-defined entities such as system services control points, physical units, and logical units. *Resource relationship identification* is the process of identifying and recording the physical and logical configuration of network resources.

*Performance and accounting management* quantifies, reports, and controls the utilization and charges associated with network components. *Response-time monitoring* measures end-user session response times and generates problem notifications if predetermined thresholds are exceeded. *Availability monitoring* reports component availability. *Utilization monitoring* keeps tabs on the utilization of network resources and the server; it generates an unsolicited problem notification if preset threshold values are exceeded. *Component delay monitoring* tracks critical component delays; it initiates an unsolicited problem notification if predetermined service levels are exceeded. *Performance tuning* is the process of modifying critical network performance parameters to improve throughput. *Performance tracking and control* is the process of recording and tracking performance events or alerts. *Accounting* records, allocates, and tracks network resources in an effort to properly allocate costs.

## NetView

To support all the tasks listed in Figure 8-5, IBM has developed a number of software and hardware tools that work with and in an SNA network. All of these were consolidated into a single product line with the introduction of NetView. The underlying theme of NetView is that a very sophisticated degree of network monitoring and control can be focused on a single location (operating on a mainframe local to that location), yet call on resources distributed throughout the network as "eyes" and "hands" to perform its functions. The NetView architecture is in general terms that of Figure 8-4. A network control center resides on a mainframe that communicates and controls network management software and hardware elements throughout the network.

NetView is intended to operate across multiple networks, where the networks may not all be SNA-based, but may include token ring LANs, X.25 packet-switching networks, and even non-IBM wide area networks. To that end, some interfaces and operating details of NetView have been published to permit other suppliers to build NetView handles and extensions into their products, so that those non-IBM products can be part of NetView's network management continuum. This concept is referred to as *open network management.*

One of the capabilities of this open system is NetView/PC, a software product that resides in an IBM personal computer or IBM PC-compatible product. NetView/PC makes it possible for the personal computer, despite running autonomous applications (from the mainframe perspective), to interface with the mainframe's network management capabilities and participate with the mainframe in the overall management of the network.

Figure 8-6 depicts the major software elements of NetView and NetView/ PC. The NetView software residing on the mainframe that acts as the network control center consists of the following key elements:

- *Control facility:* Provides the capability to operate the network. It uses NetView commands to control such network resources as modems and protocol converters.

- *Hardware monitor:* This is actually a software package that collects notifications of failures or significant events affecting physical network or computer resources. These notifications, as well as recommended actions, may be displayed.

- *Session monitor:* Collects session-related information on the resources of the logical components of the network, such as physical units (PUs), logical units (LUs), and system services control points (SSCPs). It includes measurements of response-time and session-failure data.

- *Status monitor:* Displays status information on network resources. It also automatically reactivates network resources following failures.

- *Help facilities:* Provided at several levels for commands, messages, and codes. Descriptions of displayed fields are included, and a systematic problem-solving facility guides the user through the various steps of particular network management tasks.

- *Customization facilities:* Permits a user to tailor NetView. Information not needed can be suppressed. Information can be changed to accommodate a user's procedures. Additional functions can be added to increase a user's network management capabilities.

The software just listed applies primarily to computer and data network management. In addition, an IBM host can contain software that specifically relates to the management of digital PBX and voice network resources. This latter software obtains data from the digital PBX through a NetView/PC package, described subsequently. The host software consists of the following:

- *Network billing system:* Provides the user with a clear accounting of PBX costs and usage categorized by department, long-distance carrier, and equipment.

- *Traffic engineering line organization system:* Allows the user to analyze call-detail records received from the PBX. It helps to determine cost-effective ways to configure a site's telecommunication network, both voice and data, and also helps identify such network problems as overcapacity, undercapacity, and isolated links.

- *Tariff database:* Provides tariff information for U.S. long-distance carriers.

The remaining NetView-related software resides in a personal computer and is referred to as NetView/PC. This software can be used for standalone network management. For example, NetView/PC can perform specific device tests locally and record the results in a local disk file. In addition, NetView/PC

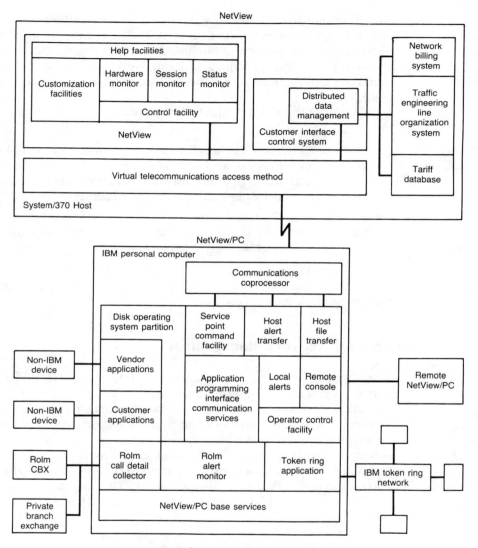

**Figure 8-6** NetView and NetView/PC.

can send information to NetView on a host, which can then take additional measures.

The two key applications that are part of NetView/PC deal with two IBM networking products: the token ring local area network and the Rolm CBX, which is a digital PBX provided by the Rolm subsidiary of IBM.

The token ring application records network errors in an event log. Other network events, such as stations joining and withdrawing from the LAN, can be recorded in the log to assist the user in problem determination. Logged events may be displayed and printed for a specified station or period of time. Alert conditions are immediately signaled to the operator by audible alarms and highlighted indicators on the display. At the same time, an alert message can be transmitted to NetView in the host. The token ring application can operate as a standalone application. In addition, NetView/PC's remote-console support allows an operator at a remote PC to use the local token ring network manager.

Control of the Rolm digital PBX is provided by two software programs in the PC:

- *Call detail collector:* Gathers information from as many as 10 PBXs or non-Rolm PBXs equipped with special software. The program provides site collection, multisite polling, and host transfer of data, which may be used for billing, capacity planning, and network analysis.

- *Alert monitor:* Detects problem conditions, gathers error and alarm information from the PBXs, and translates the information into different categories of alerts based on their degree of severity.

NetView/PC also provides documented software interfaces so that non-IBM vendors and customers can write additional network management applications and link these to the NetView scheme.

## Standards for Network Management

The International Standards Organization (ISO) has developed a standard for network management, referred to as the management framework. It specifies the functions to be performed by a network management system and defines protocols for the exchange of commands, responses, and measurement data. Although this standard is relatively new and no products are yet available, it is serving as the basis for network management systems being developed by computer and local area network vendors and so will assume increasing importance in the marketplace. Also, as with the IBM architecture, a review of the ISO framework provides a useful checklist of network management system features.

### Network Management Categories

The ISO network management framework comprises the following major categories:

- Fault management
- Accounting management
- Configuration and name management
- Performance management
- Security management

Table 8-1 provided a brief definition of each category. Note the similarity with the IBM scheme, which was shown in Table 8-3. This is reassuring because it indicates that the key functions of network management are reasonably well defined.

*Fault management* facilities allow network managers to detect problems in the communications network and the OSI environment. These facilities include mechanisms for the detection, isolation, and correction of abnormal operation in any network component or in any of the OSI layers. Fault management provides procedures to

1. Detect and report the occurrence of faults. These procedures allow a system to notify its manager of the detection of a fault, using a standardized event reporting protocol.
2. Log the received event report. This log can then be examined and processed.
3. Schedule and execute diagnostic tests, trace faults, and initiate the correction of faults. These procedures may be invoked as a result of the analysis of the event log.

*Accounting management* facilities allow a network manager to determine and allocate costs and charges for the use of network resources. Accounting management provides procedures to

1. Inform users of costs incurred, using event reporting and data manipulation software.
2. Set accounting limits for the use of managed resources.
3. Combine costs when multiple resources are used to achieve needed communication.

*Configuration and name management* facilities allow network managers to exercise control over the configuration of the network components and OSI layer entities. Configurations may be changed to alleviate congestion, isolate faults, or meet changing user needs. Configuration management provides procedures to

1. Collect and disseminate data concerning the current state of resources. Changes that are locally initiated or changes due to unpredicted occurrences are communicated to management facilities by standardized protocols.
2. Set and modify parameters related to network components and OSI layer software.
3. Initialize and close down managed objects.
4. Change the configuration.
5. Associate names with objects and sets of objects.

*Performance management* facilities provide the network manager with the ability to monitor and evaluate the performance of network and layer entities. Performance management provides procedures to

1. Collect and disseminate data concerning the current level of performance of resources.
2. Maintain and examine performance logs for purposes such as planning and analysis.

*Security management* facilities allow a network manager to manage services that protect the access to communications resources. Security management provides support for the management of

1. Authorization facilities
2. Access control
3. Encryption and key management
4. Authentication
5. Security logs

## OSI Management Architecture

The architectural model of OSI systems participating in network management is shown in Figure 8-7. The system on the left functions as a network control center; the system on the right is representative of other nodes in the network. The key elements of this architecture follow:

- *Network management application (NMA):* This application provides the mechanism for the human network manager to read or alter data, control the network, and access reports. This application could be a very simple command interpreter or an expert system requiring very little interaction with the network manager. This application is present in the network control center.

- *System management application process (SMAP):* This is the local software in a system that is responsible for executing the network management functions on a single system (e.g., host or front-end processor). It has access to an overall view of system parameters and capabilities and therefore can manage all aspects of the system and coordinate with the network management application and SMAPs on other systems.

- *System management application entity (SMAE):* This application is responsible for communication with other nodes, especially with the network management application in the network control center host. Standardized application-level protocols are used for this purpose.

- *Layer management entity (LME):* Software is embedded into each layer of the OSI architecture to provide network management functions specific to that layer.

- *Management information base (MIB):* The collection of information at each node pertaining to network management.

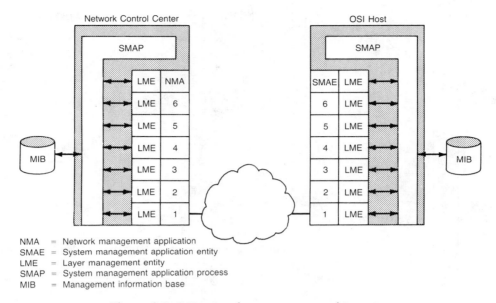

NMA   = Network management application
SMAE  = System management application entity
LME   = Layer management entity
SMAP  = System management application process
MIB   = Management information base

**Figure 8-7**  OSI network management architecture.

This structure is essentially the same as that depicted in Figure 8-4, with more detail. By defining these particular elements, ISO has created a structure within which standards relating to network management can be developed.

## Choosing a Network Management System

Customers' increasing reliance on computers from multiple vendors—coupled with the need to manage a growing variety of networks, including local area and wide area networks—makes the concept of a single, unified network management system attractive. The diversity of hardware, however, makes a unified network management difficult to achieve.

Two approaches are possible for the manager. First, and most obvious, is NetView. This is a sound choice for an SNA-based network. Even if the configuration includes a number of non-IBM devices, NetView is well established, and a number of vendors provide software to interface to NetView.

In a non-IBM environment, the logical choice would appear to be the ISO network management standard. This standard is still evolving, however, and few products exist. In anticipation of the ISO standard, a number of vendors have produced proprietary schemes that are intended to be predecessors of ISO network management and that allow migration with relative ease. Most notable of these are the offerings of AT&T and DEC. The IBM, AT&T, and DEC offerings are compared in Table 8-4, which also shows two other representative products.

**TABLE 8-4** Integrated Network Management Systems

| Vendor | Architecture | Product | Operation Platform | Database | Interfaces |
|---|---|---|---|---|---|
| AT&T Basking Ridge, N.J. | OSI-based UNMA, SNA connectivity | Accumaster Integrator, StarKeeper Network Management System, Dataphone II Level IV System Controller, Accumaster Trouble Tracker, Acculink Data Communication Services, Accunet T1.5 Information Manager | AT&T 3B2, Sun Microsystems, Inc. workstation, Unix V operating system | Central repository integrates and displays information | Cincom UNMA for SNA information—physical and logical components; OSI-based UNMA interface via NMP and NMP-based alarm interface; future single command language |
| Cincom Systems, Inc. Cincinnati | SNA, UNMA/OSI connectivity | Net/Master, Info/Master shell for custom inventory and accounting applications | MVS, MVS/XA, MVX/ESA, VM, VM/XA, VSE, NIDOS and MSP operating systems; customizable NCL APIs; ISPF-compatible user interface, color graphic split-screen windows, automated, modifiable network control center help desk | Flat file and external VSAM; automated rule-based expert system foundation; central repository integrates all screen information | NetView/PC and UNMA/Accumaster via customizable and easily modified NCL 4GL shell; Net/Master interface with Accumaster Integrator |
| Digital Equipment Corp. Maynard, Mass. | DNA-DECnet/OSI based EMA; TCP/IP, SNA connectivity | DECnet Phase IV: Network Control Program (NCP), Network Management Listener, Loopback Mirror, Event Logger; Network Management Control Center/DECnet Monitor (NMCC/DECnet Monitor) ($15,000); NMCC/VAX Ethernet Network Integrity Monitor (Ethernim) ($10,000); LAN Traffic Monitor (LTM) ($5,000); Remote System Manager (RSM) ($600 to $17,500); Remote Bridge Management System (RBMS) ($2,500); Terminal Server Management (TSM) ($1,000) | VMS, Ultrix, RSTS, RSX, MS/DOS operating systems; Advanced color graphics VMS/DECnet workstations; C- and VMS-compatible language programming; NICE protocol; X11 DECWindows | Relational/distributed, indexed, flat file; customizable 4GL programs; dynamic routing and automated configuration where practical | X.25, 802.3; Timeplex, Inc., StrataCom, Inc. and Digital Communications Associates, Inc. T-1 multiplexers; Codex Corp. modems and multiplexers; Siemens AG and TSB International, Inc. PBXs; Vitalink Communications Corp. LAN Bridges |

(continued)

| Vendor | Architecture | Product | Operation Platform | Database | Interfaces |
|---|---|---|---|---|---|
| Hewlett-Packard Co. Palo Alto, Calif. | OSI-based OpenView, SNA connectivity | Wide-area networks: NS Diagnostic Monitor (HP-3000), Data Line Monitor, Node Management Services Configurator (NMMGR), NetAssure, NS Performance Monitor, Network Command Interpreter (NetC), In-service Transmission Impairment Measurement Set (ITIMS) Manager, Local-area networks: Bridge Manager, 4972A LAN Analyzer, Business Systems Plus | Core OpenView (Microsoft Corp.-based) Windows on color HP Vectra PC (IBM Personal Computer AT-compatible); Network topology display, menu-driven application command executions, on-line help facilities | NetCI customizable shell automates command execution (CList/NCL-comparable) | X.25 and HP Private Packet Network; Dial-up, point-to-point and leased lines; FiberCom, Inc. (FDDI); Ungermann-Bass, Inc. local-area networks; Microtronics Systems, Ltd. matrix switches and T-1 multiplexers; Telindus modems, multiplexers and PADs |
| IBM Armonk, N.Y. | SNA, OSI connectivity | NetView; NetView/PC (DOS, OS/2, Personal Computer AT, Personal System/2); NetView Performance Monitor (NPM); Distribution Manager; Network Asset Manager; Info Manager | System/370—3270 terminal, DOS, OS/2 Extended Edition | Repository database not yet fully integrated | NetView/PC or non-IBM custom options |

| Vendor | Fault Management | Configuration Management | Performance Management | Accounting Management | Security Management | Pricing |
|---|---|---|---|---|---|---|
| AT&T Basking Ridge, N.J. | Physical and logical management and session control; dynamic element control and attribute reconfiguration; integrates problem ID, isolation, resolution; filtered SNA alarm, alert monitoring, reporting | Dynamic voice and data, and physical and logical reconfiguration capabilities now in development. Configuration is integrated with all functional modules. Real-time modification utilizes relational database; IBM command automation based on OSI data model; dynamic PU configuration via optional asset management in development | Comprehensive voice management; good for data management; response time monitoring | OSI application under development; OSI interface-driven | Through ACF2 or RACF only for SNA | $100,000 to $300,000 |

**TABLE 8-4** *(cont.)*

| Vendor | Fault Management | Configuration Management | Performance Management | Accounting Management | Security Management | Pricing |
|---|---|---|---|---|---|---|
| Cincom Systems, Inc. Cincinnati | Filtered alert and alarm monitoring and reporting; automated and integrated trouble ticketing; natural language diagnostics; automated problem resolution | Configuration and inventory integrated with all functional modules; multidomain monitoring and connectivity; real-time attributes modification can link or bypass database; CList/REXX command automation; dynamic PU configuration via optional asset management | Session monitor for response and utilization; automated availability monitoring via rule-based status; component delay notifications | Customized modules through Info/Master shell | RACF, ACF2, Top/Secret interfaces; network applications access control; command and partition operator authorization; combined network access log | $56,000 each year for three years, or $133,000 one-time charge |
| Digital Equipment Corp. Maynard, Mass. | User-defined alarms and alerts threshold filtration; real-time historic event report logging; test tracking and fault isolation to OSI layer, component level; automatic recovery with fault correction; decentralized but integrated view of topology | Displays mapped topology and graphs status statistics; on-line real-time attribute modification; self configuring nodes, bridges, routers; automatic database entry with reference editor | Packet size- and distance-based response time monitoring; node and resource availability cycle analysis; bandwidth utilization graphics; real-time performance tuning; capacity and contingency planning over network life cycle | Access and availability connect costing; node-resident counter reconciliation | Network segment access; denial authorization; password, proxy, dialback user account confirm; systems-application access control via account, node, classification; DEC's Ethernet Secure Network Controller encryption; native OS security log maintenance | $18,500 for local net package (includes LTM, RBMS, Ethernim, TSM components); $33,500 for package with wide-area network capability, including local net package plus DECnet Monitor, wide-area net capability alone with DECnet Monitor costs $15,000 |
| Hewlett-Packard Co. Palo Alto, Calif. | Monitors status of networked HP 3000s over wide- and local area networks (NS Diagnostic Monitor); fault isolation for telecommunications lines and devices (ITIMS); testing and troubleshooting analog lines (Data Line Monitor); local net troubleshooting and fault isolation (Bridge Manager); Ethernet/802.3 fault isolation (HP 4972A LAN Analyzer) | Displays topological map of networked HP 3000s (NS Diagnostic Monitor); data communications inventory and configuration for HP 3000 (Node Management Services); Inventory | Telecommunications line and device analysis (ITIMS); statistical information collected on links (NS Performance Monitor) | Accounting management for X.25 private packet networks | Safeguard local net security (Bridge Manager) | Vectra Windows user interface $6,000 to $8,000; Developers Kit $1,000; Status/Diagnostic Monitor $6,000; Performance Monitor $6,000; Network Command Interpreter bundled free; ITIMS $1,000 to $2,000; Bridge Manager $2,500 maximum |

| Vendor | Fault Management | Configuration Management | Performance Management | Accounting Management | Security Management | Pricing |
|---|---|---|---|---|---|---|
| IBM Armonk, N.Y. | Comprehensive SNA alarm and alert monitoring; upstream SNA device monitoring and downstream control; trouble-ticketing for problem resolution via Info Manager. Increased voice and data systems alert and accounting management | Change management via microcode download; real-time modifications bypass database; CList/REXX command automation; dynamic PU configuration via optional asset management | Performance Monitor 3270-oriented; Network Logical Data Monitor session monitor thresholds indicating availability; non-SNA devices require NetView/PC or custom-developed interfaces | (Network Assessment Management and NetView Performance Monitor); SNA device support (controllers, printers, modems and data service unit/channel service units); expanded PBX and voice support | Uses RACF/ACF2 | $48,000 each year for three years or $233,000 one-time charge. |

ACF2 = Advanced communications function 2
API = Application program interface
CList/REXX = Command list/IBM computer language
FDDI = Fiber distributed data interface
4GL = Fourth-generation language
ISPF = Interactive system productivity facility
NCL = Network control language
NCP = Network control program
NICE = Network input control entity
NMP = Network management protocol
RACF = Resource access control facility
UNMA = Unified network management architecture

Source: *Network World*, June 19, 1989.

Figure 8-8 projects the popularity of these various approaches in Fortune 1000 companies by the mid-1990s. Although NetView is expected to remain dominant in IBM sites, ISO and compatible network management schemes will flourish. Ultimately, the ISO standard will be the most widely used network management scheme.

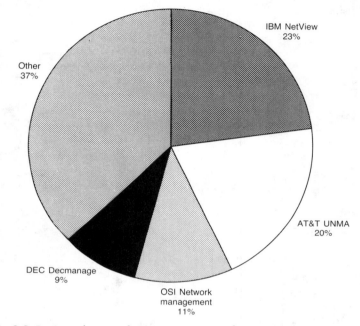

**Figure 8-8** Projected network management products in Fortune 1000 sites in 1995. *(Source: Forrester Research Inc., Cambridge, MA, July 1988.)*

# *Case Study 6*
# Ohio University[2]

## The Basic Network Approach

Ohio University has developed a large and complex configuration of LANs to serve its user community. The approach taken by the University reveals the benefits of a systematic approach to network design and the use of a limited number of homogeneous building blocks. The architecture encompasses hardware, protocol, and software considerations that are applicable to industrial as well as educational institutions.

---

[2] This case study is based on material in T. Reid, "Managing Ethernet Sprawl," *Data Communications,* May 1989.

The University, rather early on, made the decision to base their networking strategy on the use of Ethernet. This type of LAN is attractive for a number of reasons:

- The baseband technology is relatively simple (compared to broadband) and can be installed by an electrician rather than a specialist.
- Ethernet technology is one of the oldest LAN technologies. It is proven, well-understood, and provided by a number of vendors.
- Because a number of vendors provide the basic Ethernet logic on chips, Ethernet is one of the most cost-effective solutions.

All of these reasons now apply to IEEE 802.3 as well. When the network was initially installed, however, only a few of the large number of Ethernet vendors also supported the similar 802.3 specification. Ethernet is still strongly supported, and Ohio University sees no immediate need to migrate to the 802.3 standard.

Ohio University needed to support a relatively large number of users spread over many buildings on a large campus. It was clear that a single Ethernet bus would be inadequate to span the distances involved. The Ethernet specification allows the use of any number of repeaters, as long as no more than four repeaters are cascaded between any two stations. The specification also defines the concept of a remote repeater (Figure 2-12). The most common remote repeater link consists of a pair of optical fiber cables, one for transmission in each direction.

The University developed a very simple architecture based on the use of a central backbone Ethernet in the building designated as the network center. Repeaters were attached between this central backbone and 35 of the 110 on-campus buildings. Figure 8-9a shows the basic architecture. Each of the remote sites, designated a minihub, services equipment in a single building or a cluster of buildings. Thus, the architecture is a star arrangement, with a central backbone network and a number of minihub networks attached to the backbone. With this arrangement, the path between any two stations passes through no more than two repeaters (four half-repeaters).

## Internetworking Strategy

### Increasing Campus Network Capacity

The architecture described so far is logically a single Ethernet system. Thus, a packet transmitted on any one Ethernet segment appears, by way of repeaters, on every segment, and only one station on the entire network of segments can successfully transmit at a time. Thus, a total capacity of 10 Mbps is available to service all the stations on all the LANs. As the number of users grows, and as the amount of use by each user grows, this capacity is strained.

The University chose a straightforward way of nearly doubling the available capacity without changing transmission technology and without a

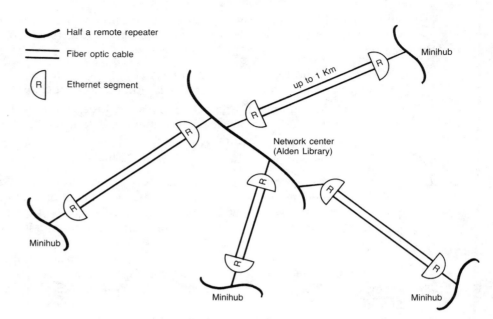

*(a)  Extended Ethernet using repeaters.*

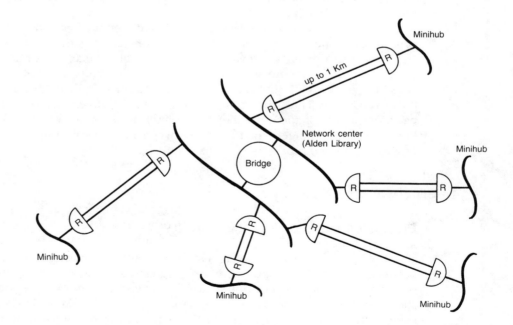

*(b)  Extended Ethernet using repeaters and a bridge.*

**Figure 8-9**  Campus Ethernet internetwork.

dramatic reconfiguration. As shown in Figure 8-9b, the backbone segment becomes two backbones connected by an Ethernet bridge. Recall that the use of a bridge does not introduce any new protocols and that it is essentially transparent to the attached stations (Figure 6-3). That is, each station continues to have a unique address and any station can address a packet to any other station just as before.

Approximately 1.5 Mbps can pass through the bridge between the two segments. Thus, the total network yields a theoretical available capacity of 18.5 Mbps (at full bridge utilization), rather than the 10-Mbps limit of a single Ethernet. To see this, suppose that the bridge is removed and the two network center segments are isolated from each other. Stations on each half of the cut configuration have a capacity of 10 Mbps, for a total capacity of 20 Mbps. However, each station can only send packets to stations on the same side of the cut. With the bridge in place, any station can transmit to any other station. If the bridge is fully utilized, it will be pumping packets from one Ethernet to the other at the rate of 1.5 Mbps. This traffic is duplicated. That is, 1.5 Mbps of traffic is generated on one side and repeated on the other. Therefore, the total capacity for traffic is 20 minus 1.5, which equals 18.5 Mbps.

Effective use of this configuration requires thoughtful load balancing. Fortunately, the following situations hold:

- The data communications requirements at Ohio University can be roughly divided into two classes: administrative and academic, and these two parts are approximately equal in load generation.

- Most of the traffic is between stations within the same class.

Each minihub services primarily one of the two classes.

These facts suggest an obvious solution. Using repeaters, attach all the administrative minihubs to one of the segments in the network center, and attach all the academic minihubs to the other segment in the network center. Because the amount of traffic between classes is significantly less than the amount of traffic within each class, the load on the bridge is kept to reasonable proportions and does not create a bottleneck.

An extra bonus of the dual-segment Ethernet design is its capability to isolate network faults at an additional level. If a malfunctioning Ethernet controller on the academic side of the network is jabbering (that is, transmitting packets in an uncontrolled, continuous fashion, causing jamming on both the academic side and across the bridge), the bridge can simply be told to stop routing traffic. This quickly cuts in half the number of clients being affected by the disruption, and makes troubleshooting easier.

At present, this architecture, together with some additional links mentioned in the following section, is sufficient to serve most of the needs of the university. Ohio University plans to ultimately replace the two network center Ethernet segments with a 100-Mbps FDDI LAN. This will provide much greater capacity for linking the stations scattered throughout the campus, but requires changing the architecture in only a single location! It is expected that the Ethernet minihubs will continue to provide adequate capacity to their direct users for quite some time. Meanwhile, when the total campus-wide load exceeds 18.5 Mbps, a change in the network center will cleanly and simply solve the capacity problem.

## Wide Area Extensions

Ohio University has five regional campuses located across southeastern Ohio in a 90-mile radius around the main campus at Athens. In keeping with their main-campus configuration, the university has come up with an architecture that is simple, uniform, and compatible with the central campus architecture; it also provides communications both within each regional campus and among all campuses.

Figure 8-10 illustrates the architecture. Each regional campus is served by a minihub. Each minihub is connected to the main campus by a pair of remote bridges (see Figure 6-4). Each pair of remote bridges is connected by a 56-Kbps link provided by a university-owned private microwave system. For emergency backup, an alternative path through 9.6-Kbps modems using dial-up telephone lines is in place. Thus, if the microwave system fails, a limited amount of connectivity can be supported using the public telephone network. If the single 56-Kbps link becomes saturated, it is possible to install an additional 56-Kbps link between the same two bridges. The units use multiple links simultaneously, load balancing between them automatically.

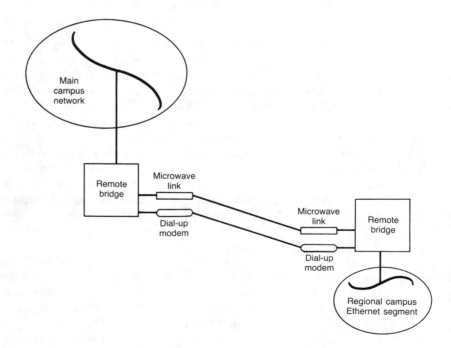

**Figure 8-10** Regional interconnection.

This scheme extends the transparent, seamless interconnection of devices to the regional campuses. In effect, the regional networks and the central system perform as a single Ethernet. Every station on the expanded network has a unique address, and any station can address any other station with no knowledge of the physical location of the other station. The consistent use of repeaters and bridges guarantees this transparency. Furthermore, the regional campuses are poised for expansion with no disruption or reconfiguration of the overall network. Any regional minihubs linked to the central network can become the central segment in a star-like expansion using repeaters and Ethernet segments, replicating the central campus architecture (Figure 8-9a). Indeed, any of the regional campuses can establish a two-segment backbone in the same manner as the central campus (Figure 8-9b). The same seamless interconnection exists no matter how much the remote network expands.

## Foreign Network Connection

There is also a requirement for connection to networks that are not part of the master Ethernet architecture and that are beyond the administrative control of the campus network managers. These include other university networks, which are controlled by various departments of other units, national shared networks, such as ARPANET, and outside information providers, such as CompuServe. All of these are viewed as foreign network connections. Once again, the managers have attempted to use simple, consistent mechanisms to achieve their objectives.

Two methods of connection to foreign networks are provided:

- *Terminal servers:* In this configuration, terminals attached to either network interface units or host systems on the network can connect to a terminal server. This approach was discussed in Chapter 5 and illustrated in Figure 5-6a. The terminal server provides a way to logically connect a user terminal to a port on a local node of an information provider (Figure 8-11a). In the case of Ohio University, the information provider is CompuServe. The local node is installed on the campus and has a 9.6-Kbps leased line into the CompuServe packet-switching network. The CompuServe node provides multiple asynchronous ports using the common RS-232C standard on the user side and performs packet assembly and disassembly functions on the CompuServe network side. As use of the network grows, so can the speed of the link and the number of ports supported by the node.

- *Routers:* More complex needs for host-to-host communications require closer links between the local network and foreign networks. For this purpose, Ohio University uses a router from Proteon Corp. The router connects to another router that is connected to both ARPANET and a supercomputer network managed by the state (Figure 8-11b). The routers can forward data units using the internet protocol that is part of the TCP/IP protocol suite and the internet capability that is part of DEC's proprietary networking architecture, DECnet.

## User Connection Options

In designing an expanded Ethernet configuration with foreign network connections, such as the Ohio University design, the nature of the user connections has an impact on both functionality and security. In what follows, we present the two connection options available to users, and focus on the implications of functionality. The issue of security is dealt with in the next subsection.

The two options for user connection are terminal server and host bus attachment. *Terminal servers* are network interface units that can support multiple terminals or personal computers functioning in a terminal-emulation mode, as was shown in Figure 5-6a and 5-6b. Figure 8-12a illustrates the attachment of terminal servers to the Ethernet system. Terminal servers allow a terminal to connect to another terminal port or to an asynchronous host port, as shown in Figure 5-6a. In this case, the server handles low-level conversion between dissimilar client ports. For instance, a terminal using a network RS-232C interface running at 19.2 Kbps with 8-bit data, no parity, and using

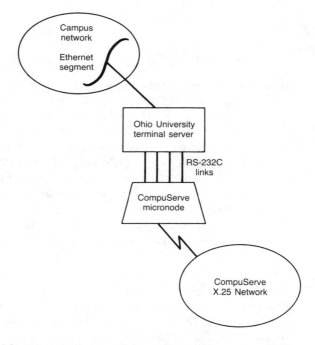

*(a) The RS-232C link provides controlled access to outside networks.*

**Figure 8-11** Foreign network connection.

X-on/X-off flow control can communicate with an IBM 3705 controller operating at only 1.2 Kbps with 7-bit data, odd parity, and no flow control.

The servers are also equipped with the TCP/IP protocols needed for remote access to host computers, including TCP, IP, and TELNET. Thus, from a terminal server, a user can log on to a host system on the extended Ethernet.

Some functional requirements can be satisfied only by *host bus attachment*. In this case, a user workstation or another computer connects to Ethernet through an interface unit. This allows host-to-host interaction at high speeds (Figure 8-12b).

## Security

With a large user community and an environment as diverse as this, security is of paramount importance. Administrators are understandably uneasy about the prospect of students gaining access to grade or test files, for example.

Security measures for the terminal server portion of the network present the least difficulties. The terminal server can be configured to restrict the computers which can be accessed. The table containing this information can be

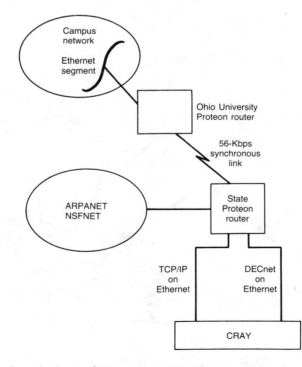

*(b)  The link to the State of Ohio supercomputer network is a bus-to-bus router.*

**Figure 8-11**  *(Cont.)*

read or altered only by a user with the appropriate password. For foreign network attachments using a terminal server, such as CompuServe, the terminal server that connects to the foreign node can screen incoming connection requests and allow access to the foreign network only to authorized users.

Direct bus attachments present greater difficulties. If a personal computer or workstation is directly connected to Ethernet, and if a user knows how to reload the software in the Ethernet interface board of the computer, there are opportunities for illicit activity. A risk exists because of the broadcast nature of a LAN: any packet can be received by all stations on the same LAN. Consider the following hacker's scenario:

1. Find an accessible, directly attached workstation.
2. Obtain Ethernet monitoring and diagnostic software (several packages are available on electronic bulletin boards).
3. Monitor network traffic by capturing a wide cross-section of packets.
4. Decode the contents of captured packets.
5. Identify addresses that conduct the type of business in which you are interested.
6. Set the diagnostic software to capture only packets addressed to targets of interest.

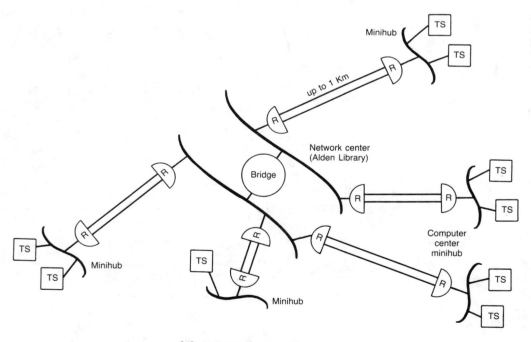

*(a) Support for terminal access.*

**Figure 8-12** Device attachment.

7. Decode captured passwords: Look for and find logon sequences and passwords for desired applications.

8. Extract and use information surreptitiously gathered.

This process can be executed by a moderately knowledgeable individual. One measure that would thwart such activity is encryption. However, Ohio University decided that applying encryption universally would be too expensive and too awkward.

The solution chosen by Ohio University has its own elements of expense and awkwardness, but like virtually every other aspect of the network design, it is simple, clean, and straightforward. Let us refer to the following as the core network:

- The two Ethernet segments that are in the network center and connected by a bridge
- All other Ethernet segments that connect to one of these two segments by means of a repeater

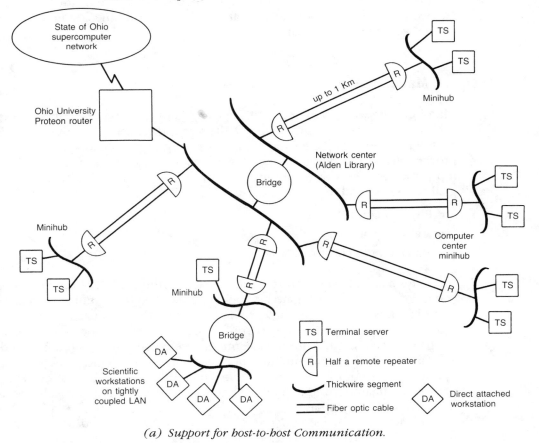

*(a) Support for host-to-host Communication.*

**Figure 8-12** *(Cont.)*

Network policy dictates that no workstations or other computers can be attached directly to the core network. Instead, such systems must be attached to an Ethernet segment, which in turn attaches to the core network by means of a bridge. All terminal servers are attached to the core network.

Now, the bridge becomes a line of defense. All traffic to and from a computer can still be observed on the core network because terminal users are on the core even though the computers they use are not on the core. The bridge can perform access control, however, and allow packets through the bridge only if they have an authorized combination of source and destination addresses. Within a subnetwork, a security risk remains because workstations and computers are all directly attached to the subnetwork. The subnetwork users are briefed regarding the inherent security risks to them of their direct attachment. As an added bonus, the total traffic on the core network is reduced.

In terms of foreign network connection, the routers to other networks also perform security functions to allow only authorized traffic to and from the university complex.

Another security feature is that all network management functions are password protected. Thus, the ordinary user cannot alter the configuration of the network or any of its parameters.

## Network Management

Although a network designed with such simplicity and homogeneity lends itself to effective network management, the size and complexity of the facility is such that there must be a substantial investment in network management to prevent chaos. The design of the network management system reflects three top priorities: network reliability, security, and versatility. To achieve these goals three general measures are used:

- Physical controls
- Software controls
- Management controls

In terms of *physical controls,* the focus is on the control of the minihubs and the network center segments. Each minihub, and the terminal servers attached to it, is housed in a single room. Lines from the terminal servers to the actual terminals pass from the controlled room to terminal locations outside the room. Each minihub room is alarmed, access controlled, and monitored. An alarm network for the minihubs notifies the network control center of out-of-tolerance conditions for temperature, humidity, smoke, loss of electrical power, and unauthorized entry. These signals tie into an alarm console that is monitored 24 hours a day.

The network management group uses a few *software control* tools to assist in network management. These support the capability to configure devices remotely, diagnose problems, and reboot terminal servers. Utilities exist for automating password changes, collecting server usage statistics, and reviewing server programmable read-only memory (PROM) revision levels.

Software is available to produce audit trails for all connections, disconnections, occurrences of queues, network faults, and other network events of significance. The audit trail helps determine needs for additional host computer connections, identify common client mistakes, and study other usage trends.

A LAN monitoring package provides cumulative information on overall Ethernet traffic. Reports, available in real time, provide information regarding peak throughput and long-term utilization trends. The information derived from the monitor helps determine expansion requirements, assists in deciding how to load balance the two halves of the core network, and generally provides a good picture of overall use and performance of the Ethernet.

The area of *management controls* encompasses the policies and procedures for managing the network, providing access, and procuring additional equipment. A central organization selects vendors to supply networking products.

The managers of the network recognized early on the value of limiting equipment to a single vendor. For example, early in their Ethernet experience, Ohio University mixed Ethernet components from two different vendors, each of which had certain strengths in terms of product features. However, this mix created chronic problems. Each manufacturer tended to quickly pinpoint the other manufacturer's equipment as the source of the intermittent (but severe) network disruptions that were being endured. Finally, for the sake of standardization, Ohio University eliminated all LAN equipment except that of a single vendor. The improvement in the reliability of the network was dramatic. Prior to the standardization, there was an average of three user-perceivable Ethernet disruptions per *day*. After standardization, the rate settled down to fewer than one disruption per *month*. This was not due to the fact that the remaining vendor was the only reliable one; it was due to the fact that there was a single point of responsibility for errors.

# Summary

As with security, the need for network management grows with the complexity and scale of a network. Network management covers a number of areas; the most important of these are

- *Fault management:* The most important function of network management is to maintain high availability of network services and resources. For this purpose, it is necessary to monitor the network for faults, isolate the faults, and recover from the faults.

- *Accounting management:* Divisions, cost centers, or projects may be charged for the use of network resources. Effective planning for network expansion requires an understanding of usage patterns. For both charges and planning, an accounting of network usage is needed.

- *Configuration and name management:* The resources of the network must be initialized and the intended relationships established for proper network operation.
- Performance monitoring: To provide efficient service with acceptable response times and throughput, it is necessary to monitor the performance of the network.
- Security management: The various schemes for security must be managed in a reliable and secure fashion.

Most LAN vendors and LAN software vendors provide network control center functions that encompass configuration, monitoring, and fault isolation. Although tools tailored to the LAN environment are clearly needed, the manager should plan for these as part of an integrated network management capability.

To satisfy all network management requirements in an efficient and practical fashion, a full-fledged network management system is needed. Software that provides network management functions should be embedded into the software suite of every node in the network. Then the software in one or more network nodes can control any hardware monitoring or controlling devices. A central network control center communicates with the network management software in all the other nodes and with any specialized hardware. A good example of a mature network management system is IBM's NetView. Recently, a standard for a network management system has been issued by ISO.

# Chapter 9

# LAN Selection

$S$O FAR, WE HAVE LOOKED AT THE REQUIREMENTS that LANs are intended to satisfy and the various hardware and software elements in the LAN market. The broad range of choices makes the selection of a LAN or set of LANs difficult. This chapter provides guidelines to aid in the selection process.[1] The suggestions are necessarily general because the requirements of each organization are unique. Nevertheless, it is hoped that this chapter will stimulate the decision maker to approach the problem in a systematic and comprehensive fashion.

We begin by looking at the overall process of planning a data processing and networking installation. We concentrate on an installation whose main goal is the provision of office automation tools. The same principles should apply in other contexts. The remainder of the chapter looks at the various elements in a selection decision.

## Planning a System[2]

In this section, we look at the process of translating the information needs of your organization into an overall plan for an office automation system. The process has three steps: (1) Define objectives, (2) Describe the system, and (3) Determine communications needs

As we proceed, you will see that the discussion is based on determining

---

[1] This chapter is a revision of material that appeared in F. Derfler and W. Stallings, *A Manager's Guide to Local Networks,* Prentice-Hall, 1983.

[2] The tables and many of the ideas in this section are adapted from an excellent publication by the National Bureau of Standards (now the National Institute of Standards and Technology), *Guidance on Requirements Analysis for Office Automation Systems,* NBS Special Publication 500-147, March 1987.

your data processing equipment needs. The focus of this book is on local area networks—purchasing them, incorporating them in your organization, and controlling their use and evolution. Because the principles are general, however, they are also useful in the broader context that includes devices that hook into the network.

## Define Objectives

The objectives for the installation or modification of an office automation system must relate to the information products of the organization. These products are the items used to gather, store, present, and analyze information needed for the operation of the organization. Table 9-1 provides a representative list of such products.

**TABLE 9-1**    Typical List of Information Products

| | |
|---|---|
| Correspondence | Letter |
| | Memorandum |
| | Message |
| Reports | Budget initiatives |
| | Case study |
| | Fiscal |
| | Management |
| | Material deficiency |
| | Personnel |
| | Project status |
| | Technical |
| | Trip |
| | Weekly activities |
| Documents | A76 cost comparison |
| | Action item list |
| | Administrative notice |
| | Change order |
| | Configuration change status report |
| | Contract funds status report (CFSR) |
| | Contract management systems checklist |
| | Cost estimate |
| | Data management report |
| | Delivery order |
| | Engineering change proposal (ECP) |
| | Environmental assessment |
| | Independent cost analysis (ICA) |
| | Invitation for bid |
| | Integrated logistics support plan (ILSP) |
| | Life-cycle cost study |
| | Military construction program reporting |
| | Procurement directive |
| | Procurement plan |
| | Program management directive |
| | Program management plan |

**TABLE 9-1** *(cont.)*

|  |  |
|---|---|
|  | Quarterly resources report |
|  | Request for proposal (RFP) |
|  | Sole source justification |
|  | Staff meeting agenda (and report) |
|  | Statement of work (SOW) |
|  | System safety program plan |
|  | Technical evaluation and report |
|  | Training plan |
| Forms | Data item description |
|  | Inspection and acceptance document |
|  | Military order |
|  | Personnel action request |
|  | Position description |
|  | Printing request |
|  | Purchase request |
|  | Report of survey |
|  | Security classification guide |
|  | Time card |
|  | Travel request |
|  | Work order request |
| Services | Electronic bulletin board |
|  | Information tracking |
|  | Response to inquiry |
|  | Technical assistance |
| Reviews and Briefings | Business strategy panel meeting |
|  | Command or senior officer briefing |
|  | Division advisory group (DAG) review |
|  | EEO review |
|  | Executive management review (EMR) |
|  | Financial management board review |
|  | Internal management review |
|  | Periodic program review |
|  | Program management review (PMR) |
|  | Quarterly financial review |
|  | Scientific advisory board (SAB) meeting |
| Audiovisual Aids | Briefing board |
|  | Briefing text |
|  | Graphic aid |
|  | Vugraph |
|  | 35mm slide |

By considering how these products are produced and used, you can probably see several ways to improve the productivity of your information workers. But first, you must be more specific. You must be able to answer in quantitative terms the question: What is the information movement and processing system supposed to do?

It is best to begin by defining some productivity goals. The goals must be quantitative and must relate to information creation, storage, transfer, and reporting. General categories include timeliness, responsiveness, convenience, and workload. The goals you set must be based on the situation you have today and where you think improvements are needed. For example, suppose it is important to get reports or documents quickly; also suppose that these documents are usually revised because of an internal review cycle. A productivity goal would be to reduce revision typing time. Another example: Only certain key professionals can produce briefing materials or reports, and this is draining too much of their time. A corresponding productivity goal would be to reduce the effort required of the professional staff during the information creation phase.

These goals should be as quantitative as possible. Think in terms of how many documents need to be produced by how many people, the time it should take to prepare charts, and so forth.

At this stage, don't limit the number of things you look at. Consider all your information products. Table 9-1 can be used as a checklist. Consider the feasibility and significance of your goals. Propose goals in practical areas where there is room for significant improvement. If certain activities are already accomplished efficiently, leave them be.

One particularly effective way of formulating goals is to survey the concerns of senior management. This has the added benefit of creating a climate in which reasonable and effective improvements will more readily receive management approval. For certain key information products, determine the concerns that management considers important. Table 9-2 presents a list of possible management concerns and goals. For example, if timeliness was identified as a primary concern for a key product, the suggested product goal may be to reduce delays in the preparation and distribution of information. If responsiveness was cited as a primary concern, the suggested product goal may be to reduce the amount of "telephone tag" among professionals.

**TABLE 9-2**   Key Product Goals

| Management Concern | Desired Goals |
| --- | --- |
| Timeliness | Reduce preparation delays |
| | Reduce distribution delays |
| Responsiveness | Reduce "telephone tag" |
| | Improve query response time |
| | Reduce float |
| Convenience | Improve information input/output methods |
| Efficient use of resources | Increase office automation system usage |
| | Improve training |
| | Reduce user resistance |
| Organizational effectiveness | Reduce need for reprocessing |
| | Reduce duplication of effort |
| | Provide access to organizational database |
| Managerial effectiveness | Improve decision-making process |
| | Improve quality of presentation |
| Cost of labor and overhead | Reduce costs, waste, and overtime |

From these product goals, it is possible to derive more specific system requirements that will guide product selection. Table 9-3 lists examples of system requirements for the product goals cited in Table 9-2.

**TABLE 9-3** Examples of System Requirements

---

Produce documents locally

Access or download data from organizational databases

Edit and revise documents easily

Transfer documents among offices within and outside the organization

Perform interactive file queries by office users

Send and receive messages electronically

Produce compound documents (text, spreadsheets, and graphics)

Perform "what if" scenarios quickly

Conferencing (by computer and telephone)

Output presentation and letter quality documents

Transfer word processing skills across offices

Send and receive documents by facsimile

Use electronic calendars and scheduling tools

Integrated, easy-to-use office automation systems

Train users to realize full capabilities of systems

Develop policies and procedures for system usage, information storage and disposition, security, and system operations

Streamline paper handling

Enable the staff to be responsible for administrative and operational needs of office information resources

---

## Describe the System

Now you have some specific goals. The next thing to do is to list some options for moving closer to achieving those goals. As a manager, you know that not all improvements come from buying equipment. Consider three interrelated methods of achieving improvement: organizational, procedural, and technological. Perhaps things are being done by the wrong group (organizational), or in the wrong way (procedural), or with inadequate equipment (technological). Table 9-4 gives some idea of how these three factors can be used to improve productivity.

These factors affect each other. A technological change may dictate an organizational change. For example, if it becomes quick and easy to produce charts using presentation software on a personal computer, perhaps the charts should be produced by the professional staff rather than a support group.

Our focus is technological. We need to determine what additional equipment can be beneficial. We can group our options into four categories: input,

**TABLE 9-4**   System Design Model

| Organizational | Procedural | Technological |
|---|---|---|
| Work group A will be responsible for initial compilation of budget data | All budget computations will be performed using spreadsheet software | Personal computers |
| Work group B will be responsible for researching program data | All intraoffice memos will be sent by electronic mail | Software applications including: word processing, spreadsheet, communications, and database management systems |
| Work group C will replace work group A in the review of key products relating to grant applications | Key products will be developed on personal computers and electronically transferred to support personnel for final processing | Laser printers and letter quality printers |
| Professional staff in work group C who are responsible for budget compilation will be reassigned to work group A | Support staff will be designated as product distributors | Electronic typewriter with OCR fonts |
|  | Final drafts will be microfilmed rather than filed | Minicomputer |
|  |  | Microfilm reader-printer |
|  | Training classes will be available to all personnel | Modems |
|  |  | Electronic messaging system |
|  | Policies on usage, information management (including storage and disposition), operation of systems, and security will be updated semiannually | Local area network and software support |

production, output, and distribution. Table 9-5 lists representative equipment in each category, together with a description of benefits and drawbacks and an estimate of productivity improvement. This will allow you to assess the impact of various pieces of equipment.

## Determine Communications Needs

You know what information equipment your organization has. You have tentatively decided what the creation, processing, and storage equipment should achieve in terms of productivity. The last element is the information movement equipment—the local area network. To be truly effective and efficient, your collection of equipment must become a system capable of moving information as well as creating, processing, and storing it. The process of selecting a LAN or a set of LANs begins with a specification of requirements. These boil down to two considerations: compatibility and capacity.

**TABLE 9-5**  Productivity Citings for Representative Equipment Types

**Input Phase**

| Equipment | Benefits | Drawbacks | Citings |
|---|---|---|---|
| Dictation | Input is four times faster than longhand<br>Transcription is twice as fast as reading longhand or shorthand<br>Any secretary can transcribe<br>Priority work can be handled<br>24-hour input is allowed | Clarity of thought and expression is required<br>Pre-organization of material by dictator is necessary<br>Many originators resist dictation | 6.25–12% time savings/day—Herbert M. Kaplan, *Words*, International Word Processing Association, June—July 1980, pp. 40–43 |
| Electronic typewriter with OCR font | Correction time is reduced<br>Input by OCR reader into production equipment is possible | No text editing is possible<br>No storage capacity is available<br>Input into production equipment is off-line | See optical character recognition citing |
| Optical character recognition | Every typewriter with an OCR font can be a low-level input device for text editing and data manipulation<br>Re-keyboarding of input text and data is eliminated<br>Production equipment is freed for word or data processing<br>Work distribution is enhanced | Generally only a limited number of fonts can be read<br>Scanning errors are possible<br>Specific input formats may be required<br>Accuracy depends upon ribbon, strike, paper, and other variables | 600% increase in throughput, Compuscan sales literature, AW-5B-018.0 |
| Personal (professional) terminal | Data entry, access, and retrieval time can be reduced<br>Paper and supplies can be saved through electronic capture of keystrokes<br>Can be expanded, reconfigured, or networked as applications expand and new requirements evolve | Training is required<br>CPU downtime can affect the use of the terminal<br>Response degradation may occur during peak periods | 50% productivity rise, Emerick G. Zouks, *Business Week*, April 7, 1980, pp. 81–82 |

*(continued)*

**TABLE 9-5** *(cont.)*
**Production Phase**

| Equipment | Benefits | Drawbacks | Citings |
|---|---|---|---|
| Blind automatic word processor | Correction time is reduced<br><br>Light-change text editing is handled | Text editing functions are limited<br><br>Large amounts of text cannot be manipulated<br><br>Storage may be limited | Average 48–69% productivity improvement if used for original and revision typing; average 69–98% if used for revision only; NARS standards |
| Standalone display text editors | Extensive text editing is easily handled<br><br>Input and formatting is facilitated by a CRT<br><br>Saves paper and supplies through electronic capture of keystrokes | Some are unprogrammable<br><br>Large databases may not be manipulated<br><br>Storage may be limited | Average 75–133% productivity improvement if used for original and revision typing; average 104–181% if used for revision only; NARS standards |
| Shared logic word processor | Extensive text editing is easily handled<br><br>Input and formatting is facilitated by a CRT<br><br>Saves paper and supplies through electronic capture of keystrokes<br><br>Different tasks may be performed at the same time<br><br>Some are programmable by the user | CPU downtime can be a problem<br><br>Specially trained personnel may be necessary to administer the system<br><br>Response degradation may occur during peak periods<br><br>System backup may be limited | Average 84–89% productivity improvement if used for original and revision typing; average 115–122% if used for revision only; NARS standards |
| Minicomputer | Can be expanded, reconfigured, or networked as applications expand and new requirements evolve<br><br>Performs many different tasks at the same time<br><br>Can support simultaneous users<br><br>Is programmable<br><br>Paper and supplies can be saved through electronic capture of keystrokes | Early obsolescence on large investment is a risk<br><br>System backup may be limited<br><br>CPU downtime can be a problem<br><br>Response degradation may occur during peak periods | Same statistics as for shared logic word processors<br><br>Data processing figure totally dependent on each application |

| Equipment | Benefits | Drawbacks | Citings |
|---|---|---|---|
| Data processing system | Handles many applications<br>Is programmable<br>Can be expanded, reconfigured, or networked as applications expand and new requirements evolve<br>Performs many different tasks at the same time<br>Can support a large number of users<br>Handles large amounts of text or data | CPU downtime can be a problem<br>Specially trained personnel may be necessary to administer the system<br>May be susceptible to response degradation during peak periods<br>System backup may be limited<br>Techniques and procedures usually are alien to the office environment | Same statistics as for shared logic word processors<br>Data processing figure totally dependent on each application |

**Output Phase**

| Equipment | Benefits | Drawbacks | Citings |
|---|---|---|---|
| Word processing impact printer | High quality print is produced<br>Carbon copies can be created<br>Automatic single sheet feeder or continuous form paper may be used | Changing printwheels can be time-consuming<br>Inserting paper may be required | 15 to 55 characters per second burst speed, *Datapro Reports on Word Processing*, April 1980.<br>148–533% faster than electric typewriter capability |
| Word processing nonimpact printer | High quality print is produced<br>Automatically feeds paper<br>Typestyles are changed electronically within the printer | Usually prints no carbon copies | 77 to 92 characters per second burst speed, *Datapro Reports on Word Processing*, April 1980<br>770–918% faster than electric typewriter capability |
| Data processing printer | Prints at high speeds<br>Carbon copies can be created<br>Usually incorporates an automatic paper feed | Print quality is usually unacceptable for word processing output | 40–120 characters per second (matrix), *Auerbach Computer Technology Reports #31*, 1978, p. 13<br>1184–3554% faster than electric typewriter capability<br>150–2000 lines per minute (line), *Auerbach Computer Technology Reports #31*, 1978, p. 13<br>4813–6417% faster than electric typewriter capability |

*(continued)*

**TABLE 9-5** *(cont.)*

| Equipment | Benefits | Drawbacks | Citings |
|---|---|---|---|
| Photocomposers | Word processors may serve as a means of keyboarding for preparing photocomposer input<br><br>User can save between 30–40% in the final required number of pages<br><br>OCRs may be used to generate photocomposer tapes<br><br>Document preparation time may be decreased | May be less expensive to procure this service from outside vendors<br><br>Compatibility with other systems may be a problem | 20–80 lines per minute, *Datapro Reports on Office Systems*, September 1979<br><br>641–2566% faster than electric typewriter capability |
| Micrographics | Recording on microfilm consumes as little as 2% of the space occupied by the same records on paper<br><br>Only seconds are involved in retrieving one of a million records filed within reach of a seated operator<br><br>Duplicate microfilm files kept off premises to protect against loss of vital information<br><br>Magnetic-tape data is made readable on microfilm in a fraction of the time required for printing out on paper<br><br>Microfilm records retention cost is considerably lower than paper records systems | Archive quality of film images is questionable<br><br>Quality control and inspection procedures must be maintained during the filming, processing, and storage activities<br><br>Complexities exist when indexing for automated retrieval<br><br>High costs may be associated with conversion of existing paper files to microfilm images | 25% (Commander Lloyd C. Burger) to 62% (Reuben Donnelly) access/retrieval time savings, *Modern Office Procedures*, May 1977, p. 60 |

## Distribution Phase

| Equipment | Benefits | Drawbacks | Citings |
|---|---|---|---|
| Intelligent copiers | Document storage can be reduced<br><br>Speed of document communications can be enhanced<br><br>Scope of document communications can be enhanced<br><br>Acts as a convenience copier | Copier may be used as a printing press with increased per page costs<br><br>Potential exists for excess copying<br><br>Potential exists for nonbusiness copying | 75–600 characters/second transmission speed, IBM 6670 literature (G54 1006)<br><br>When 600 cps compared to 2 days for mail to arrive, 3927 times faster for page with 50 lines (65 characters/line) |

| Equipment | Benefits | Drawbacks | Citings |
|---|---|---|---|
| Facsimile (FAX) | Electronically sends text, graphic data, photographs, drawings, or charts with little difficulty | Line costs are relatively high | 30 sec- 6 min. to transmit 8½ x 11 page, *Datapro Reports on Office Systems* #2, June 1980 |
| | | Compatibility with receiving device must exist | |
| | Documents transfer much faster than mail, messenger, and so on | Sizes of sending and receiving documents are limited | When 6 min. compared to 2 days for mail to arrive, 480 times faster |
| | | Certain devices require station-to-station coordination | |
| | | Quality of received documents may not be acceptable | |
| Executive telephone | Reduces staff time in using the telephone | Difficult to cost justify | No citing available |
| | Provides arithmetic capabilities | | |
| Word processing data processing system with communications feature | Increased speed of document or data communications | Possible compatibility problems with mainframe or minicomputer | 40% reduction in dissemination time, *Report on Electronic Mail*, 4th Quarter 1978, Yankee Group, p. 13 |

These sample productivity improvement citings have been derived from representative sources available as of March 1, 1989. New technological developments are rapidly changing the productivity to be derived from the use of these representative equipment types. Therefore, the information needs to be continuously researched and updated.

Several items are listed here that we have not discussed before. A blind automatic word processor is a unit without a display, with text usually stored on magnetic cards or tape. An executive telephone is a combination telephone and calculator. Features may include call pickup, automatic dialing, automatic dialing, one-line display, calculating, clocking, and appointment calendaring.

After selecting some candidate equipment, you need to judge the benefit of any item compared to its cost. Then you can trim the list to those things you are prepared to buy.

Although this is a preliminary list, it gives you and any potential vendor a clear idea of your requirements.

*Compatibility* is the easier of the two to specify, but the harder to achieve. You simply need to determine which devices need to exchange data. For example, if you intend to combine data from an accounting system with text from a word processor, there must be an electrical path from the accounting system to the word processor, and the word processor must be able to accept and process the received data.

The second part, *capacity,* is more difficult to pin down but, paradoxically, easier to satisfy. In fact, you don't need to be very accurate in estimating capacity. LANs have tremendous capacity; this is one of their chief advantages. For example, the National Institute of Standards and Technology has a LAN that uses a baseband cable, with a 1-Mbps data rate and CSMA/CD protocol. By today's standards, this is a system with modest capacity and performance characteristics. Over 200 devices in twenty buildings are connected, with an overall extent of 1.5 kilometers. This is not a prototype or experimental system; it is in daily use by a staff with data processing needs as least as great as those of the average office. Yet, the utilization of the network's information movement capacity is under 2 percent!

So, for this part, don't worry about making precise estimates. To determine the required LAN capacity, all that a network designer needs is a general idea of the workload and performance demands of the network. Table 9-6 summarizes the information needed to design a network. Again, you do not need exact numbers for this checklist; rough estimates will be sufficient.

First, estimate the workload that the various devices on the LAN will generate. Table 9-7 will give you an idea of the kind of workload generated by various devices on a local area network. These estimates were prepared by the IEEE 802 standards committee.

It is useful at this point to know the nature of the information exchanges that will take place. We can group these exchanges into two broad categories: file transfer and transaction (Figure 9-1). A file transfer is primarily a one-way movement of data, such as the transfer of a word processing file to a printer or an image to a facsimile machine. Transactions are typically responses to inquiries or requests for data. In the first case, you are more concerned with *throughput:* the amount of data to be transferred in a given time. In the second case, you are more concerned with *response time:* how long it takes to get an item after it is requested.

Next, you need to look at the total capacity demand. On average, how many information exchanges will take place at a time? What is the peak? For file transfers, you can now add up the individual loads to get an idea of the overall throughput demand on the network. For transactions, it is better to express your needs in terms of a performance goal. For example, for a certain type of transaction, you might specify that you want 90 percent of the transaction to have a response within three seconds.

Finally, you need to look at future growth. If your organization is growing, someday you will want to buy more equipment. Your total file size will grow. You may add new functions to the network. The network should be designed to accommodate growth. Given the capabilities of today's LANs, you should be

**TABLE 9-6**  Capacity Checklist

| | |
|---|---|
| For each type of information exchange | Initiator device and location<br>Responder device and location |
| For file transfers | Amount of data for transfer<br>Time allotted for transfer |
| For transactions | Amount of data requested<br>Response time |
| For total system | Average loading<br>Peak loading<br>Performance goals |
| Future growth | Number of devices<br>File size<br>Added functions |

**TABLE 9-7**  Workload Generated from Each Source Type

| Type of Source | Peak Data Rate (Kbps) | Duty Cycle (%) |
|---|---|---|
| Heat, vent, air conditioning, alarm, and security | 0.1 | 100 |
| Line printer | 19.2 | 50–90 |
| File server or block transfer | 20,000 | 0.1 |
| File server or file transfer | 100 | 10–30 |
| Mail server | 100 | 30–50 |
| Information server or calendar | 9.6 | 1.5 |
| Information server or decision support | 56 | 20–40 |
| Word processor | 9.6 | 1–5 |
| Data entry terminal | 9.6 | 0.1–1.0 |
| Data enquiry terminal | 64 | 10–30 |
| Program development | 9.6 | 5–20 |
| Laser printer | 256 | 20–50 |
| Facsimile | 9.6 | 5–20 |
| Voice, immediate | 64 | 20–40 |
| Voice, store and forward | 32 | 30–50 |
| Video, noncompressed | 30,000 | 50–90 |
| Video, freeze frame | 64 | 50–90 |
| Video, compressed | 400 | 20–40 |
| Graphics, noncompressed | 256 | 1–10 |
| Graphics, compressed | 64 | 10–30 |
| Optical character reader | 2.4 | 50–90 |
| Gateway | 1,000 | 0.1–1.0 |
| Host, 0.5 MIPS | 128 | 20–40 |
| Host, 5 MIPS | 1,000 | 20–30 |

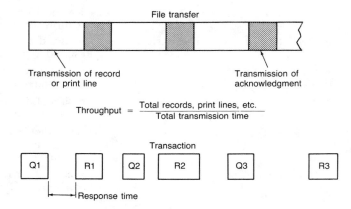

**Figure 9-1** Types of information exchange.

able to install a network now that will not need to be replaced in the near future. Furthermore, with tiered LANs, any future growth can be absorbed partly by an additional load on existing LANs and partly by the addition of new LANs.

# General Selection Criteria

Having gone through the process of planning a system, you can translate your needs into a statement of network requirements. The preceding section developed your requirements from a user or application point of view. That should help you answer the question: What is the system supposed to do? The next step is to answer the question: What features must the local area network have to meet my system requirements?

Keep in mind two points as you go through the rest of this chapter. First, we are not trying to teach you how to design your own network; we just want you to be able to hold your own in dealing with experts and would-be experts. Second, the emphasis is still on what the network will do, not how the network will do it. The *what* is the customer's responsibility; the *how* is the vendor's responsibility. Don't make the mistake of precluding a cost-effective solution by telling the vendor how to do his or her job. In this section, we give you some general selection criteria to keep in mind as you consider various vendors (Table 9-8). These are the features you should look for and compare.

The first criterion is cost. If the cost exceeds what you perceive as the expected savings in increased productivity, the system isn't worth the price.

Second, the system has to meet the requirements you have established. Although there are always compromises, the system must match the basic requirements. Related to this is the concept that the network should be expandable with only incremental cost. That is, expanding the system later should not be overly expensive or complicated. This allows you to start small, at low risk, and gradually expand the network to meet more of your requirements.

**TABLE 9-8**   Vendor Selection Criteria

| | |
|---|---|
| Total cost | |
| Meets requirements | |
| Expandable incrementally in cost | |
| Capable of interfacing with equipment supplied by multiple vendors | |
| Ease of | Installation |
| | Maintenance |
| | Reconfiguration |
| | Interconnection |
| Software | Servers |
| | Security |
| | Network management |

Along with expandability, your system needs reliability. The system should be designed to prevent total network failure. In addition, the network should be capable of interfacing with equipment supplied by more than one vendor. We explore this issue at the end of this chapter.

You want a network that is easy to install, maintain, and occasionally reconfigure. Flexibility is important. You want to be able to connect your equipment to the network easily, with no impact on hardware or software.

Finally, there are software issues, such as the need for servers, security, and network management. These can be supplied in an integrated fashion with the LAN or purchased separately. The former solution may mean that you have fewer vendors to deal with and simpler training. The latter solution may give you more flexibility in your choices.

## Specific LAN Requirements

Let us consider specifically what you will require of a network. Much of the information was discussed in the beginning of the chapter, and a knowledgeable consultant or vendor can work with that sort of information. This section will give you a better idea of what to ask for, a checklist of what has to be provided.

We can group our concerns into five areas:

- Services
- Traffic
- Reliability
- Growth
- Installation, maintenance, and training

## Services[3]

The functions performed by the network that are most visible to users and management are referred to as *network services*. A primary consideration in developing network services is the physical network environment. Is the network all in one building or spread over several? If the latter, must the buildings be linked together? Where is the equipment located? What space is available for network components? What false ceilings, conduits, and buried cable runs exist for wiring? Are there any special environmental problems?

Next, what type of equipment will be supported? This consideration leads to the question of interfaces. Some devices, such as terminals, may require a standardized communications interface, such as RS-232C. Others, such as personal computers and workstations, may interface to the network through a communications board mounted in the chassis of the computer. Only resources that need to be shared should be on the network. For example, if you have a special plotter that must be driven by the software in one and only one computer, hook the plotter to that computer—don't make them communicate over the network.

There is also the software interface to consider. For example, what protocols are provided to allow terminals to communicate with a variety of computers? The discussion in Chapter 5 on terminals is relevant.

Next, consider the type of information to be transmitted over the network. This is the whole point of having a network. For data, your primary concern is compatibility. Given the types of equipment you will have and the types of data to be transmitted, the network and the software in the attached devices must provide the communications software needed for full compatibility. Issues of communications architecture (Chapter 3) and server software (Chapter 5) need to be addressed.

Security and privacy are a concern. When multiple user groups have access to the network, the network must provide means for isolating information and restricting access to it. Similarly, unauthorized users should be kept off the network altogether.

Another concern is remote communications. You may want to link two installations by a satellite data channel and routers or bridges. Or you may want to augment your in-house processing capability with outside services, available over a packet-switching network such as Telenet or Tymenet. You may also want to provide dial-in ports on a modem server so that personnel who are traveling can enter the network from anywhere in the country.

Finally, one service is absolutely essential to the successful operation of a network: network management. Some level of monitoring and control, as described in Chapter 8, is needed.

---

[3] Many of the ideas in this section are adapted from another excellent publication by the National Bureau of Standards (now the National Institute of Standards and Technology), *The Selection of Local Area Computer Networks,* NBS Special Publication 500-96, November 1982.

# Traffic

The network must have the capability to meet the expected traffic load. This was explored previously in this chapter. Throughput and response-time requirements must be specified. Especially important are peak-load requirements.

How does this translate to a specific LAN capacity? A good guideline is to estimate the total load and then purchase a LAN with at least 10 times that capacity. That figure may seem excessive, but it is not. First, you are more likely to underestimate than overestimate your capacity needs. Second, demand will grow.

# Reliability

The network must be available to its users a very high percentage of the time: there must be a long period between component or network failure, and a minimal period before repairs are completed. A useful measure of reliability is *mean time between failure (MTBF).* For the transmission medium, which includes the cable, amplifiers, taps, and so on, an MTBF of 175,000 hours is reasonable. For intelligent network devices, such a bridges or network interface units (NIUs), an MTBF of 30,000 hours is a good goal.

Another aspect of reliability is the *error rate* of transmitted information. This is usually expressed as the rate of bit errors. There are two types of error rates to be concerned about: undetected and detected. An undetected error is discovered the hard way: The numbers didn't balance, or someone didn't get a paycheck. Detected errors are those discovered by the communications logic and automatically corrected, usually through a retransmission. Undetected errors are obviously unacceptable, and the communications software used across a LAN should be able to prevent these, or at least reduce them to an acceptable minimum. Detected errors are not as bad, but they do cause unnecessary network overhead.

Good reliability values are a detected-error rate of 1 bit in $10^9$ and an undetected-error rate of 1 bit in $10^{12}$. Detected-error rates are easily monitored. Undetected-error rates must be estimated from off-line tests using artificial traffic.

# Growth

No matter how good your analysis of current requirements, you cannot expect to satisfy all your local area network needs once and for all. For example, you may anticipate that your word processing staff will double in the next three years. You should be able to attach these additional stations to the network easily, with no disruption of network operations. Also, the network must have the capability to handle the increased traffic generated by the new stations.

New types of applications or devices might be added to the network (for example, a facsimile machine). This will require new protocols. If such growth is to be possible, the network hardware and software must be capable of easily accommodating new protocols. This is most easily done with an OSI-based architecture because virtually all work on new protocols is in that framework.

## Installation, Maintenance, and Training

The preceding criteria had to do with the capability and capacity of the network. This subsection speaks to an equally important consideration: the service provided by the vendor. First, the vendor must plan, with your cooperation, the layout of the network. This includes the physical placement of all cable (including taps, splitters, and amplifiers) and wiring and the location of all network components. The vendor must assure that the layout meets all fire and building codes.

Following installation, maintenance of the network is an ongoing responsibility, divided between you and the vendor. How that responsibility is divided varies; the next few paragraphs present an example.

The customer has the following responsibilities for the network hardware:

- Maintain a permanent survey of the network through the use of logging files and traffic statistics.
- When a problem occurs, perform diagnostics to attempt to localize the fault, using vendor-supplied test equipment and diagnostic software.
- When the fault is localized, reconfigure the network, if possible, to provide continued service.
- When the vendor has corrected a failure, assist the vendor in checking the network.

Customer personnel will require training from the vendor to perform these tasks.

The vendor's maintenance responsibilities follow:

- Cross-check customer diagnostics, if necessary.
- Replace failed components. (To minimize lost service time, faulty components are replaced rather than repaired.)
- After correcting a failure, check the network.

If the network includes substantial software, which is likely, software maintenance becomes quite complex. This should be left entirely to the vendor.

Training is closely related to maintenance. As mentioned, some customer personnel need training to participate in maintenance activities. One or more individuals will need to be trained in network management functions and perhaps security functions. End users, in general, should require little or no training. At most, the application user should have to learn a logon procedure. Beyond that, the network should be transparent to the user.

# Type of Vendor

One final point to consider is the type of vendor. There is a broad spectrum here, but we will group vendors into two categories to clarify the issue: the network vendor and the data processing vendor.

The network vendor's primary business is to sell local area networks. Typically, network vendors are independent companies or subsidiaries of firms other than computer companies. Network vendors make their money from the sale of the network.

The data processing vendor, on the other hand, is in business to sell data processing equipment. A LAN is a means of meeting a customer's need for linking equipment purchased from the vendor.

Which type of vendor is preferable? If you already have or are planning to purchase most of your data processing equipment from one vendor and that vendor offers a LAN, it makes sense to get the LAN from the same vendor because it simplifies maintenance responsibilities. Otherwise, you might be better off with a LAN vendor because LANs are the vendor's specialty.

# *Case Study 7*
# The World Bank[4]

The World Bank was established in 1945 to help raise living standards in developing countries by channeling financial resources, in the form of loans, from more fortunate countries. Although it differs from ordinary commercial banks in many ways, the fundamental functions related to approving and administering loans are similar to those of other banks.

From the late 1970s through the early 1980s, the bank experienced a data processing growth that is unfortunately all too common. There was no centrally coordinated master plan for the acquisition of data processing equipment. No requirements for automated support of bank functions were defined. Instead, various division-level and department-level managers acquired equipment out of their own budgets, while information systems executives reporting to top management acquired mainframe-based capability to support the bank's databases. Links to outside data sources, information services, and networks were acquired haphazardly. By 1983, expenditures on information processing were in excess of $20 million per year, with over $11 million in installed equipment. This included over 750 word processors, 100 microcomputers, and about 1500 terminals. Various mainframes and minicomputers were also installed. Much of this equipment was unable to communicate with other equipment because of incompatibilities and the plain lack of physical

---

[4] This case study is based on material in M. Mathov, "The World Bank: Choosing a Path to Interconnection," *Data Communications,* January 1986.

connections. It was clear that the bank was not getting its money's worth from its equipment and ongoing expenditures.

The bank set up a program to rationalize its information processing function. Two separate teams were commissioned. The first would decide on a single workstation to perform all functions not to be supported by central shared systems. That is, the central mainframes and minis would continue to host the bank's databases and any large number-crunching applications, but all other applications, such as word processing, electronic mail, and terminal handling, were targeted to the new workstation. After the workstation was approved, managers would be encouraged to migrate to this equipment as quickly as possible. The second team was responsible for defining a local area networking strategy. Although a final decision of a LAN strategy would depend on the selection of a workstation, much could be done to define requirements and set up an evaluation procedure. Thus, the two teams worked in tandem to reach the goal as quickly as possible.

The networking team followed the step-by-step procedure summarized in Table 9-9. The first step was to interview users to determine their networking requirements. The needs of three major functional groups in the bank had to be addressed: operations (loan granting and management), finance (money management and accounting), and personnel and administration, which includes such services as data processing, medical, and payroll.

The interviews were informal rather than structured; at this stage, the team was concerned with gathering as much information as possible. After some analysis of the results, and some follow-up interviews, the networking team concluded that one type of work group, although not invariable, was typical of the way work was conducted at the bank. The usual size of a work group in the bank is about 20 people, comprising a manager plus secretarial and professional staff members. Although the tasks performed by various work groups differed, the following requirements were common:

- Sharing certain peripherals, mainly disk storage and printers, within the work group.
- Staff access to the bank's electronic resources from outside locations (for example, their homes or overseas locations), both to retrieve and to send electronic mail and files.
- Ease of use, including an effective network data management capability. For example, there is a need for automatic file backup without user intervention.
- Synchronous communication from the workstation to the IBM mainframe.
- Asynchronous communication from the workstation to access other mainframes and minis in the bank and external information sources.
- High system availability.

The team decided that the most straightforward configuration would involve a separate LAN for each work group. With approximately 6,000 employees and an average of 20 users per work group, about 300 LANs would be

---

**TABLE 9-9**   Step-by-Step Network Selection

---

The procedure followed by the World Bank to link its users may be useful to any organization undertaking a similar project:

- Interview users and determine their basic needs.
- Define geographical distribution and constraints.
- Define the typical work group and its major tasks.
- Determine physical restrictions, if any.
- Visit installations in other organizations and try to get an idea about basic problems and solutions.
- Develop an ideal configuration.
- Select potential vendors.
- Match user requirements against potential products and eliminate those that do not fulfill them.
- Develop a checklist of technical characteristics.
- Pilot test the products still being considered, evaluating them in terms of the characteristics on the checklist.
- Define a standard configuration for all vendors.
- Start compiling cost figures for each alternative.
- Select the critical characteristics.
- Prepare and complete an evaluation.
- Visit the premises of the best-rated vendor(s).
- Visit installations similar to the one you will implement in your corporation.
- Make a decision.
- Negotiate an agreement with the vendor(s).
- Prepare an implementation plan.
- Have the decision and implementation plan approved by top management.
- Cross your fingers.
- Good luck.

---

Source: *Data Communications,* January 1986.

---

required. In some cases, several small work groups could share the same LAN. However, it would be easier to control access and system growth if in most cases each work group had its own LAN.

Figure 9-2 shows the layout of a typical LAN, as envisioned by the networking team. Each LAN would support about 20 workstations, a file server for information of interest primarily in the work group, a printer server for shared access to a high-quality printer, communication servers for synchronous and asynchronous access, and an inter-LAN connection box. Assuming that a uniform LAN strategy was adopted, the latter could be a simple bridge. The typical layout was defined to provide a reference configuration against which various LAN hardware and software vendors could be evaluated.

By this time, the workstation group had narrowed their selection to three possibilities. This allowed the networking group to begin intensive vendor evaluation, concentrating only on vendors who could support one or more of the candidate workstations. The networking team prepared a checklist of desirable

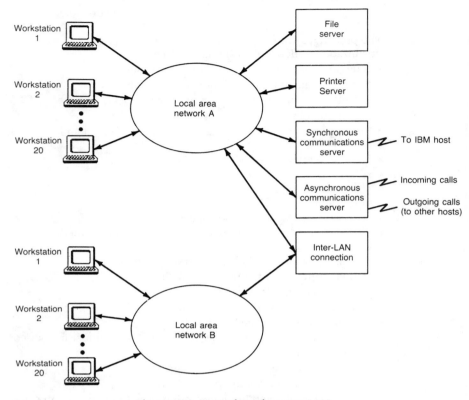

**Figure 9-2** Typical work group LAN.

features to be used in characterizing each vendor (Table 9-10). The checklist was used not to rate or evaluate vendors, but simply to create an inventory of features from each vendor. If a vendor was missing any critical features and was unwilling to develop them, that vendor could be eliminated at this stage.

**TABLE 9-10**   Checklist of Network Features

| | YES | NO | | | YES | NO |
|---|---|---|---|---|---|---|
| 1. User Interface | — | — | 1.5 | Network displays status information on each user's workstation | — | — |
| 1.1 Menu-based access to network services | — | — | 1.6 | User-defined default options | — | — |
| 1.2 Experienced user may bypass basic steps | — | — | 1.7 | Error messages are explicit and understandable | — | — |
| 1.3 Mid-session help available | — | — | 2. File Sharing | | | |
| 1.4 User may terminate any activity at any point | — | — | 2.1 | All users can share the server's hard disk(s) | — | — |

**TABLE 9-10**   *(cont.)*

| | | YES | NO | | | | YES | NO |
|---|---|---|---|---|---|---|---|---|
| 2.2 | Hard disk(s) can be partitioned | — | — | 3.2 | Types of printers supported: | | — | — |
| 2.3 | Volume size can be variable | — | — | | 3.2.1 | Parallel printers | — | — |
| 2.4 | Upper limit of volume size is user-defined | — | — | | 3.2.2 | Serial printers | — | — |
| | | | | | 3.2.3 | Laser printers | — | — |
| 2.5 | Disk drives are virtual to the users (that is, to the user, the server disk seems to be connected directly to the workstation) | — | — | | 3.2.4 | Graphics plotters | — | — |
| | | | | | 3.2.5 | High-speed (9.6 Kbps) printers | — | — |
| 2.6 | One volume may occupy more than one drive | — | — | | 3.2.6 | Low-speed (300 bps) printers | — | — |
| 2.7 | Multiple virtual drives can exist | — | — | 3.3 | Print job manipulation allowed: | | | |
| 2.8 | Password protection at volume level: | | | | 3.3.1 | Print-file spool | — | — |
| | 2.8.1 Private volume | — | — | | 3.3.2 | Print-file queue | — | — |
| | 2.8.2 Group volume | — | — | | 3.3.3 | Print-file priority | — | — |
| | 2.8.3 Public volume | — | — | | 3.3.4 | Print file abort/delete | — | — |
| 2.9 | Disk-to-tape backup available: | | | | 3.3.5 | Start/stop jobs in print queue | — | — |
| | 2.9.1 By volume | — | — | | 3.3.6 | By the user | — | — |
| | 2.9.2 By file | — | — | | 3.3.7 | By the network administrator | — | — |
| | 2.9.3 Incremental | — | — | 3.4 | Default printer setup | | — | — |
| | 2.9.4 Automatic (programmable) | — | — | 3.5 | Usage statistics available | | — | — |
| 2.10 | Restore tape-to-disk available: | | | 3.6 | Diagnostic tools for maintenance available | | — | — |
| | 2.10.1 By volume | — | — | **4. Communications Server** | | | | |
| | 2.10.2 By file | — | — | 4.1 | Share communications links among all users | | — | — |
| 2.11 | File names located in a directory/subdirectory | — | — | 4.2 | Types of communications links supported: | | | |
| 2.12 | Multiple file servers allowed in one local area network | — | — | | 4.2.1 | 3270 binary synchronous communications | — | — |
| 2.13 | Usage statistics available | — | — | | 4.2.2 | 3270 systems network architecture | — | — |
| 2.14 | Diagnostic tools for maintenance available | — | — | | 4.2.3 | ASCII asynchronous dial-out | — | — |
| **3. Printer Server** | | | | | | | | |
| 3.1 | Network printers can be shared by all users | — | — | | | | | |

**TABLE 9-10**   *(cont.)*

| | | | YES | NO | | | | YES | NO |
|---|---|---|---|---|---|---|---|---|---|
| | 4.2.4 | ASCII asynchronous dial-in | ___ | ___ | 5.13 | Automatic printing of messages for nonregistered users (to be delivered by hand) | | ___ | ___ |
| | 4.2.5 | ASCII asynchronous dedicated lines | ___ | ___ | 5.14 | If user is on, the arrival of a message is noticeable to the user | | ___ | ___ |
| | 4.2.6 | X.25 | ___ | ___ | 5.15 | If user is on, the arrival of a message does not interrupt process | | ___ | ___ |
| | 4.2.7 | VT-100 emulation | ___ | ___ | 5.16 | Message received may be printed on request | | ___ | ___ |
| | 4.2.8 | Burroughs poll/select | ___ | ___ | 5.17 | Old messages may be purged/deleted | | ___ | ___ |
| 4.3 | | Interface with the bank's CODEX data switch | ___ | ___ | 5.18 | A user may have multiple mailboxes | | ___ | ___ |
| 4.4 | | Automatic dial-out capability | ___ | ___ | 5.19 | Reply to current message defaults to sender's name | | ___ | ___ |
| 4.5 | | Easy to use | ___ | ___ | 5.20 | Messages can be forwarded to other users | | ___ | ___ |
| 4.6 | | Usage statistics available | ___ | ___ | 5.21 | Messages can be filed | | ___ | ___ |
| 4.7 | | Diagnostic tools for maintenance available | ___ | ___ | 5.22 | User-generated distribution lists allowed | | ___ | ___ |
| **5. Electronic Mail** | | | | | 5.23 | Unread messages highlighted | | ___ | ___ |
| 5.1 | | Menu-driven | ___ | ___ | 5.24 | Unanswered messages highlighted | | ___ | ___ |
| 5.2 | | Preformatted screens for different types of documents | ___ | ___ | 5.25 | Unsent messages highlighted | | ___ | ___ |
| 5.3 | | Supports directory with up to 6,000 users | ___ | ___ | 5.26 | Date/time of messages automatically included | | ___ | ___ |
| 5.4 | | Word processing-type editor for message creation | ___ | ___ | 5.27 | User-defined priority for outgoing messages | | ___ | ___ |
| 5.5 | | Return-receipt option available | ___ | ___ | 5.28 | User-defined priority for incoming messages | | ___ | ___ |
| 5.6 | | Message broadcast available | ___ | ___ | 5.29 | Possibility to withdraw messages already sent (but not yet read) | | ___ | ___ |
| 5.7 | | Predefined groups for message broadcast | ___ | ___ | 5.30 | Usage statistics available | | ___ | ___ |
| 5.8 | | Urgent-message handling | ___ | ___ | **6. Network Calendaring** | | | | |
| 5.9 | | Merging of text and data files allowed | ___ | ___ | 6.1 | Network calendaring available for all users in a LAN | | ___ | ___ |
| 5.10 | | Display list of all messages created | ___ | ___ | | | | | |
| 5.11 | | Display list of all messages sent | ___ | ___ | | | | | |
| 5.12 | | Display list of all messages received | ___ | ___ | | | | | |

## TABLE 9-10 (cont.)

| | | YES | NO | | | YES | NO |
|---|---|---|---|---|---|---|---|
| 6.2 | Network calendaring available throughout all interconnected LANs | ___ | ___ | 9. LAN-to-LAN Interconnection | | | |
| 6.3 | Appointment-scheduling password protected | ___ | ___ | 9.1 | Nearby LANs can be interconnected | ___ | ___ |
| 6.4 | Automatic scheduling of multiple-user meetings | ___ | ___ | 9.2 | Remote LANs can be interconnected | ___ | ___ |
| 6.5 | Automatic resource scheduling (such as meeting rooms) | ___ | ___ | 9.3 | Users on one LAN may transparently access resources on another LAN | ___ | ___ |
| 6.6 | Usage statistics available | ___ | ___ | 9.4 | Files can be transferred between LANs | ___ | ___ |
| 7. Compatibility Required with Application Software | | | | 9.5 | Global electronic mail throughout LANs | ___ | ___ |
| 7.1 | dBASE II | ___ | ___ | 9.6 | Heterogeneous LANs can be interconnected | ___ | ___ |
| 7.2 | dBASE III | ___ | ___ | 9.7 | Inter-LAN traffic statistics available | ___ | ___ |
| 7.3 | Personal computer focus | ___ | ___ | 10. IBM PC Compatibility | | | |
| 7.4 | Personal computer model 204 | ___ | ___ | 10.1 | IBM PCs may coexist on the same LAN | ___ | ___ |
| 7.5 | Lotus 1-2-3 | ___ | ___ | 10.2 | Files may be transferred between a user and an IBM PC | ___ | ___ |
| 7.6 | Multiplan | ___ | ___ | | | | |
| 7.7 | Visicalc | ___ | ___ | 10.3 | Electronic mail may be sent to an IBM PC | ___ | ___ |
| 7.8 | Multimate | ___ | ___ | 10.4 | Compatibility at the data level | ___ | ___ |
| 7.9 | Wordpro | ___ | ___ | | | | |
| 7.10 | Wordstar | ___ | ___ | 10.5 | Compatibility at the program level | ___ | ___ |
| 8. Data Transmission within the LAN | | | | 10.6 | File-format translation required and available | ___ | ___ |
| 8.1 | File transfer between workstations | ___ | ___ | 11. Security | | | |
| 8.2 | File transfer between file server and workstations | ___ | ___ | 11.1 | Access to individual LANs password-protected | ___ | ___ |
| 8.3 | File transfer with a centralized office environment, such as all-in-one from Digital Equipment Corp. (DEC) | ___ | ___ | 11.2 | Access to interconnected LANs password-protected | ___ | ___ |
| | | | | 11.3 | Access to volumes password-protected | ___ | ___ |
| 8.4 | Workstations that may be used in the LAN: | ___ | ___ | 11.4 | Access to files password-protected | ___ | ___ |
| 8.4.1 | Data General's Desktop | ___ | ___ | 11.5 | Password change easy to perform | ___ | ___ |
| 8.4.2 | DEC's Professional | ___ | ___ | 11.6 | Automatic file-closing when user turns off workstation | ___ | ___ |
| 8.4.3 | IBM Personal Computers (PCs) | ___ | ___ | | | | |

**TABLE 9-10**    *(cont.)*

| | YES | NO | | | YES | NO |
|---|---|---|---|---|---|---|
| **12. Network Administration** | | | | 12.10.1 Dial-in | —— | —— |
| 12.1 Easy add/delete of users, printers, and so on | —— | —— | | 12.10.2 From an interconnected LAN | —— | —— |
| 12.2 Control access to the network | —— | —— | | **13. Documentation** | | |
| 12.3 Usage statistics provided | —— | —— | | 13.1 Installation guide available | —— | —— |
| 12.4 Service start/shutdown controlled | —— | —— | | 13.2 Network administration guide available | —— | —— |
| 12.5 Disk-to-tape backup: | | | | 13.3 User's guide available | —— | —— |
|    12.5.1 Prescheduled | —— | —— | | 13.4 Planning guide available | —— | —— |
|    12.5.2 On demand | —— | —— | | 13.5 Maintenance guide available | —— | —— |
|    12.5.3 Unattended | —— | —— | | 13.6 Training aids available | —— | —— |
| 12.6 Network management console | —— | —— | | 13.7 Mid-session help available | —— | —— |
| 12.7 Network recovery from power failures: | | | | **14. Environmental Specifications** | | |
|    12.7.1 Automatic | —— | —— | | 14.1 Air conditioning is required | —— | —— |
|    12.7.2 Attended | —— | —— | | 14.2 Noise generated is less than 50 dB | —— | —— |
| 12.8 Adding/deleting network resources does not interfere with service | —— | —— | | 14.3 Space requirements are less than —— (fill in) | —— | —— |
| 12.9 Remote maintenance capability: | —— | —— | | 14.4 Heat generation is less than 400 watts | —— | —— |
|    12.9.1 Dail-in | —— | —— | | 14.5 Electrical power consumption is less than —— (fill in) | —— | —— |
|    12.9.2 From an interconnected LAN | —— | —— | | | | |
| 12.10 Remote-administration capability | —— | —— | | | | |

Source: *Data Communications,* January 1986.

Next, cost analysis was done. Each candidate vendor was asked to price a reference configuration consisting of the following:

- Five workstations, each with a 10M hard disk and a floppy disk drive
- Fifteen workstations with floppy drives only
- Twenty standard-carriage dot matrix printers (one for each workstation)
- One file server with a capacity of about 40M and cartridge tape backup
- One printer server with one wide-carriage dot matrix printer and one laser printer
- One synchronous communications server with a minimum capacity of eight simultaneous IBM 3270 terminal sessions

- One asynchronous communications server with a minimum capacity of four asynchronous lines

Table 9-11 shows the costing table. Five vendors submitted proposals, and the data was entered into a spreadsheet with this format. The results, in terms of an average cost per workstation, ranged from $4,500 to $15,000.

The final stage in the selection process involved the use of an evaluation sheet for each vendor (Table 9-12). The evaluation consisted of a simple numerical score ranging from 0 to 4 for a number of features. These features were divided into those considered more important for the bank (critical factors) and those thought less important (noncritical factors). No attempt was made to weight the factors. A simple summation of the critical and noncritical factors was produced. This, together with the price information and the checklist, provided the network team with sufficient information to make a recommendation.

**TABLE 9-11**  Cost Analysis Spreadsheet

|  | Vendor _____ | | | |
| --- | Qty | Description | Unit Cost | Total Cost |
| --- | --- | --- | --- | --- |
| Workstation (WS) | | | | |
|   With hard disk | ____ | _____ | ____ | ____ |
|   Floppy drive only | ____ | _____ | ____ | ____ |
|   Printer | ____ | _____ | ____ | ____ |
| **Subtotal (WS) | ____ | _____ | ____ | ____ |
| Local Area Network (LAN) | | | | |
| File Server | ____ | _____ | ____ | ____ |
|   Tape backup | ____ | _____ | ____ | ____ |
| Printer Server | ____ | _____ | ____ | ____ |
|   Matrix printer | ____ | _____ | ____ | ____ |
|   Letter-quality printer | ____ | _____ | ____ | ____ |
| Communications Server | ____ | _____ | ____ | ____ |
|   Asynchronous | ____ | _____ | ____ | ____ |
|   3270 | ____ | _____ | ____ | ____ |
| Other LAN Hardware | | | | |
|   Transceiver cable | ____ | _____ | ____ | ____ |
|   Network cable | ____ | _____ | ____ | ____ |
|   Adapter cards | ____ | _____ | ____ | ____ |
|   Components | ____ | _____ | ____ | ____ |
|   Console | ____ | _____ | ____ | ____ |
|   LAN interconnectors | ____ | _____ | ____ | ____ |
| LAN Software | | | | |
|   LAN-to-LAN connection | ____ | _____ | ____ | ____ |

**TABLE 9-11**    *(cont.)*

| | Vendor | | Unit | Total |
| | Qty | Description | Cost | Cost |
|---|---|---|---|---|
| Disk sharing | —— | ———— | —— | —— |
| Printer sharing | —— | ———— | —— | —— |
| Electronic mail | —— | ———— | —— | —— |
| Asychronous communications sharing | —— | ———— | —— | —— |
| 3270 communications sharing | —— | ———— | —— | —— |
| **Subtotal (LAN) | —— | ———— | —— | —— |
| Total cost (WS + LAN) | —— | ———— | —— | —— |
| Average cost per WS | —— | ———— | —— | —— |

Source: *Data Communications,* January 1986.

**TABLE 9-12**    Evaluation Card

| | Vendor A | Vendor B | Vendor C | Vendor D | Vendor E |
|---|---|---|---|---|---|
| **Critical Factors** | | | | | |
| User interface | 4 | 2 | 3 | 3 | 0 |
| File sharing | 3 | 4 | 1 | 3 | 0 |
| Printer server | 2 | 3 | 2 | 3 | 4 |
| Communications server | 2 | 1 | 3 | 1 | 1 |
| Inter-LAN communications | 4 | 0 | 1 | 2 | 1 |
| IBM PC compatibility | 4 | 4 | 4 | 1 | 1 |
| Wiring flexibility | 4 | 2 | 1 | 0 | 0 |
| Subtotal 1 | 23 | 16 | 15 | 13 | 7 |
| **Noncritical Factors** | | | | | |
| Intra-LAN communications | 2 | 2 | 2 | 3 | 3 |
| Performance | 2 | 3 | 3 | 3 | 1 |
| Security | 3 | 4 | 1 | 3 | 3 |
| LAN administration | 4 | 2 | 2 | 3 | 3 |
| Documentation | 2 | 2 | 2 | 2 | 2 |
| Environment | 3 | 3 | 2 | 2 | 3 |
| Maturity reliability | 2 | 3 | 4 | 3 | 0 |
| Subtotal 2 | 18 | 19 | 17 | 19 | 15 |
| Total score | 41 | 35 | 32 | 32 | 22 |

0 = Does not meet requirements or is not available
1 = Poor
2 = Fair
3 = Good
4 = Excellent
Source: *Data Communications,* January 1986.

# Summary

There are some general selection criteria to keep in mind when making a LAN decision. The most important are total cost and your network requirements. Other criteria are expandability, capability to handle a variety of equipment, and ease of management.

The network must meet some specific requirements. These can be grouped in the following categories: services, traffic, reliability, growth, and installation and maintenance.

# Chapter 10

# The Visual Revolution

$I$N TERMS OF REQUIREMENTS, TECHNOLOGY, APPLICATIONS, and product implementations, this book has so far addressed what might be referred to as contemporary local area networks. This chapter is oriented to future requirements for LANs, although the future has become very short term in this context. Specifically, the technological ingredients are falling into place for a revolutionary shift in the form of information used by organizations. A much more substantial reliance on image (fixed) and video (moving image) forms is already taking place. By the mid-1990s, this change will transform the way information is used in organizations. This "visual revolution" has substantial implications for LANs developed in the near future.

We begin this chapter by summarizing the key technological developments that are making the visual revolution possible. We then look, in turn, at image and video communications. In both cases, typical applications and the implications for communications requirements are examined. The chapter closes with some thoughts about the types of future LANs needed to support these applications.

# Technological Trends

In a few years, millions of office workers (and free-lancers, too) will be able to capture, store, change, merge, send, receive, and display pictures, graphs, illustrations, and just about any other image in ways unimagined just a short time ago. At the same time, video will go from a passive, distribution-oriented service to an interactive tool of business in a host of applications.

A number of technological trends have combined to make possible the visual revolution:

- *Transmission capacity:* It has never been greater, and of course it is still growing. Yesterday's 10-Mbps Ethernet is today's 100-Mbps FDDI LAN. LANs with higher capacity will appear soon. In addition, the use of high-capacity long-distance communications facilities is increasing.

- *Processing power:* Workstations and PCs are beginning to have the processing power to handle fixed images and even moving images with some facility. The hardware is continuing to get faster, and the software is not far behind. For example, OS/2, which is the operating system for IBM's new line of PS/2 personal computers, was designed so that device manipulation can bypass the traditional, and cumbersome, operating system mediation that can place unnecessary limits on the fastest of machines.

- *Storage:* Nonerasable and erasable optical media have achieved densities that put massive storage at the command of small office machines.

Thus, the cost of dealing with visual information has dropped, and the processing power and capacity of handling that information has risen. The result is a dramatic increase in the use of visual information.

## Image Communications

In 490 B.C., the Greek runner Pheidippides ran 22 miles in just over 3 hours to bring news of the Greek victory over the Persians at the town of Marathon. His average speed was slightly over 7 miles per hour. Today, the amount of time to communicate a meaningful amount of data has shrunk to almost nothing (Figure 10-1a). And yet, the human ability to make decisions on the basis of incom-

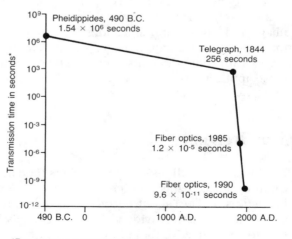

*(a)*

**Figure 10-1** The information explosion.

ing data has not significantly changed in 2500 years. Not only can data be delivered much faster than before the advent of computers and telecommunications, but the amount of data that can be generated and stored has increased tremendously (Figure 10-1 b, c). The question becomes: Is it possible for the user to make effective use of all this information?

If data is available only in the form of text and numerical data, the answer to the preceding question must be, clearly not. But this information cannot be simply ignored. Managers must have effective access to information for their businesses to remain competitive. The solution is to present information in the form of graphic images. The eye can take in graphic information at rates equiv-

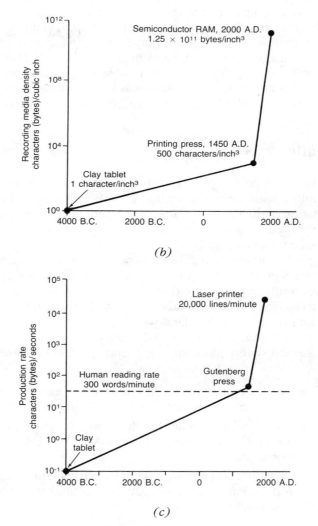

*(b)*

*(c)*

**Figure 10-1** *(Cont.)*

alent to 72 million words per minute—more than 200,000 times as fast as an average reader of text.

The type of image information we are referring to includes pictures, diagrams, and graphical displays of numerical information (bar graphs, pie charts, and so on). In addition, another type of image information is useful in business: an electronic image of a document. Even if the document contains only text, with no graphics, there is an advantage in handling that document electronically as an image. For example, a manager receives a letter from a customer and wants to transmit that letter to a number of individuals in the organization in geographically dispersed locations. One option is to duplicate the letter and send it by mail. Another option is to have someone type the letter into a computer and send it by electronic mail. Both of these options are clumsy and time-consuming. A better approach is to capture and transmit an electronic image of the paper. This is the function of facsimile.

Image information takes many forms and is used in many applications in business. In this section, we look at a sampling, focusing on three areas with particular relevance for business information communications: facsimile, interactive computer graphics, and enhanced audio teleconferencing.

## Facsimile

In its simplest form, a facsimile machine is a device that electronically transmits a visual image of the information on a sheet of paper. A bit-map representation of the image—which can include text, graphics, or pictures—is created. Facsimile has a number of advantages over other forms of document or message transmission. In addition to printed text, facsimile can transmit pictures, graphs, drawings, handwritten notes, and anything else that can be put on paper. Signatures transmitted by facsimile are considered legally binding. Also, facsimile saves preparation time because information does not have to be entered into a message system through a keyboard. The paper itself is scanned for patterns of light and dark, which are transmitted to the receiving end.

Although facsimile was developed in 1843, it is only since the mid-1970s that the system has come into common use. That use is now growing rapidly, thanks to a number of factors:

- Until recently, legal restrictions in some countries inhibited the use of the public telephone network for facsimile transmission.
- The development and widespread acceptance of international standards are making compatible interworking of facsimile possible on an international scale.
- Facsimile technology has advanced, bringing higher speed, better quality, reduced machine size, reduced machine and transmission costs, and simpler machine operation.

Facsimile systems can be classified as either *photographic facsimile,* in which the original copy is reproduced with black, white, and intermediate grey scales, or *document facsimile,* in which only black and white are used. The primary interest in office and telecommunication applications has been in document facsimile.

Traditionally, facsimile equipment operates by a local scan of a page, the transmission of an electronic version of the scanned information to a remote counterpart, and the printing of the same image at the remote location (Figure 10-2). In earlier designs, the scanning and printing processes are synchronized; there is little or no signal storage between the scanner and the printer. In more recent digital designs, buffered facsimile equipment has appeared. This allows the connection of machines that work at different data rates.

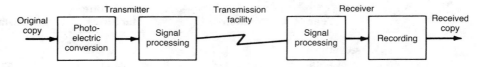

**Figure 10-2** Facsimile: Generic block diagram.

Not only is the range of applications for facsimile expanding, but the variety of equipment is also growing. Figure 10-3 shows what is becoming a typical configuration. A personal computer can be equipped with a facsimile communications board and linked by a networking or communications facility to a standalone facsimile machine. Documents can be entered into the remote facsimile machine by scanning, and the resulting image is transmitted and displayed on the personal computer. The computer can also be attached to a facsimile machine or a graphics printer (such as a laser printer) or both. Table 10-1 indicates the projected growth of the facsimile market.

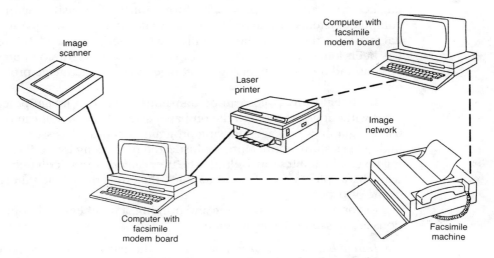

**Figure 10-3** Example facsimile configuration.

**TABLE 10-1**  The U.S. Fax Market

| | In Millions of Dollars | | |
| Year | Boards | Standalone Machines | Total |
|---|---|---|---|
| 1987 | 9 | 1071 | 1080 |
| 1988 | 35 | 1313 | 1348 |
| 1989 | 74 | 1445 | 1519 |
| 1990 | 127 | 1520 | 1647 |
| 1991 | 177 | 1472 | 1649 |

| | In Thousands of Units Sold | | |
| Year | Boards | Standalone Machines | Total |
|---|---|---|---|
| 1987 | 11 | 365 | 376 |
| 1988 | 33 | 490 | 523 |
| 1989 | 70 | 605 | 675 |
| 1990 | 151 | 655 | 806 |
| 1991 | 228 | 715 | 942 |

Source: *Data Communications,* March 1988.

## Image Processing Systems

The most recent advance in facsimile technology is the use of digital techniques for storing and transmitting the facsimile image. The advent of the digital facsimile allows a page of information to be easily manipulated by computer systems, stored on disk or tape, and encrypted for security. With digital facsimile, the role of the facsimile has broadened. Indeed, this technology has been joined with the display capabilities of modern computer terminal screens and the capacity of digital storage to create the image processing system.

In digital form, pages can be transmitted between image processing devices without going through the on-paper stage. A document can be prepared using a graphics package, drawing program, or word processor, then handled in digital facsimile form. More sophisticated processing is possible by combining text and graphics capabilities. The user can create and edit text, combine it with charts, pictures, and other graphics, then treat the whole thing as an electronic or paper image.

Beyond document scanning and printing, a number of additional applications are possible. These include

- *Image-based electronic mail:* As an alternative to traditional electronic mail systems.

- *Storage and retrieval from an image database:* Documents, created with a graphics processor, can be stored for remote printing later.
- *Format conversion:* From one facsimile standard to another.
- *Optical character recognition (OCR) and analysis of graphic data:* Images can be transmitted in bit-map form for later processing using pattern recognition and other image-processing techniques.

Figure 10-4 indicates the factors driving the image-processing market. Although the benefit of paper reduction is often stressed by vendors to sell their systems, it comes in third in the ranks of what users really want.

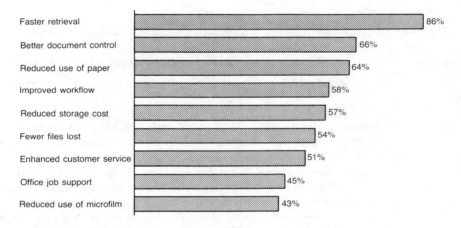

| | |
|---|---|
| Faster retrieval | 86% |
| Better document control | 66% |
| Reduced use of paper | 64% |
| Improved workflow | 58% |
| Reduced storage cost | 57% |
| Fewer files lost | 54% |
| Enhanced customer service | 51% |
| Office job support | 45% |
| Reduced use of microfilm | 43% |

**Figure 10-4** Benefits of image processing, as perceived by users. *(Source: The Yankee Group, based on a survey of 596 IS managers, July 1989.)*

Figure 10-5 shows that image-processing systems of all sizes are projected to experience healthy growth, with medium-size systems seeing the biggest jump. More buying decisions are being left to individual departments, and it appears that most managers want to avoid getting stuck with a system that is too small and may therefore purchase systems that exceed current needs, anticipating future growth in system use.

Finally, Figure 10-6 indicates where the market for image processing is growing. Government, which gave the image-processing market its first real boost, will not expand as rapidly as other market sectors. Manufacturing and insurance will be the main players in a widely diversified field. Other vertical markets, such as health and utilities, will begin to account for a notable share by 1992.

In the remainder of this section, we look at one of the most promising image-processing applications, medical image processing. Some of the most innovative work in the use of image processing is being done in medical health science centers, such as university medical school and hospital complexes. Communications users in these centers are often early experimenters with leading-edge technologies. They cooperate with vendors to develop ca-

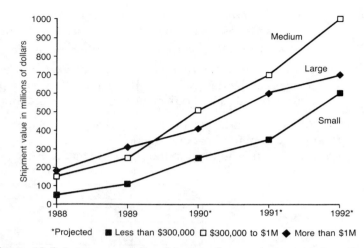

**Figure 10-5** Image processing shipment forecast by system size. *(Source: The Yankee Group, July 1989.)*

pabilities that benefit the medical care, teaching, and research environments. Image capture and analysis—in the form of X rays, ultrasound, nuclear medicine, tomography, and magnetic resonance imagery (MRI)—are essential for quality medical care and state-of-the-art biomedical research.

Typically, the medical health science center encompasses all the functions of both university and hospital: clinical care (both outpatient and inpatient), academic research, teaching, and administration. Image communications developments have tended to focus on enhancing the quality and efficiency of clinical care, with some transfer into the teaching and curriculum development area as well.

Major areas of activity in image communications include

- Picture archiving and communications systems (PACS) and teleradiology, which involves the transmission and management of diagnostic images and the linkage of textual medical records with image files

- Biovisualization, which is the creation and manipulation of three-dimensional databases to model surgical procedures, aging processes, and prosthetic devices

- Image-oriented computer-aided instruction on such topics as pathology and anatomy, paced to the student's learning rate

The major components of a medical image processing system include

- Image acquisition devices such as computer-based radiography and X-ray

- Viewing stations such as nursing stations and multiscreen diagnostic lab stations

- Archiving and data management systems such as optical disk storage

- Shared peripheral devices such as film digitizers and laser printers

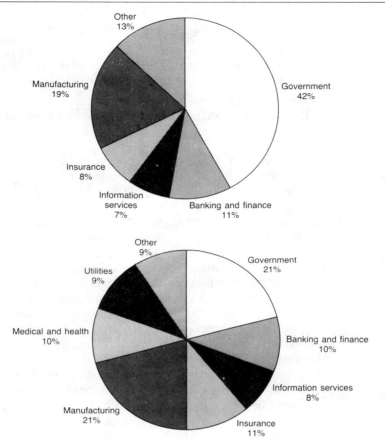

**Figure 10-6** Image processing market share by shipment value.

Over the next ten years, medical centers hope to benefit from image processing systems through

- Medical records consolidation and management
- Reduced film purchasing, processing, and storage
- Distributed access for consultations and referrals
- Improved information sharing among research institutions
- Facilitation of problem-based computer-aided pathology and anatomy instruction

## Interactive Computer Graphics

Interactive computer graphics refers to a range of applications with the following characteristics:

- The user interacts with a computer using a keyboard and screen.
- The display consists of two-dimensional images that can be referenced or manipulated by the user. Often, the user's terminal is equipped with a mouse, a light pen, or another pointing device to allow ready reference to objects or positions on the screen.
- The displayed image changes at a rate that is comparable to the response time in a conversation.

Until recently, interactive computer graphics was experienced by only a handful of workers, mainly scientists and engineers engaged in computer-aided design, data analysis, and mathematical modeling. Now the privilege of exploring real and imaginary worlds through the looking glass of the computer is becoming increasingly common. Indeed, graphics is well on its way to being the standard form of communication with computers.

There are several reasons for this change. First, dramatic improvements in the price and performance of computer graphics hardware have made sophisticated graphics terminals and graphics-based personal computers widely affordable. Corresponding improvements in graphics software have greatly increased the range of applications that can be handled pictorially. New software packages for business applications, for example, make it possible to display data in the form of charts and graphs even on inexpensive home computers. In addition, standard high-level software packages for graphics are becoming widely available, making it easier for new application programs to be written and transported from one make of computer to another.

Currently, over a quarter of a million computer graphics workstations are installed. But, with over eight million engineers, scientists, and technicians worldwide, the market for these devices is huge. Figure 10-7 is a projection.

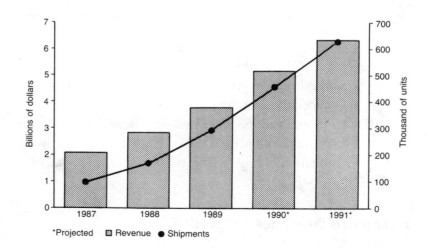

**Figure 10-7** Worldwide shipments of graphics workstations. *(Source: Dataquest, Inc., March 1988.)*

In the remainder of this section, we look at one of the most important interactive computer graphics applications, computer-aided design and manufacturing. Computer-aided design (CAD) systems have become almost universal in engineering design applications and are one of the largest specialized markets for computer systems. Such systems use interactive computer graphics in the production of engineering drawings for everything from automobiles to microchips. Initially, these applications performed little more than simple automated drafting. But, as computer hardware and software became more powerful, additional capabilities were added. CAD systems now permit the user to perform a much wider range of geometric manipulations and sophisticated analyses. For example, civil engineering packages have knowledge of the strength of materials and automatically check that the design is within a specified tolerance for the materials used.

One of the most fruitful areas for the use of CAD is in manufacturing. A user at a CAD graphics terminal can design a part, analyze stresses and deflection, study mechanical action, and produce engineering drawings automatically. These systems have a dramatic impact on productivity because, with or without computers, graphic information is an essential element of the engineering design process. Figure 10-8, which is based on a survey of engineers, illustrates this point. Note that text is important at the beginning and end of an engineering development process. For example, project plans and specifications begin most projects, and documentation dominates at the end. However, graphics maintains its importance throughout the process.

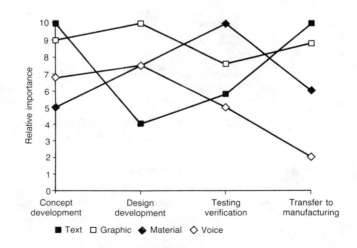

**Figure 10-8** Importance of different forms of communication in an engineering project. *(Source:* IEEE Communications, *February 1988.)*

The output of a CAD system can be used as input to another interactive graphics application, computer-aided manufacturing (CAM). Some of the tasks that can be performed with CAM are producing instructions for programmable devices (known as numerical control devices), generating process plans, programming robots, and managing plant operations. These two technologies can be integrated into a CAD/CAM system. With this system, a design is created and the manufacturing process is controlled and executed with a single computer system sharing a common database. An idealized system is illustrated in Figure 10-9.

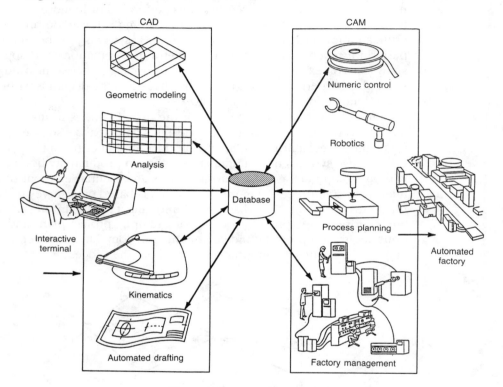

**Figure 10-9** CAD/CAM system.

## Enhanced Audio Teleconferencing

As in any other business endeavor involving communications, audio teleconferencing can be enhanced by the use of image information. Some of the possibilities include

- *Facsimile:* Each conference room can be equipped with a facsimile machine. Previously prepared graphics and hand-drawn figures generated during the teleconference can be transmitted to the other participants.

- *Electronic graphics:* A computer graphics system for teleconferencing permits the immediate creation, alteration, transmission, and remote viewing of graphic images. In its simplest form, one-way transmission is supported.

A user at one site can create images on a local computer graphics computer. The image displayed on the user's screen can be transmitted to one or more sites and displayed on remote display terminals. Thus, for a given period, the remote displays are "slaved" to the originating terminal. With an interactive system, teleconferencing participants at distant locations can be given control of the image so that they can create or alter the graphics, with the image visible at all locations as it takes form. A more restricted type of equipment requires predistribution of graphics but permits interactive electronic pointing with a spot of light.

- *Electronic blackboard:* An electronic blackboard looks like a conventional blackboard but has embedded sensors that can follow the tracings of chalk on the board. The sender writes on the board with regular chalk, and the chalk strokes are converted to electronic signals. These can be displayed on local and remote display screens. The sensors can also respond to a conventional eraser to permit selective erasure. The system can be one-way or interactive. In the latter case, users at all location can draw and selectively erase images.

Audio teleconferencing enhanced with images provides a powerful teleconferencing capability, yet one with relatively low cost and relatively modest communications demands (compared to video teleconferencing). Graphics improve retention when used with the spoken word and aid comprehension when substituted for text. A simple diagram or graph can help a speaker communicate an idea more rapidly.

## Communications Implications

The various configurations by which image information is used and communicated do not fundamentally differ from the configurations used for text and numerical data. The key difference is in the volume of data. A page of text may contain 300 words, which can be represented with about 13,000 bits (assuming 8 bits per character and an average of 5.5 characters per word). The bit image of a good-quality personal computer screen, such as that of the Macintosh, requires over 300,000 bits. A facsimile page with a resolution of 200 points per inch (which is an adequate but not unnecessarily high resolution) generates 3,740,000 bits. Thus, for image information, a tremendous number of bits is needed for representation in the computer.

In medical image processing (discussed previously), even conservative forecasts, which assume a very gradual transition of physicians' diagnostic preferences and the use of local optical storage to reduce network transit of images, quickly lead to peak hour transmissions that require fiber-based LANs with speeds in the FDDI range. A single MRI image, which may be 256 points by 256 points by 12 bits deep, can be transmitted across an Ethernet in five seconds. A single chest X ray, which may be 2000 points by 2000 points by 12 bits deep, requires 100-Mbps FDDI speeds to provide adequate transmission times.

Figure 10-10 shows a projection for a typical 500-bed medical center hospital, generating 120,000 image exams of varying types. This could generate peak-hour LAN demands in excess of 20 Mbps. Larger institutions concentrating in high-resolution diagnostic areas or using three-dimensional images would generate even greater bandwidth requirements.

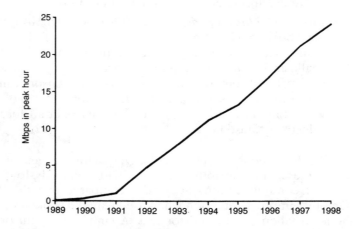

**Figure 10-10**  Projected network load for image traffic. *(Source: Northeast Computing Resources, Boston, July 1989.)*

The number of bits needed to represent an image can be reduced by image compression techniques. In a typical document, whether it contains text or pictorial information, the black and white areas of the image tend to cluster. This property can be exploited to describe the patterns of black and white in a manner that is more concise than simply listing black and white values, one for each point in the image. Compression ratios (the ratio of the number of points in the image to the number of bits in the representation) from 8 to 16 are readily achievable.

Even with compression, the number of bits transmitted for image information is large. The two concerns are response time and throughput. In some cases, such as a CAD/CAM application, the user is interactively manipulating an image. If the user's terminal is separated from the application by a communications facility, the communications capacity must be substantial to give adequate response time. In other cases, such as facsimile, a delay of a few seconds or even a few minutes is usually of no consequence. However, the communications facility must still have a capacity great enough to keep up with the average rate of facsimile transmission. Otherwise, delays on the facility will grow over time as a backlog develops.

# Video Communications

Perhaps the most exciting possibility for improved business information use is in the area of video. With the increasing capability of telecommunications systems, a greatly expanded use of video will take place in the next few years. We can divide the types of video information services available to the business user into four categories:

- Distribution services
- Retrieval services
- Messaging services
- Conversational services

## Distribution Services

Distribution services are also referred to as broadcast services. They provide a continuous flow of information distributed from a central source to an unlimited number of authorized receivers connected to the network. Each user can access this flow of information but has no control over it. In particular, the user cannot control the starting time or order of the presentation of the broadcasted information. All users simply tap into the flow of information.

The most common example of this service is broadcast television. Currently, broadcast television is available from network broadcast by means of radio waves and cable television distribution systems. Private broadcast capabilities can be used for educational, training, and corporate communications. For these applications, the organization uses a broadcast studio to transmit a program, which can be received and shown on television screens at various employee locations.

## Retrieval Services

Retrieval services provide the user with the ability to retrieve information stored in information centers that are, in general, available for public use. This information is sent to the individual user on demand only.

A simpler service is Videotex. This interactive system services both home and business needs. It is a general-purpose database retrieval system that can use the public telephone network or an interactive metropolitan cable TV system. Figure 10-11 depicts a typical system. The Videotex provider maintains a variety of databases on a central computer. Some of these are public databases provided by the Videotex system; others are vendor-supplied services, such as a stock market advisory. Information is provided in the form of pages of text and simple graphics.

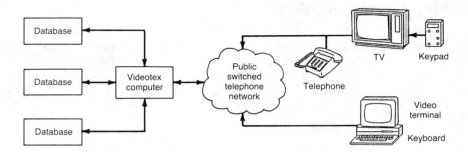

**Figure 10-11** A typical Videotex system.

*Broadband videotex* is an enhancement of the existing Videotex system. The user can select sound passages, high-resolution images, and short video scenes, in addition to the current text and simplified graphics. Examples of broadband videotex services follow:

- Retrieval of encyclopedia entries
- Results of quality tests on consumer goods
- Computer-supported audiovisual entries
- Electronic mail-order catalogs and travel brochures with the option of placing a direct order or making a direct booking, respectively

An example of an operational broadband videotex system is the video response system (VSR) in use at Kanto Teishin Hospital in Japan (Figure 10-12). The system is used by doctors, nurses, pharmacists, patients, and patients' family members. It provides text, graphics, and video segments in three areas: information to assist medical examination and treatment, counseling and educational information, and guidance information.

Another retrieval service might be called pure video retrieval. With this service, a user can order full-length films or videos from a film and video library facility. Because the provider may have to satisfy many requests, only a small number of different video transmissions can be supported at any one time. A realistic service would offer perhaps 500 movies or videos for each two-hour period. The provider tells the user when the film will be available to be viewed or transmitted to the subscriber's video recorder.

## Messaging Services

A new form of messaging service made possible by technical advances is *video mail,* which is analogous to today's electronic mail (text and graphic mail) and voice mail. Just as sending electronic mail replaces mailing a letter, sending video mail replaces mailing a video cassette. This may become one of the most powerful and useful forms of message communication.

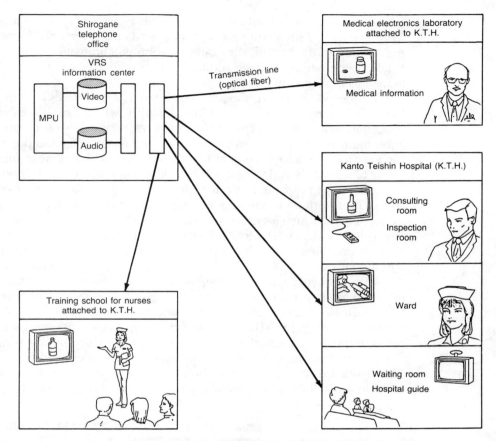

**Figure 10-12** System outline of Kanto Teishin Hospital's video response system (VRS).

## Conversational Services

Conversational services provide the means for two-way dialogue between two users or between a user and a service-provider host. These services support the transfer of data specific to a given user application. That is, the information is generated by and exchanged between users; it is not "public" information.

This category encompasses a wide range of applications. Perhaps the most important of these services is video telephony. Video telephony simply means that the telephone instrument includes a video transmit and a receive and display capability so that dial-up calls include both voice and live picture. The first use of this service is likely to be in the office. It can be used in any situation where the visual component of a call is advantageous, including sales, consulting, instruction, negotiation, and the discussion of visual information, such as reports, charts, and advertising layouts. As the cost of videophone terminals declines, it is likely that this will be a popular residential service as well. The cost of such equipment will depend on the required picture quality and the size of the screen. For example, computer animation that represents a detailed engineering design requires much higher resolution than ordinary human-to-human conversation.

Another video conversational service is *videoconference*. The simplest form of this service is a point-to-point capability, which can be used to connect two conference rooms. This differs from videophone in the nature of the equipment used. A point-to-point videoconference uses additional features such as facsimile and document transfer and special equipment such as electronic blackboards. A different sort of videoconference is a multipoint service. This allows participants to tie together single videophones in a conference connection, without leaving their workplaces, using a video conference server in the network. Such a system supports a small number of simultaneous users (typically less than ten). Either one participant would appear on all screens at a time, as managed by the video conference server, or a split screen technique could be used.

Although videoconferencing is more expensive than other forms of teleconferencing, businesses are beginning to recognize the value of this facility. Figure 10-13 reports the results of one of the most comprehensive studies of videoconferencing. The user success stories now appearing in the trade press simply reiterate and validate the benefits outlined by this study.

A third variant of the video conversational service is video surveillance. This is not a distribution service because information delivery is limited to a specific subscriber. This form of service can be unidirectional; if the informa-

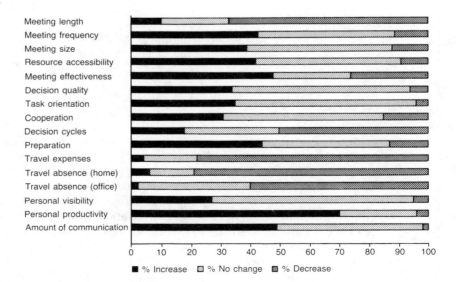

**Figure 10-13** Effects of videoconferencing as perceived by users. *(Source: Business Horizons, November/December 1984.)*

tion is simple video images generated by a fixed camera, the information flow is only from video source to subscriber. A reverse flow would come into play if the user had control over the camera (change orientation, zoom, and so on).

## Communications Implications

As might be expected, the communications capacity requirements for video transmission far exceed those for any other form of information we have described. Two complementary approaches are used to reduce capacity requirements:

- Use data compression techniques that remove redundancy or unnecessary information
- Permit distortions that are least objectionable to the eye

Knowing what information is necessary and the types of acceptable distortion requires an in-depth understanding of the image source to be coded and human vision. With this knowledge, one can apply various coding techniques and engineering tradeoffs to achieve the best image possible.

What is acceptable in terms of image quality and data rate is a function of application. For example, videophone and videoconferencing require both transmission and reception. To limit the engineering requirements at the subscriber site, we would like to drastically limit the video transmission data rate. Fortunately, the resolution required for videophone, especially in conversational applications, is modest. And for both videoconference and videophone, the rate of change of the picture is generally low. This latter property can be exploited to produce very powerful compression techniques.

The CCITT standards organization has defined five levels of quality for video images, as shown in Table 10-2. The table also indicates the data rate currently required for the transmission of such images.

**TABLE 10-2**  Data Rates for Compressed Video Transmission

| Service Quality | Description | Data Rate (Mbps) |
|---|---|---|
| A | High definition television (HDTV) | 92 to greater than 200 |
| B | Digital component-coding signal | 30/45 to 145 |
| C | Digitally coded NTSC, PAL, SECAM for distribution | 20 to 45 |
| D | Reduced spatial resolution and movement portrayal | 0.384 to 1.92 |
| E | Highly reduced spatial resolution and movement portrayal | 0.064 |

The bottom two categories (D and E) are often referred to as low bit rate encoding systems, which are defined as systems that transmit at data rates of about 2 Mbps or less. These quality levels are targeted at videoconference and videophone applications. For quality level D, there is reduced resolution compared to broadcast television and reduced capability to track movement. In general, this produces acceptable quality, but rapid movement in the scene being televised will appear as jerky, discontinuous movement on the viewer's screen. Furthermore, the resolution on the screen may be inadequate for the transmission of a high-resolution graphics image. To overcome this latter problem, the transmitter should be capable of switching between a full-motion, lower-resolution transmission and a freeze-frame, higher-resolution transmission at the same data rate.

The choice between quality levels D and E for videoconferencing is simply a tradeoff between cost and quality. Table 10-3 indicates the 1988 prices of the necessary equipment. (Note the substantial drop in prices over a five-year period.)

**TABLE 10-3**   Declining Cost of Videoconferencing

|  | Speed | 1983 | 1988 |
|---|---|---|---|
| Fully equipped room (includes one video monitor, one still frame graphics machine, and speakers) | High (348 Kbps to 1.544 Mpbs) | $500,000 | $95,000 |
|  | Low (56 to 64 Kbps) | Not available | $49,500 |
| Video transmission (measured from San Francisco to New York) | High (768 Kbps) | $1,500/hour | $450/hour |
|  | Low (56 Kbps) | Not available | $45/hour |
| Video compression coders/ decoders | High (348 Kbps to 1.544 Mbps) | $151,000 | $68,000 |
|  | Low (56 to 64 Kbps) | Not available | $30,000 |

Source: Compression Labs, Inc., San Jose, CA, June 1988.

Returning to Table 10-2, quality level C corresponds to the quality of broadcast television today. Quality level B is known as digital component coding or extended definition television. This system provides improved quality but retains the same number of lines and ratio of screen height to width as current broadcast television standards. The development of this system was undertaken with the direct-broadcast satellite application in mind, but it is certainly appropriate to business video applications.

Finally, the highest quality standard is high-definition television (HDTV). This system is comparable in resolution to 35-mm film projection and will put the quality of TV reception in the home and office at the level of the cinema. With HDTV, not only is the resolution greater, but the system supports wider screens, more along the lines of cinema screens in height-width ratio.

For these higher quality video transmission technologies (A through C), there is, as yet, little business use. By the mid 1990s, however, greatly expanded transmission capacity will be in place to support business video applications. As this capacity becomes available, the exploitation of video applications will grow.

# LANs for the Visual Revolution

The prospect of a dramatic increase in the use of image and video in distributed applications threatens to swamp existing LANs. In many cases, the manager who has built a solid base of knowledge about contemporary LANs and their use to satisfy existing applications may find that carefully laid plans for managing the growth of local communications are wildly off-target.

The problem is a complex one, and it is difficult to predict the course of technical and product evolution. One way to view the problem is as a race between compression technology and application demand. If the shrinking of digital representations of images continues at its recent pace, much of the increased demand for visual communication will be soaked up by the increased capability to compress images for storage and transmission. However, it is very doubtful that compression technology can fully keep pace. What we can hope is that compression technology will give the manager some breathing room, so that image- and video-based applications can be brought on-line gradually. Then, as higher speed LANs become available, more applications can be supported.

The two types of contemporary LANs that are most useful in coping with the visual revolution are broadband coaxial cable LANs and FDDI. A broadband LAN has plenty of bandwidth to support traditional analog video transmission. Typically, a broadband LAN can provide a bandwidth in the neighborhood of 400 MHz. A typical capacity used for both video channels and data channels is 6 MHz. Thus, even if the LAN has several data channels, dozens of channels are available for video transmission. For digital data transmission, which is needed in image processing and computer graphics applications, the 100-Mbps capacity of FDDI provides some early support.

That these applications will outrun FDDI is without doubt. For example, full-color animation, which can be useful in a host of applications, requires a data rate of 3 megabytes per frame at about 10 frames per second. That means a data stream of 30 megabytes per second, or 240 Mbps. Compression can reduce that number; nevertheless, it gives you some idea of what you will be faced with.

A number of technical trends and standardization efforts offer a clue about the direction the market will take. One hopeful standard is the high-speed channel (HSC), which was originally conceived at Los Alamos National Laboratory and is now being developed by the American National Standards Institute. HSC technology uses a 32-bit parallel medium operating at 800 Mbps. A number of vendors are already working on HSC-based interfaces and networks.

Even higher speed LANs are being developed. For example, Ultra Network Technologies is testing a 1 gigabit-per-second (Gbps) network called Ultra-Net. Networks with capacities of this magnitude are the next generation after FDDI. Driven by the need to handle image and video information, these networks will soon begin to spread into the office environment.

# Case Study 8
# Maimonides Hospital[1]

As with any hospital, Maimonides Medical Center in Brooklyn struggles against a sea of paperwork. Admissions records, diagnostic reports, dietary information, and reports from attending physicians are kept for every person admitted to this 700-bed hospital.

The hospital's search for a system to automate information handling was motivated by two concerns. The first concern was the problems of dealing with paper. Paper is bulky, fragile, and difficult to share. In many cases, the records associated with a patient are handled over and over. Even if these files remained in perfect order, they quickly become difficult to work with. Plus, if one hospital employee has a medical record, no one else can get at it. Because an average of 60 patients are admitted each day, and because New York State law requires that these records be kept for six years, the hospital desperately needed an efficient and cost-effective way to handle patient records.

The second concern was a financial one. The billing department must keep track of every charge every patient incurs from the moment of admission; all charges are listed on the discharge bill, which the department sends to the patient's insurance company. The faster the bill goes out, the faster the hospital is paid.

The hospital acquired an image-processing system that meets their needs admirably. Figure 10-14 illustrates the essential components of the system. The heart of the system is the file server, which manages a variety of secondary-storage media. The most important form of storage is the write-once, read-many (WORM) optical disk system[2]. This storage provides exceptionally high capacity with absolute data integrity. After data is written to the disk, it can

---

[1] This case study is based on material in P. Schnaidt, "WORM Networks: Maimonides Hospital Reduces Paper with Optical Disks," *LAN Magazine,* August 1988.

[2] For a discussion of WORM and CD-ROM technology, see William Stallings, *Computer Organization and Architecture, Second Edition,* Macmillan, New York, 1990.

never be erased or altered. When a record is changed, it is stored as a new file, automatically leaving a trail of who changed what and when.

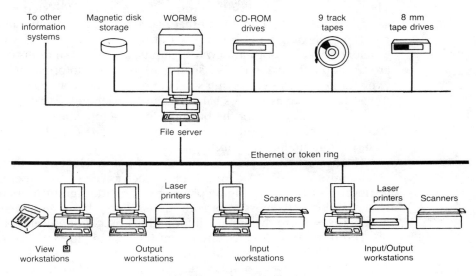

**Figure 10-14** LAN elements.

The file server connects to an Ethernet LAN, which also supports a number of user workstations. The workstations perform six principal functions:

- *View:* Records from the optical database can be retrieved and displayed.
- *Record input:* Hard-copy records are scanned into the system. The exact image of the paper is preserved, including any handwritten notations.
- *Record:* Laser printers provide high-quality output, which reproduces the image.
- *Modify:* A form or record in optical storage can be modified by positioning a cursor to the correct position and entering data. This creates a new version of the file, which is stored separately from the older version.
- *Voice input:* A physician can record a diagnosis and have the recording stored with a link to the appropriate medical record. To record, the physician picks up the telephone attached to the workstation, selects the audio record function, and begins to speak. His voice input is digitized and recorded with high sound quality.
- *Voice output:* To retrieve a diagnosis, a user enters the appropriate access code, picks up the telephone, and hears the recording.

The system has external as well as internal uses. For example, seriously delinquent accounts can be transferred from WORM storage to a CD-ROM disk using special equipment at the vendor site. The CD-ROMs are then sent to the collection agency, which uses the less expensive (compared to WORM) CD-ROM input equipment.

# Summary

The explosive growth in the volume of computer-generated and computer-stored data is so overwhelming that managers and decision makers face two choices in dealing with this vast sea of data: Ignore most of it or find more efficient ways to absorb it. Because graphic and pictorial forms of information are far more effective for this task, the use of image information is increasing. Even for documents consisting solely of text, there is often significant benefit to handling them as images using facsimile machines. Although image information provides relief for the business information consumer, the large number of bits required to represent an image means that the communications facility requirements are substantial.

The newest mode of information—and potentially one of the most important for business—is video. Applications such as video teleconferencing, video retrieval, and video messaging promise to provide significant benefits in efficiency and effectiveness in organizations. Video, however, places strong demands (even more than image information) on communications facilities.

The result of the increasing use of image and video is that today's LANs, even FDDI, will soon prove inadequate in many environments. The alert manager needs to be aware of this situation and prepared to move to higher capacity LANs, as applications dictate and technology allows.

# Glossary

**Amplifier**  An analog device designed to compensate for the loss in a section of transmission medium. It increases the signal strength of an analog signal over a range of frequencies.

**Asynchronous transmission**  Transmission in which each information character is individually synchronized, usually by the use of start elements and stop elements.

**Availability**  The percentage of time that a particular function or application is available for users.

**Bandwidth**  The difference between the limiting frequencies of a continuous frequency band.

**Baseband**  Transmission of signals without modulation. In a baseband local area network, digital signals (1s and 0s) are inserted directly onto the cable as voltage pulses. The signal uses the entire spectrum of the cable. This scheme does not allow frequency-division multiplexing.

**Bridge**  An internetworking device that connects two similar local area networks that use the same LAN protocols.

**Broadband**  In local area networks, the use of coaxial cable for providing data transfer by means of analog (radio-frequency) signals. Digital signals are passed through a modem and transmitted over one of the frequency bands of the cable.

**Bus**  A LAN topology in which stations are attached to a shared transmission medium. The medium is a linear cable; transmissions travel the length of the medium and are received by all stations.

**Byte**  A group of eight bits that represent a character of data.

**Carrierband**  A transmission scheme in which the entire spectrum of the cable is devoted to a single transmission path; frequency-division multiplexing is not used.

**Cheapernet**   A baseband local area network that uses a thinner cable and less expensive components than Ethernet or the original IEEE 802.3 standard. Although the data rate is the same (10 Mbps), the network span and maximum number of taps allowed is less for Cheapernet.

**Coaxial cable**   A cable consisting of one conductor, usually a small copper tube or wire, within and insulated from another conductor of larger diameter, usually copper tubing or copper braid.

**Collision**   A condition in which two packets are transmitted over a medium at the same time. Their interference makes both unintelligible.

**Communications architecture**   The hardware and software structure that implements the communications function.

**CSMA/CD**   Carrier sense multiple access with collision detection. A medium access control technique for bus and tree LANs. A station wanting to transmit will first sense the medium and transmits only if the medium is idle. The station ceases transmission if it detects a collision.

**Cyclic redundancy check (CRC)**   An error-detecting code in which the code is the remainder resulting from dividing the bits to be checked by a predetermined binary number.

**Data compression**   The process of eliminating gaps, empty fields, redundancies, and unnecessary data to shorten the length of records or blocks.

**Data link layer**   Layer 2 of the OSI model. Converts an unreliable transmission channel into a reliable one.

**Differential manchester encoding**   A digital signaling technique in which there is a transition in the middle of each bit time to provide clocking. The encoding of a 0 is represented by the presence of a transition at the beginning of the bit period; a 1 is represented by the absence of a transition.

**Distributed data processing**   Data processing in which some or all of the processing, storage, and control functions, in addition to input and output functions, are dispersed among data processing stations.

**Dual cable**   A type of broadband cable system that uses two separate cables: one for transmission and one for reception.

**Electronic mail**   Correspondence in the form of messages transmitted between workstations over a network.

**Encrypt**   To convert plain text or data into unintelligible form by means of a reversible mathematical computation.

**Error-detecting code**   A code in which each data signal conforms to specific rules of construction, so that departures from this construction in the received signal can be automatically detected.

**Error rate**   The ratio of the number of data units in error to the total number of data units.

**Ethernet**   A 10-Mbps baseband local area network specification developed jointly by Xerox, Intel, and Digital Equipment. It is the forerunner of the IEEE 802.3 CSMA/CD standard.

**Facsimile**   A system for the transmission of images. The image is scanned at the transmitter, reconstructed at the receiving station, and duplicated on paper.

**Fiber distributed data interface (FDDI)**   A standard for a 100-Mbps optical fiber ring local area network.

**File server**   A computer that each computer on a network can use to access and retrieve files that can be shared among the attached computers. Access to a file is usually controlled by the file server's software rather than by the operating system of the computer that accesses the file.

**File transfer facility**   A distributed application that transfers files and portions of files between computers.

**Frame check sequence**   An error-detecting code inserted as a field in a block of data to be transmitted. The code checks for errors upon reception of the data.

**Frequency-division multiplexing (FDM)**   Division of a transmission facility into two or more channels by splitting the frequency band transmitted by the facility into narrower bands, each of which constitutes a distinct channel.

**Frequency-shift keying (FSK)**   A digital-to-analog modulation technique in which two different frequencies are used to represent 1s and 0s.

**Frequency translator**   In a split broadband cable system, an analog device at the headend that converts a block of inbound frequencies to a block of outbound frequencies.

**Full-duplex transmission**   Transmission of data in both directions at the same time.

**Gateway**   An internetworking device that connects two computer networks that use different communications architectures.

**Half-duplex transmission**   Data transmission in either direction, one direction at a time.

**Headend**   The endpoint of a broadband bus or tree local area network. Transmission from each station is toward the headend. Reception by each station is from the headend.

**Header**   System-defined control information that precedes user data.

**IEEE 802**   A committee of the Institute of Electrical and Electronics Engineers organized to produce local area network standards.

**Internet**   A collection of communication networks interconnected by bridges, routers, or gateways.

**Internet protocol**   An internetworking protocol that executes in hosts and routers to interconnect a number of packet networks.

**Internetworking**   Communication among devices across multiple networks.

**Layer**   In a network architecture, a group of services, functions, and protocols that is complete from a conceptual point of view, that is one out of a set of hierarchically arranged groups, and that extends across all systems that conform to the network architecture.

**Local area network (LAN)**   A communications network that provides interconnection of a variety of data communicating devices in a small area. It makes use of a shared transmission medium and packet broadcasting. A packet transmitted by one station is received by all other stations. Typically, a LAN has a bus, tree, or ring topology.

**Manchester encoding**   A digital signaling technique in which there is a transition in the middle of each bit time. A 0 is encoded with a high level during the first half of the bit time; a 1 is encoded with a low level during the first half of the bit time.

**Medium access control (MAC)**   For a local area network, the method of determining which station has access to the transmission medium at any time. CSMA/CD, token bus, and token ring are common access methods.

**Modem (*modulator/demodulator*)**   A device that converts digital data to an analog signal that can be transmitted on a telecommunication line and converts the analog signal received to data.

**Multiplexing**   In data transmission, a function that permits two or more data sources to share a common transmission medium such that each data source has its own channel.

**Network interface unit (NIU)**   A communications controller that attaches to a local area network. It implements the LAN protocols and provides an interface for device attachment.

**Network layer**   Layer 3 of the OSI model. Responsible for routing data through a communication network.

**Open systems interconnection (OSI) reference model**   A model of communications between cooperating devices. It defines a seven-layer architecture of communication functions.

**Optical fiber**   A thin filament of glass or other transparent material through which a signal-encoded light beam is transmitted by means of total internal reflection.

**Packet**   A group of bits that includes data plus control information. Generally refers to a network layer (OSI layer 3) protocol.

**Packet assembler/disassembler (PAD)**   A functional unit that enables data terminal equipment not equipped for packet switching to access a packet-switched network.

**Packet switching**   A method of transmitting messages through a communications network in which long messages are subdivided into short packets.

Each packet is passed from source to destination through intermediate nodes. At each node, the entire message is received, stored briefly, and passed to the next node.

**Physical layer**  Layer 1 of the OSI model. Concerned with the electrical, mechanical, and timing aspects of signal transmission over a medium.

**Presentation layer**  Layer 6 of the OSI model. Concerned with data format and display.

**Private branch exchange (PBX)**  A telephone exchange on the user's premises. Provides a circuit-switching facility for telephones on extension lines within the building and access to the public telephone network.

**Protocol**  A set of semantic and syntactic rules that determines the behavior of functional units in achieving communication.

**Protocol data unit (PDU)**  Information that is delivered as a unit between peer entities of a network and contains control information, address information, or data.

**Remodulator**  In a split broadband cable system, a digital device at the headend that recovers the digital data from the inbound analog signal, then retransmits the data on the outbound frequency.

**Repeater**  A device that receives data on one communication link and transmits it, bit by bit, on another link as fast as the data is received, without buffering.

**Ring**  A LAN topology in which stations are attached to repeaters connected in a closed loop. Data is transmitted in one direction around the ring and can be read by all attached stations.

**Response time**  In a data system, the elapsed time between the end of transmission of an inquiry message and the beginning of the receipt of a response message, measured at the inquiry terminal.

**Router**  An internetworking device that connects two computer networks. It uses an internet protocol and assumes that all attached devices on the networks use the same communications architecture and protocols.

**Service access point (SAP)**  A means of identifying a user of the services of a protocol entity. A protocol entity provides one or more SAPs, for use by higher-level entities.

**Session layer**  Layer 5 of the OSI model. Manages a logical connection (session) between two communicating processes or applications.

**Spectrum**  Refers to an absolute, contiguous range of frequencies.

**Splitter**  Analog device for dividing one input into two outputs and combining two outputs into one input. Used to achieve tree topology on broadband LANs.

**Star wiring**  A method of laying out the transmission cable installed for a local area network. All cables are concentrated in a wiring closet, with a dedicated cable run from the closet to each device on the network.

**Subnetwork**   Refers to a constituent network of an internet. This avoids ambiguity because the entire internet, from a user's point of view, is a single network.

**Synchronous transmission**   Data transmission in which the occurrence of each signal representing a bit is related to a fixed time frame.

**Systems network architecture (SNA)**   The communications architecture used by IBM. It is also implemented on many other computers from other vendors to provide connection to the IBM world.

**Tap**   An analog device that permits signals to be placed on or removed from a transmission medium.

**Teleconference**   A conference between persons remote from one another but linked by a telecommunications system.

**Terminal emulation**   The capability of a personal computer to operate as if it were a particular type of terminal linked to a processing unit.

**Token bus**   A medium access control technique for bus and tree LANs. Stations form a logical ring, around which a token is passed. A station receiving the token may transmit data and then must pass the token to the next station in the logical ring.

**Token ring**   A medium access control technique for ring LANs. A token circulates around the ring. A station may transmit data by seizing the token, inserting a packet onto the ring, then retransmitting the token.

**Topology**   The way in which the end points, or stations, attached to a network are interconnected. The common topologies for LANs are bus, tree, and ring.

**Transmission medium**   The physical medium that conveys data between data stations.

**Transport layer**   Layer 4 of the OSI model. Provides reliable, sequenced transfer of data between endpoints.

**Tree**   A LAN topology in which stations are attached to a shared transmission medium. The medium is a branching cable emanating from a headend, with no closed circuits. Transmissions propagate from any station to the headend and then throughout the medium, and are received by all stations.

**Twisted pair**   A transmission medium that consists of two insulated conductors twisted together to reduce noise.

**Videoconference**   A teleconference involving video. The video may be full-motion video or some lesser quality scheme.

**Virtual circuit**   A packet-switching mechanism in which a logical connection (virtual circuit) is established between two stations at the start of transmission. All packets follow the same route, need not carry a complete address, and arrive in sequence.

**Voice mail**   A computerized system for recording and delivering recorded telephone messages.

**Wiring closet**   A specially designed closet used for wiring data and voice communication networks. The closet serves as a concentration point for the cabling that interconnects devices, and as a patching facility for adding and deleting devices from the network.

# Index

# The William Stallings Books on Computer and Data Communications Technology

## TEXT/REFERENCE BOOKS ON DATA COMMUNICATIONS AND COMPUTER ARCHITECTURE

*(Available from Macmillan, Inc.)*

### Data and Computer Communications, Second Edition

A broad but detailed survey, covering four main areas: (1) data communications, including transmission, media, signal encoding, link control, and multiplexing; (2) communication networks, including circuit- and packet-switched, local, packet radio, and satellite; (3) communications architecture, including the OSI model and related protocols; and (4) ISDN.

### Local Networks: An Introduction, Third Edition

An in-depth presentation of the technology and architecture of local networks. Covers topology, transmission media, medium access control, standards, internetworking, and interface issues.

### Computer Organization and Architecture, Second Edition

A unified view of this broad field. Covers fundamentals such as CPU, control unit, microprogramming, instruction set, I/O, and memory. Also covers advanced topics such as RISC and parallel organization.

### ISDN: An Introduction

An in-depth presentation of the technology and architecture of integrated services digital network (ISDN). Covers the integrated digital network (IDN), ISDN services, architecture, signaling system no. 7 (SS7), and detailed coverage of the 1988 CCITT standards.

### Business Data Communications

A comprehensive presentation of data communications and telecommunications from a business perspective. Covers voice, data, image, and video communications and applications technology, and includes a number of case studies.

---

*All of these books include a glossary, a list of acronyms, homework problems, and recommendations for further reading. These books are suitable as references, for self-study, and as textbooks.*

*See first page for additional Stallings titles.*